The Islamic World and the Mediterranean

This collection investigates the conflictual relationship between the Islamic world and Western civilization, looking at its history as key to understanding its present. The historical narrative starts from the controversial encounter that took place at the close of the 18th century, the effort being to improve our understanding of that engagement and its current implications, focusing in particular on how it has affected law, philosophy, and religion. The subsequent age of 19th-century colonialism is analysed with a view to understanding the currents of mutual influence that throughout that era ran between Islam and the Western world, looking at the law and the institutions, as well as at different strains in the culture. This discussion provides the backdrop against which the book turns a critical eye on current Euro-Mediterranean relations, highlighting the need to move beyond the conditionality principle that has traditionally been a cornerstone of European policy toward Arab Muslim peoples and to set this relationship on a new foundation, one that recognizes the interdependency between these two areas, making it possible to open up a Mediterranean space of mutual recognition among all its peoples. The book will be of interest to researchers and academics working in the areas of legal and political history, comparative law, legal philosophy, law and religion, and Islamic studies.

Gustavo Gozzi is Alma Mater Honorary Professor at the University of Bologna, Italy.

The Islamic World and the Mediterranean

From Colonial Legacy to Political and Cultural Interdependence

Edited by Gustavo Gozzi

Routledge
Taylor & Francis Group
LONDON AND NEW YORK

First published 2025
by Routledge
4 Park Square, Milton Park, Abingdon, Oxon OX14 4RN

and by Routledge
605 Third Avenue, New York, NY 10158

Routledge is an imprint of the Taylor & Francis Group, an informa business

British Library Cataloguing-in-Publication Data
A catalogue record for this book is available from the British Library

Library of Congress Cataloging-in-Publication Data
Names: Gozzi, Gustavo, 1947– editor.
Title: The Islamic world and the Mediterranean : from colonial legacy to political and cultural interdependence / edited by Gustavo Gozzi.
Description: Abingdon, Oxon [UK] ; New York, NY : Routledge, 2025. | Includes bibliographical references and index.
Identifiers: LCCN 2024042179 (print) | LCCN 2024042180 (ebook)
Subjects: LCSH: Islamic law—Philosophy. | Islamic law—Political aspects. | Islamic law—Mediterranean Region. | Feminism—Religious aspects—Islam. | Colonies—Law and legislation.
Classification: LCC KBP144 .I857145 2025 (print) | LCC KBP144 (ebook) | DDC 909/.09822081—dc23/eng/20240910
LC record available at https://lccn.loc.gov/2024042179
LC ebook record available at https://lccn.loc.gov/2024042180

ISBN: 978-1-032-55561-4 (hbk)
ISBN: 978-1-032-55563-8 (pbk)
ISBN: 978-1-003-43120-6 (ebk)

DOI: 10.4324/9781003431206

Typeset in Galliard
by Apex CoVantage, LLC

This book has been published with the support of the King Abdulaziz Chair for Islamic Studies (http://kais.unibo.it), Alma Mater Studiorum—University of Bologna.

Copyediting by Filippo Valente, who has also translated Chapter 1 from the Italian and Chapter 6 from the French.

Contents

Contributors

Raja Bahlul is Professor of Philosophy in the Philosophy Programme of the Doha Institute for Graduate Studies.

Abdelmajid Charfi is a member of the Académie Tunisienne Beit Al-Hikma.

Siham Cherif is *Maitre de Conférence* and Researcher at the Laboratory for Religion and Society at the University of Algiers 2.

Erhan Doğan teaches political science and international relations at the Marmara University Department of International Studies (Turkey).

Nacer-Eddine Ghozali is Professor of Public International Law and International Relations at the University of Paris XIII, formerly a judge at the OPEC Fund Administrative Tribunal and formerly Vice President of the Académie Internationale de Droit Constitutionnel.

Gustavo Gozzi has been Full Professor at the University of Bologna, Italy, teaching the history of political thought and the history of international law. He is currently an Alma Mater Honorary Professor at the same university.

Hande Orhon Özdağ serves as a political advisor in the Turkish Grand National Assembly and is also a part-time lecturer on regional studies, current issues in world politics, and political communication.

Alessandro Romagnoli is Professor at the University of Bologna, Italy, where he teaches business economics, economic development in the Middle East and North Africa, and economic-systems analysis.

Lana Sirri—academic, author, activist—is a postdoctoral researcher (NWO-Veni 2022 Laureate) at the Amsterdam Institute for Social Science Research.

Editor's Introduction

Islam and Western Civilization

Gustavo Gozzi

This book analyses the relation between Islam and Western civilization, underscoring the multifaceted complexity of this relation through its history over a period that spans from the end of the 18th century to the contemporary age. The complexity of this relation comes through in the plurality of questions addressed in the book. And though it may not be immediately apparent how these questions connect in that plurality, there is a unifying theme that runs across the entire book: the theme of the manifold ways in which imperialist Europe engaged in a mutual exchange with the colonized regions but at the same time also acted to subjugate and exploit them. And out of this dynamic and intersection comes the complex relationship laid out in the three sections into which the book is organized.

Thus Part I analyses the current debate unfolding in the Muslim world in regard to religion. This debate bleeds into the debate on the Western construction and representation of Islamic feminism, which is critically scrutinized in making the argument that this representation reproduces the Orientalist discourse of the West and Islam.

Then, against the same background of the imperialist interchange, Part II analyses (a) the colonial legacy in the colonized countries after their independence; (b) the current debate on religion, democracy, and human rights in Islam; and (c) the case of current Algeria as an oligarchic system where the constitutional scheme underpins a practice divorced from its ostensible ideals.

Finally, Part III turns to the present embodiment of that past history in the form of current Euro–Mediterranean relations, where the discussion is organized under the main theme of the different levels of development between the northern and southern shores of the Mediterranean, with the imbalances this disparity entails, and migration is analysed as one of its consequences.

In short, the different topics and issues addressed in the book revolve around some core ideas which are developed against a historical background and which in turn offer a starting point from which further research may be developed.

The historical narrative starts out from the controversial encounter that took place in the 18th century between Islam and Western civilization, where

DOI: 10.4324/9781003431206-1

the effort will be to add to our understanding of that encounter and its current implications—or how it has affected law, philosophy, and religion.

The subsequent age of 19th-century colonialism is analysed with a view to understanding the currents of mutual influence that throughout that era ran between Islam and the Western world, looking in particular at the law and the institutions, as well as at different strains in the culture.

The book analyses Islam's encounter with Western civilization, highlighting a contradiction which cuts to the heart of that civilization and which becomes especially apparent in its self-image. For this civilization typically understands or portrays itself as universal, and yet it generally only acknowledges its Greco-Roman and, in recent years, its Judeo-Christian heritage, without necessarily acknowledging that it has greatly benefited from other cultures as well, including Islamic culture. An argument for this broad view has been advanced by Abdelmajid Charfi,[1] who gives them a clear and compelling statement in "Missed Opportunities in Islam's Relations with Western Civilization," serving as a sort of opening manifesto for the entire book.

It was in the 19th century that the relationship between Islam and secularism first emerged as a specific question within the broader frame of the encounter between Islamic and Western civilization.

According to some scholars, such as Abdou Filali-Ansary (1999, 126), there are two characteristics of Islam that predispose it to welcome the secular approach: the demythologizing of religious conceptions and the explicit appeal to rationality in representation and in legislation. The first characteristic concerns Islam's rejection of miracles, fetishes, and the whole symbolic dimension—a rejection which can loosen the hold that the idea of divine transcendence may have on individual consciences. This clears a path toward a conception of secularism that conceives religiosity as a personal matter rather

1 On the contested relationship between the West and Islamic societies, whose outlook on the West swings back and forth between hostility and fascination, see Charfi 2004, 10ff. Charfi argues that Islamic societies have not known a modernity engendered by a home-grown evolution. It is therefore not surprising that modern values have been perceived as *forced* onto them by a dominant power. To Muslim eyes, the introduction of modern thinking has appeared as an attempt to undermine Islam (ibid., 214). Modernity, Charfi acknowledges, is certainly a Western development, and certainly among its core values is the idea of the human being as a free and self-determined person rather than as an individual embedded in a community. But Qur'anic ethics are incompatible with certain aspects of Western society—notably the decoupling of customs and morals and the cult of the individual at the expense of solidarity—and Muslim societies can hardly experience these aspects in the same way. If the Islamic sciences are informed by the values of ancient societies, these sciences need to be rebuilt on new foundations suited to the values that shape the current context (ibid., 217). In particular, it needs to be recognized that Muslims, like all human beings, possess inalienable and non-negotiable rights. This makes it necessary to upend the traditional view of Muslims as *duty*-bound, above and beyond any rights they may enjoy. Hence the need to become fully aware of this modern vision, a vision to realize which it is in turn essential to refashion education by breaking with the ideas received from the past so as to emphasize the legitimate aspirations for more freedom, justice, equality, and human dignity (ibid.).

than as a force shaping the whole of social and political life. The second characteristic consists in a strong current among Islamic theologians who argue that religious law finds its justification in the purposes recognized by reason.

But resistance to secularism stems primarily from the aggression that Muslim peoples have suffered at the hands of Western powers. And conspiring with this legacy and cultural force is the resistance that stems from the association between secularism and national belonging. This is in contrast with Islam, which has made it possible for political entities to emerge and coalesce not around an idea of nationhood but around a community's adherence to a creed (Filali-Ansary 1999, 130). Can Islam overcome its resistance to secularism? The question remains open and highly contested.

In Chapter 1, "Islam: A Changing Religious Institution in the Era of Globalization," Charfi analyses Islam's relationship with the West by discussing the transformations that Islam as a religious institution underwent in the process of globalization. As Charfi argues, with globalization comes the privatizing of faith, where faith-based movements no longer respond to states, as they are supported by private groups that operate according to a transnational logic and contribute to a dismantling of public space. But, above all, globalization involves a breakdown of traditional ties, which in turn leads to a loss of community, creating a climate where it becomes easier to adhere to totalitarian and violent movements such as the Islamic State of Iraq and the Levant (ISIL/Da'esh). These are movements that place the good of the group above the good of the individual.

This brings to light the difficulty faced by traditional Islamic religious institutions, which show themselves to be ill-equipped to adapt to the transformations of globalization and to respond to the needs of so-called modernity. To be sure, this difficulty could be explained by pointing to the Islamic resistance to Westernization and secularization, but in reality it betrays the inability of Islamic religious thought to renew its categories. This is why Islam as a religious institution no longer finds in public opinion the support it used to enjoy. And as Charfi argues, this in turn points to the impelling urgency of updating Islamic thought.

Some of the chapters collected in this book pay close attention to particular aspects of Islamic culture, bringing out the complexity of the current debate.

In particular the chapter by Lana Siri—"Islamic Feminism: The Politics of Representation in Germany" (Chapter 3)—uses Germany as a case study through which to shed light on the Western construction and representation of Islamic feminism. The argument is made that this representation reproduces the Orientalist discourse of the West and Islam as inherently distinct geographies and that this construction ushers in a neo-Orientalist discourse that homogenizes and essentializes both Islam and Muslim women by ignoring the heterogeneity of Muslim women's voices, limiting discussions on Islam and women to discussions about gender, and looking at women's rights only through a Western feminist lens. Western feminism fails not only to identify the heterogeneity of women's lives, their experiences, and their self-identification but also to recognize this heterogeneity as a strength. The Western epistemological traditions produce *purportedly objective* knowledge about the world, but this knowledge is detached from its context. The reality that needs to be acknowledged, by contrast, is the diversity and plurality that exists within the world of Islam, which encompasses a full range of socio-cultural and political traditions. In this regard we can recall Sousa Santos's work, which challenges the hegemony of Western systems of knowledge and points to the need to recognize the different forms of knowledge created in non-Western cultural communities.

The chapter finally argues that in order for there to be an honest and genuine exchange of ideas among feminists, it is necessary to move beyond a certain neocolonialist feminist discourse that is prevalent in the West and tends to stoke anti-Islamic sentiment.

In Chapter 2 ("Civilizational Thought and the Building of Societies"), Siham Cherif dissects some key cultural issues in Islam by comparing the work of two eminent Islamic scholars: Malek Bennabi and ʿAli Shariʿati. Bennabi put forward a new approach to Islam, at once historical and spiritual, on which basis to analyse Muslim civilization, address the causes of its crisis, and identify the paths to a possible renaissance. Bennabi also analysed the relation between the tradition of orthodox Muslim reformism and the commitment to fight for national liberation from colonialism.[2] Cherif compares Bennabi's conception of civilization with that of ʿAli Shariʿati,[3] an Iranian sociologist, philosopher, and political militant who sought to achieve a synthesis between Islamism and revolutionary nationalism. On this basis he developed an independent view on the two blocs that clashed in the Cold War. He was also very close to some anticolonial authors, such as Frantz Fanon.

The question of colonialism is a central topic in this book, one that is frontally addressed in Chapter 4 ("Colonial Law and Muslim Law"), where Gustavo Gozzi underscores the two levels on which this historical phenomenon unfolded: on a basic ground level there was the traumatic encounter of Islam with the brute force and violence of Western rule, and running parallel to it was the layering of an ideological and institutional framework whose legacy exerted its influence on Western and Muslim countries alike.

More to the point, colonialism in Chapter 4 is analysed through the paradigm of colonial law, which comprised three elements: metropolitan law, consisting of that part of the mother country's law which was carried over and

2 Worth pointing out in this regard is that Bennabi (2017, 92ff.) identified and criticized the colonial effort to break up the network of social and cultural ties among Muslim countries.

3 On Shariʿati's work see Black 2011, 310–14. On the one hand Shariati followed Marxism and on the other he attempted to set in motion a revolution within Islam itself, in a way that linked these two projects. As he argued (Shariʿati 1986, 21, 44, 99–100, 109–12), from a Qur'anic perspective the achievement of knowledge and victory over the oppressed are one and the same project (cf. Black 2011, 311). Shariʿati (1979, 101–9) merged the Islamic philosophy of history with Marxist philosophy, predicting a final victory of the oppressed classes.

applied to the colonies; special law, a body of law that the metropolitan and colonial authorities established specifically for the colonies; and local law (see Bras 2015, 18), that is, the Muslim law of the country under colonial rule. Muslim law consisted of all the nonmetropolitan local law that governed the native population. Particularly significant in clarifying the relation between local Muslim law and the legal principles of metropolitan law is the Algerian case. Colonial policy in Algeria pursued a dual aim: to govern Muslim *property* under French law, while maintaining the Islamic law of *personal status*. This gave rise to a dual-track system of law: while *local* Muslim law was rewritten in keeping with the concepts and principles of French law, personal status continued to be governed under a kind of *transitional* Muslim law that was meant to dissolve by *assimilation* into French law. Hence the basic contradiction inherent in this dual-track system. On the one hand, Algerian Muslim law denied the supposed universality of French law, recognizing that the Algerian people had their own culture and identity but of a different or "other" sort that justified their unequal treatment. On the other hand, it was understood that this otherness would eventually wash away through a gradual "civilizing" process of assimilation into French culture and law. What clearly comes to light here is the most disturbing and violent aspect of the colonial legacy, which has given rise to an assimilationist ideology that in French society lingers on to this day, with its unwillingness to recognize the cultural identity of its immigrant population by imposing French culture as a condition for gaining full French status.

A related aspect underscored in Chapter 4 is the abiding power of the colonial legacy. This, too, was a dual legacy, at once institutional and ideological, and the point is that it survived in the postcolonial era. It did so not only in the former colonies (in Algeria as well as in the Tunisian protectorate and elsewhere) in the form of a centralized administrative structure but also in the metropole, where in the French case it took the form of an ideology of assimilation maintained as the basis on which to hold together what would become the current multicultural society.

Algeria can be taken as a kind of colonial laboratory, an on-the-ground case study, and it is as such that it is analysed in the book. That is the case with the chapter by Nacer-Eddine Ghozali, "The Inadequacies of the Algerian Political System, or the Impossibility of a Democratic Transition" (Chapter 6), where it is pointed out that, even if on the eve of independence Algeria had everything it needed to enter as a full participant in the concert of nations—a national consensus born of the war of liberation, an international aura owing to the nationalist fight, coherent administrative structures, a perennial agriculture, and promising oil resources—the country is currently paying the consequences of an oligarchic system that had become entrenched even before independence, considering the lack of any lasting counterweight to the leadership of the National Liberation Front (FLN) and the National Liberation Army (ALN), whose hold on power was therefore not competitive and which was consequently beset by conflicts of interest.

This oligarchic system actually has a basis in the constitution, whose only real function is therefore to legitimize the regime. In fact, the constitution does not allow much scope for party pluralism: it is not designed for a truly competitive democracy, since it only favours those parties that have the backing of the regime. And the same goes for the judicial system, which lacks an independent judiciary. Judges are constantly at the mercy of various interferences that prevent them from serving their judicial function. They are often compelled to submit to political decisions, so much so that the entire system has been characterized as one of "instrumentalized justice."

When the 2019–2021 Algerian protests, or Hirak Movement, broke out, the regime's response was swift and effective, and by February 2019 it had already reinstated the authoritarian order with a sweeping and unprecedented repression campaign targeting Hirak leaders, the judiciary, opposition parties, journalists, trade unionists, lawyers, students, and activists.

The Algerian case illustrates the complex situation confronting postcolonial countries as they each try to chart their own path toward democracy. And here, too, the difficulty is a legacy of the colonial system, whose political institutions and administrative machinery were superimposed onto social relations ill-suited to that apparatus: therein lies the cause of these countries' fitful path toward democracy.

The relation between Islam and democracy is addressed from a broader perspective in the chapter by Raja Bahlul, "Religion, Democracy, and Human Rights: The Example of Islam" (Chapter 5). Bahlul observes that the concepts of religion, democracy, and human rights are related in many complex but not necessarily harmonious ways. He seeks to clarify these complex relationships by setting out two models of Islamic democracy and exploring how tensions arise and how they may be resolved. He argues that these tensions can be resolved by viewing human rights as a secularized version of a religion that has been made to live up to its vision of a humanity endowed with rights in the context of a democratic regime. He also suggests that such harmony cannot be achieved solely by intellectual argument and discussion. Attitudes and concepts need to evolve, such that nothing short of a historical process can ultimately lead to this resolution, a process through which it is recognized that democracy and human rights are both grounded in the idea of self-government.

Bahlul deals with the question of democracy by analysing in particular the relation between religion, human equality, and human dignity. As he did in a previous essay (Bahlul 2000), he takes up Joseph Schumpeter's conception of democracy, according to which democracy is procedural—a decision-making method—and is not defined by any end to be pursued. This democratic method is therefore value-neutral and can be applied in different historical and cultural contexts. Bahlul argues that this value-neutral conception of democracy is compatible with two models of Islamic democracy, one moderate and the other liberal, the former associated with thinkers such as Rashid al-Ghannushi and Mohammad Khatami, the latter with thinkers such as Ali Abdel Razeq and Abou al-Fadl. According to Ghannushi, democracy is the best method by which to realize Islamic values. Razeq, by contrast, thought of Islam as a spiritual call and of democracy as the political order that Muslims should seek to establish. Liberal Islamists accept the concept of human rights, while moderate ones are critical of human rights. Bahlul acknowledges that human rights, rejected by moderate Islamism, are a constitutive element of a liberal-constitutional democracy. Consistent with the liberal tradition, he also argues that in order for human rights to be fully recognized and protected, there must be a clear separation between political life and religion, and that the latter must become a private affair. This is the conception of human rights that liberal Islamists endorse but moderate ones reject.

For the foreseeable future, societies can be expected to continue to be deeply divided along religious, philosophical, and moral lines. Bahlul suggests that conflicts among religious traditions can only be resolved over the long arc of history, with liberal Islamists carrying forward what he argues to be a more advanced understanding of Islam compatible with the idea of human rights. This outlook is very close to that espoused by Adullahi An-Naim, who offers an interpretation of Qur'anic revelation that can serve as a basis for building a conception of human rights consistent with the Western conception. "There is thus role for history to play," he comments, striking a positive note in looking to history as a force in its own right.

What emerges through these considerations is the complexity of the relationship between the Islamic and Western civilizations and the need to identify a possible common foundation.

The Mediterranean can be seen as being at the same time a geographical area and a cultural space in which different civilizations and their multiple cultures have historically met (see Brague 1992). And it can now once more act as a cultural space enabling an interchange between the Islamic and Western civilizations. But in order to get there, we need to rethink and redesign the different development models in operation in the Mediterranean Islamic countries and in the European Union. This is the thrust of the argument that Alessandro Romagnoli makes in Chapter 8 ("Islamic Economics Versus Euro-Mediterranean Partnership Policies: On Economic Upgrading in the Mediterranean Space"), where a fundamental contrast is pointed out between these two models: while the Mediterranean Islamic countries are pursuing a development process fashioned around the idea of a social contract, the European Union is pushing an agenda of "free-market fundamentalism." It is not just that the two models express different ideas, but the principles on which they are based are incompatible. Indeed, Islamic economics reject the idea of a free-market system and are instead designed to hew to the sources of Islam, from which there can be no departure. In the Qur'an, the basic principles governing economic activity are modelled on an idea of social justice: they are principles of *mutual responsibility*—under which everyone is to act consistently with the needs of the community—and *social balance*, which rests on individual donation and on the state's responsibility to meet the needs of all members of the community. Islamic economics are in this sense ethical, being grounded not in free enterprise and capitalist individualism but in the need to sustain the life of the community. And yet the argument can be made that, over time, these Islamic economics can lead to economic development as measured by criteria such as the creation of new social classes and the emergence of new labour conditions, making it possible to speak of an *Islamic model of capitalism*.

The Mediterranean area can be classified into three groups of countries—EU Mediterranean countries, the Balkan-Anatolian countries, and the southeast Mediterranean countries—among which the main divide is that between developed economies and developing ones. This divide has resulted in an uneven bargaining power among countries in these three groups, in a process under which the economically stronger position of the EU countries has helped to establish the hegemony of an economic model that denies the peculiarities which distinguish the developing countries from developed ones. And yet some of the structural differences between these two groups of countries are worth taking into account. This goes in particular for their different rates of demographic growth, which could be made to work complementarily under a cooperation programme through which to successfully manage some problems common to the entire Mediterranean area.

This brings us to the chapter by Hande Orhon Özdağ and Erhan Doğan, "Redefining Ourselves So as to Make the Mediterranean a *Mare Nostrum*" (Chapter 7). As Orhon Özdağ and Doğan argue, only by moving beyond the free-market fundamentalism of the EU countries and respecting the cultural identity of the southern Mediterranean countries will it be possible to make this historical, cultural, and geopolitical area an authentic *mare nostrum*. As Fernand Braudel (1949) showed, the geography of the Mediterranean has historically had a profound influence in shaping the diversity of the civilizations that have sprung up around it. And the question now arises how, despite this diversity, it might be possible to build something like a collective identity shared by these civilizations. In tackling this question and identifying the conditions under which it may be possible to achieve such a shared identity, Orhon Özdağ and Doğan close in on some of the points of friction: the bilateral disputes among littoral states, the subregional fragmentation, the flow of migration from south to north, and the question of resource distribution. In this connection, they also point to European Mediterranean policies, underscoring how, far from achieving the objective of "peace, stability, and prosperity" proclaimed in the Barcelona Declaration of 1995, they have instead been used to strengthen security.

What they argue, in view of that background, is that if the Mediterranean is to be reshaped into a genuine *mare nostrum*, it will be necessary to rectify the economic imbalances between the littoral states, bringing political stability to the region and fostering an environment conducive to people-to-people interaction.

In conclusion, there is a multiplicity of topics that this book addresses: the transformations that Islamic religious institutions have undergone in the process of globalization, Islamic feminism, the legacy of colonialism, the problem of democracy and its relation to Islam, the differing conceptions of development adhered to in the West and in the Muslim world, and the problem of cultural and economic relations in the Mediterranean area. What these lines of investigation underscore is the complexity of the relation between Islam and the West, and what they offer is a glimpse of possibility, outlining some attainable conditions under which these two great civilizations might be able to interact in working toward a brighter future of common prosperity.

Works Cited

Bahlul, Raja. 2000. "People vs. God: The Logic of 'Divine Sovereignty' in Islamic Democratic Discourse." *Islam and Christian-Muslim Relations* 11 (3): 287–97. https://doi.org/10.1080/713670332.

Bennabi, Malek. 2017. *Naissance d'une société: Le réseau des relations sociales*. Éditions Benmerabet.

Black, Antony. 2011. *The History of Islamic Political Thought: From the Prophet to the Present*. 2nd ed. Edinburgh: Edinburgh University Press.

Brague, Rémi. 1992. *Europe, la voie romaine*. Paris: Criterion.

Bras, Jean-Philippe. 2015. "Introduction." In *Faire l'histoire du droit colonial: Cinquante ans après l'indépendance de l'Algérie*, edited by Jean-Philippe Bras, 9–22. Paris: Karthala.

Braudel, Fernand. 1949. *La Méditerranée et le Monde méditerranéen à l'époque de Philippe II*. Paris: Librairie Armand Colin.

Charfi, Abdelmajid. 2004. *L'Islam entre le message et l'histoire*. Paris: Albin Michel.

Filali-Ansary, Abdou. 1999. *L'Islam est-il hostile à la laïcité?* Casablanca: Éditions Le Fennec.

Shariʿati, ʿAli. 1979. "The Philosophy of History: Cain and Abel." In *On the Sociology of Islam*, translated by Hamid Algar, 97–118. Berkeley, CA: Mizan Press.

Shariʿati, ʿAli. 1986. *What Is to Be Done: The Enlightened Thinkers and an Islamic Renaissance*. Edited by Farhang Rajaee. Houston, TX: The Institute for Research and Islamic Studies (IRIS).

Preface

Missed Opportunities in Islam's Relations with Western Civilization

Abdelmajid Charfi

There was a time, in ancient and medieval history, when relations between opposing powers on the southern and northern shores of the Mediterranean were not too unequal: despite wars and other forms of conflict, the two sides knew that the supremacy of one side or the other would only be temporary, even if *temporary* could mean several centuries, as was the case with Carthage and Rome, the Crusades, and the Muslim presence in Sicily and Spain.

In the modern age, these relations are no longer on an equal playing field. The Western world has gained a historic lead in every field—not only military but also, especially, scientific, technical, and even political and social.

It is an error to say that all civilizations are the same. There are cycles where one civilization gains the upper hand and surpasses the others, benefiting from those that preceded it. Modern civilization, born in Europe, has now become universal, but even if it generally only acknowledges its Greco-Roman and, in recent years, its Judeo-Christian heritage, it has benefited from a variety of previous cultures, including Islamic culture.

Imperialist Europe certainly brought some material progress to the colonized regions, but it also brought subjugation and exploitation, which undeniably outweighed the progress. In this sense, this civilization has not been true to its own values—freedom, equality, and human rights, among others. Colonialists even fostered the most archaic structures, such as Maraboutism and the outdated Sharia law.

To be sure, some attempts were made to move in the opposite direction, the most famous of which was the somewhat chimeric project of the "Arab Kingdom," supported by Napoleon III under a policy aimed at Arab-French cooperation. But these attempts all came to naught.

What has often been concealed is that colonization blocked numerous attempts at modernization in the southern Mediterranean countries. The best-known example was the effort to create a textile industry in Egypt, an initiative that was nipped in the bud to avoid competition with the British industry.

In Tunisia, the foreign powers representing French and European finance could have acted less as raptors by refraining from knowingly supporting

DOI: 10.4324/9781003431206-2

corrupt politicians, this just as an undeniable modernist movement was getting underway in a whole range of fields, including science and culture.

Even after the political decolonization of the 1950s and 1960s, French and European powers hardly fostered the development of a North-African industry, seeing the Maghreb and the rest of the Arab world as no more than a market for their manufactured goods and a source of energy and recently as a roadblock to sub-Saharan migration.

Among the former colonial powers there persists a neocolonialist mentality, as is evidenced not only by the invasion of Iraq but also by the blatant support for Islamists in Syria and the ambivalent support for the civil war in Algeria and especially in Tunisia after the Jasmine Revolution of January 2011.

There is, then, no lack of missed opportunities in the encounter with Western civilization, and among them one cannot fail to mention the unconditional support for Israel in its dispossession of the Palestinian territories, so much so that challenging the legitimacy of the Zionist entity and of its alleged right to existence in the northern Mediterranean countries is taboo, for fear of being accused of antisemitism.

Where does Islam stand in all this? From Islam—as well as from all religious traditions, especially monotheistic ones—we should expunge all essentialist visions. We would then realize that internal or external conflicts fought in its name—or in the name of illegitimate Zionist myths—do not have a religious origin. Its problems, like those of other traditions, stem from the difficulty it faces in adapting to a world that is very different from the one it was born in and in which its theology and cultural and social practices developed.

Today, with globalization and the rise of China and India, it is time to rethink relations between an aging Europe and its southern neighbours, so that the latter can let go of their reservations about their northern neighbours, who in turn can help them rid themselves of their strife and their anachronistic political and social structures and resolve the Israeli-Palestinian conflict in compliance with all international resolutions. Unfortunately, decision-makers on both shores are a long ways from this way of thinking.

Part I

Islam and the Encounter with Western Civilization

1 Islam

A Changing Religious Institution in the Era of Globalization*

Abdelmajid Charfi

1. Introduction

The topic of discussion here is one that generally sits silent, because when it is broached it meets with opposition. In fact, on more than one occasion we have heard the simple existence of a religious institution in Islam being flatly denied.

Because space is short, I will not expound on the characteristics of the religious institution in Islam, considering as well that I believe these characteristics to be familiar, at least in broad outline. I will instead begin by illustrating a distinction of great significance to our present era, and I am not making a historical point here. This is the distinction between religion as an institution in Islam and in Christianity, particularly in the Catholic Church, where it is clearly structured as a hierarchical institution.

Throughout the West, particularly in France, a core concern of the modern state, its idée fixe, was to escape the hegemony of the religious institution. The struggles between the Church and political regimes revolved around the question of who took precedence in governing public affairs. In the Islamic religious landscape, in Sunnism in particular, things are very different, considering that political power largely succeeded—and continues to succeed—in taming the religious institution. As a result, the struggles we see in our time are the converse of those that took place in the West. At the root of these struggles is not a desire to break free from the hegemony of the Church; rather, it is the religious institution that is seeking a form of independence from political power. The difference is not insignificant, and in my opinion it goes a good way toward explaining the challenges faced by this institution, which is not structured on the hierarchical model of the Church. This is evident at the political level, but it is at bottom a social and cultural reality.

* This is a translation of Abdelmajid Charfi, "Le mutazioni dell'istituzione religiosa islamica nell'era della globalizzazione," in *Raccontarsi e lasciarsi raccontare: Esperimenti di dialogo islamo-cristiano*, ed. Andrea Pacini, Kindle ed. (Venice: Marsilio, 2018), in turn a translation, by Martino Diez, of "Tahawwulāt al-mu'assasa al-dīniyya fī zaman al-'awlama," a talk that Charfi delivered in Tunis on 29 November 2014 at a conference on religious institutions and globalization organized by the association Mu'minūn bilā hudūd (Believers without Borders). All footnotes are by Martino Diez.

DOI: 10.4324/9781003431206-4

2. The Decline of the Ulema

There is no historical model or example that we can look to today in the attempt to body forth the religious institution in Islam today, and this lack of precedents is among the most serious difficulties this institution faces in claiming independence or freedom from control of the state and from political power. This is especially true if we consider that since at least the last six centuries, since the time of Ibn Khaldūn,[1] this institution has been losing its original moral suasion and force, with which it could exert influence in the political sphere. Ibn Khaldūn makes it clear that while men of religion—the ulema of his time, the representatives of Islam as a religious institution—received great praise on public occasions, that is all they received. In other words, political governance moved on regardless of their opinions.

Of course, when it came to organizing social life, particularly personal statuses, the ulema enjoyed great prestige and influence. However, the weight they carried in the life of society itself gradually waned as political power looked to other models, different from those of religion. As Hmida Ennaifer has commented, while the representatives of the religious institution exerted a *sense-making* influence, at least among the people, its influence in political life was nonexistent.

In our age, even before the rise of modern media, the ulema's diminishing credibility and influence has taken an even greater hit, and it has done so for one fundamental reason: positive law has begun to supplant the norms of Islamic jurisprudence (*fiqh*), such that the fundamentals of social life have to a considerable extent been removed from the control of religious leaders. These leaders have been facing competition from parliaments and state institutions that legislate without regard to the substantive norms of Islamic jurisprudence. Of course, enacted positive law may *formally* make reference to religious sources, but most of the laws enacted in Islamic countries are just that, namely, positive law. The only exception is the law of personal status, but even here the extent of that exception varies across regions and political contexts. There is no doubt that this state of affairs adds to the difficulty of wresting oneself free of political tutelage. In other words, if the Islamic religious institution could still significantly influence social life through Islamic jurisprudence, perhaps it would have greater leeway and could engage with political leaders and power on an equal footing. But that is not how things stand today.

3. Traditional Islam and Islamism: Competition, Rivalry, Imitation

The picture just outlined isn't complete until we note that the official religious institution faces competition as well from other institutions, formations, and social structures (such as parties, associations, and various organizations) which

1 This is the great 14th-century Arab historian, philosopher, and sociologist (1332–1406).

also speak in the name of Islam but which have different reference points than the religious official institution. All the movements we call "Islamist," "activist Islam," and the like are in competition with the official religious institution. Here it is well worth underscoring the basic difference between the religious learning propagated by these new currents and the real yet mostly fossilized learning offered by traditional institutions. We very well know that the ulema of the Azhar, Zaytāna, and Qarawiyyìn schools,[2] unlike their students, staunchly defended a type of teaching almost exclusively confined to commenting and glossing and were unwilling to renew the textbooks, whether in content or in expository form. But even if the teaching they worked to preserve was traditional and largely frozen—as there was no possibility of adding to what the ancients had said—it still allowed the various expressions of religion or religiosity to be relativized. For this reason, the positions defended by this traditional elite were tolerant toward divergent opinions, this in contrast to the newer structures and institutions born in particular with the Muslim Brotherhood movement of the 1920s: these institutions were not distinguished by any profound knowledge of religious texts, or by any solid and direct mastery of the modern human and social sciences, or finally by any ability to relativize the truths they upheld. So they did not embody anything like the spirit of tolerance usually demonstrated by the leaders of the traditional religious institution. As I see it, this difference is very important, because it explains the reasons for the fracturing the religious institution is seeing today.

The observations so far made in reality apply to both the modern age and our own time. But with globalization comes another phenomenon that is not always given due attention: the phenomenon of "privatization." In ancient times, as we have seen, the political institution and the religious institution coexisted, and even though they were not always cooperating, they both recognized that the state is entrusted with organizing collective life. With globalization, which was initially economic but then ended up infesting every aspect of life, we have begun to see nonstate entities come into the picture—capital, multinational corporations, and external forces, regional and international, encroaching on the sphere of the religious institution so as to make it an instrument or at least an executor of their policies. This can only further chip away at the already low credibility of the religious institution.

If, for example, we compare the state of affairs twenty or thirty years ago with the state of affairs today, in both the Islamic and the Christian world, we will notice that religious associations and organizations have sprung up that are very well resourced, equipped with modern means of influence, and skilled at using all forms of media, behind which lie economic forces. This is clearly illustrated, for example, by evangelical Christian movements. In Latin America, once considered a stronghold of Catholicism, evangelical movements

2 These are the three great traditional centres of Islamic study, based in Cairo, Tunis, and Fes, respectively.

represent 30 percent of believers and are backed by multinational corporations and the American right. Their influence is also noticeable in Africa. They do not believe in the nation-state, and they serve capitalist interests, which do not know any geographic boundaries.

The same exact phenomenon can be observed in the Islamic world, in which there are at work faith-based movements that do not necessarily answer to any state. A case in point is Wahhabism, which is among the most active faith-based movements in Africa, and even if its birthplace and traditional home is the Arabian peninsula and it is the dominant faith in Saudi Arabia, the support it gets does not always come directly from the Saudi government; rather, the bulk of the support comes from businessmen and wealthy men from Saudi Arabia and the other Gulf states backing Wahhabite religious organizations and institutions that act in competition with traditional ones in service of privatizing and fracturing the public space—and little does it matter whether the service is witting or unwitting. These groups recognize existing states in a purely formal way, in effect operating on a transnational basis.

4. A Hybrid Religiosity

Among the most significant consequences of the state of affairs just outlined is that of "spiritual bricolage": in the Islamic countries and regions where this brand of preaching is spreading, those who adhere to it, following the teachings of the new preachers, find themselves having to simultaneously draw on what the leaders of traditional religious institutions say, while also bringing in a third component from outside the Islamic space. This results in tripartite forms of *hybrid* religiosity whose features are no longer the neatly defined ones of traditional religiosity, in which we can clearly distinguish white from black. These forms of religiosity are also stereotyped, with much emphasis placed on rituals, which need to be at once proper to each form and collective, eliciting fear of failure to perform them correctly, for they do not distinguish between fundamental cultic prescriptions, such as prayer and fasting, from practices of social religiosity, such as the proper manner of bathing the dead and burying them or the obligation for women to cover their hair and their separation from male society.

At the same time, globalization also means loss of meaning. Which is to say that, sometimes as a consequence and sometimes as a cause, the fracturing just mentioned intersects with the loss of meaning experienced by many social classes, particularly those who undergo sudden processes of urbanization, as a result of which they lose their traditional ties and become elusive to the social control which the Islamic religious institution played such an important part in exercising. And the loss is even more damaging considering that the sense of attachment to this institution was constitutively bound up with their sense of identity. This loss of meaning explains why so many flock to the new movements and institutions. Compounding the sense of loss is the digital revolution and the spread of modern means of communication, whose effect is to facilitate the plurality of ideas and opinions and the ways of expressing them, inevitably leading to an unconscious bricolage and confusion in the minds of young people, who find themselves losing their bearings among competing and discordant opinions. In extreme cases this clears the ground for them to join violent totalitarian movements, especially religious ones.

One such institution that has no connection with the official religious institution is the Islamic State of Iraq and the Levant (ISIL/Da'esh). These institutions of contestation, proselytizing, revolution—call them what you will—are far removed in their aims and practices from the characteristics of the traditional religious institution, be it official or oppositional. If we take a look at the practices of the Islamic State—such as the barbaric use of corporal punishment, the torture of dissidents, the beheadings, and the enslavement of women—it wouldn't be too much of an exaggeration to regard them as expressions of a newfangled religion that has detached itself from the main strain of Islam, in the manner of the Bahāʾī Faith, to take one example.[3] This newfangled religion of the Islamic State sits at the opposite end of the spectrum from the historical institutions of Islam. There is no better demonstration of this than the fact that a good proportion of those who rally under the banner of this "state" are not Muslims by birth but have joined this movement from all corners of the earth to escape the loss of sense and marginalization they experienced at home.

5. Antimodern Forces

A peculiarity that seems noteworthy to me is that, like the traditional religious institution, all the nontraditional movements we have been considering place the primary emphasis on the communal dimension, on what they consider to be the good of the group and of the Islamic community as a whole, rather than on the individual and the authenticity of individual feeling and sentiment in matters of faith. This means that these institutions run inherently counter to the general trend of our age toward individualism—not to be confused with self-interest. In this sense they can be said to act as countervailing forces against the central role that in our time is broadly accorded to the individual and to the values of individual choice and of diversity.

We are therefore dealing with a complex situation, in which there is no longer the clear divide between opposing camps that was characteristic of ancient times. This in itself is already a sign of the challenge that religious institutions face in meeting the demands of our age, of what we call modernity, namely, the model of civilization in which there is no separation between the new values associated with human rights—such as freedom, equality, and democracy—and material achievements. These achievements are unquestioningly embraced, sometimes even unwittingly, by the institutions we are talking

3 The Bahāʾī Faith grew out of an Islamic context in the mid-19th century and eventually developed into an independent religion. Of course, Charfi is not comparing the practices of the Bahāʾīs—who *reject* violence—to those of the Islamic State. The point of commonality here is simply that both movements originated in Muslim lands.

about, so much so that I couldn't point to any objection that has been raised against them. At the same time, however, these very institutions reject almost unreservedly the gnosiological demands and values that form an essential part of modern civilization. This rejection is justified under the guise of resistance to Westernization, opposition to secularism, the need to protect against the threat to self-identity, and the like. I will not enter into the merits of these charges, which are well known, but I will point out that behind this rejection—whatever its justification and however contradictory it may be—lies a deliberate stance that comes through very clearly, and that is precisely the stance taken against the values of our age and its material achievements.

I can thus, in conclusion, home in on an important consequence: the difficulties experienced by religious institutions—official, traditional, and novel—stem from the difficulty that Islamic religious thought has been experiencing for the past two centuries in renewing its categories. The foundations of traditional religiosity are still standing, and all these movements are struggling to revise some of the postulates of the past, that is, to develop a constructive critique of traditional knowledge, whether it is aimed the age of decadence or at the practices of the so-called pious ancestors (*al-salaf al-ṣāliḥ*).[4] The starting point is always the glorification of some part of the religious tradition in the name of a supposedly lost purity, and this is why in our age the Islamic religious institution, in all its variety, fails to connect with the public as a whole, no longer commanding the allegiance it once did. To be sure, the institution does show itself to be capable of polarizing groups, small and large alike, by attracting staunch adherents to itself, but in relation to Muslim believers as a whole it remains a collection of divergent and sometimes conflicting movements and institutions, incapable of offering Muslims as a whole a model in which they can find an answer to the new and unprecedented challenges of our time, specifically when it comes to the need for values and knowledge.

A renewal of Islamic thought may perhaps make it possible to transcend this fractured condition and advance toward a state of affairs in which regular Muslims are generally self-satisfied and psychologically at ease, leaving behind the feeling of being threatened and the sense that their faith may go astray at any moment in the face of the powerful forces that are driving the new globalization. We are well aware that this hoped-for religious renewal stands in a dialectical relation to the modernization of a whole range of structures—economic, political, educational, and the like—but there is no way to proceed other than by taking on the challenges as a whole, without isolating one at the expense of the others. Otherwise, modernization will remain irreparably stunted—limited and largely unsuccessful—as has been the experience of Arab and Muslim societies over the past two centuries.

4 These are the first three generations of Muslims, whose model is held up as an ideal—and is idealized—in matters of religious faith and practice.

2 Civilizational Thought and the Building of Societies

A Comparison Between Malek Bennabi and ʿAli Shariʿati

Siham Cherif

1. Introduction

When the idea of an Islamic renaissance was introduced as a label for a new phase in Arab and Islamic life in 1798 (during the Egyptian expedition), it was mixed in its structure and content, with an implicit form that sees this renaissance as a global "intellectual coup" in Arab and Islamic life, even if it has a diluted form called restoration, a form through which the idea was subsequently once more renewed. The idea expresses a demand that Arab and Islamic culture be developed into a new culture with its own components and a fresh global vision, as is the case with secular and liberal demands, however heterogeneous they may be. But the point here is not to criticize the different intellectual demands that sprang from this vision but rather to analyse the intellectual backgrounds and perspectives that resulted from the dominant form of this renaissance.

So, what is the reality of that implicit intellectual form that made the Islamic renaissance look like a global intellectual coup in Arab life, even as the concept of a renaissance is logically based on a historical and civilizational fulcrum that elevates the nation by contributing to its historical and civilizational sustainability? Every intellectual practice is based on direct or implicit elements contributing to a global vision that fashions this practice into a model capable of giving life a particular meaning. These elements are complementary, converging into a historical and philosophical vision and system under which existence gains a continuity of time and place.

What in the 19th century led to the renaissance form referred to, with all its characteristics—a renaissance at once praised and attacked—was a failure of the Arab and Islamic system. Out of this failure there emerged a new concept of time and a new philosophy of history. This dynamic lies at the core of Arab life, whose volatile cycles of intellectual production and political ideology lay the groundwork for the social revolutions of the next phase.

The elements of Western culture that created modernization amount to what in the Islamic renaissance literature is referred to as a shock. This is because in the renaissance phase there was no single point from which to tap into the Arab and Islamic intellectual system in such a way as to make it possible to settle on any single concept of development.

DOI: 10.4324/9781003431206-5

Western civilization is based on a multifaceted system of knowledge and values that established the modern world: the system is plural, but its elements complete one another to form a coherent picture in which the human being figures as a source of existence and of absolute value. In the modern intellectual context, human existence is an alternative to the divine that occupies a central place in ancient civilization.

In the Arab and Islamic world, access to modernization meant access not to a selection of loosely related ideas but to an entire system of thought with radical ideas that would contribute to a big transformation in modern Arab ideology. The first reformers offered various solutions to a range of social, political, and religious questions. This is the context in which we need to fit the conceptions developed by Malek Bennabi and ʿAli Shariʿati: their work and thought is critical and innovative, considering that, like their predecessors, they revisited a range of concepts, principles, and situations in an attempt to effect reforms through which to address the problem of the Islamic world coming apart at the seams.

2. Two Different but Like-minded Individuals

2.1. Who Is Malek Bennabi?

Malek Bennabi was born in 1905 in Tébessa, Algeria. He attended primary and secondary school in Tébessa and Constantine. He wrote a memoir in which he cast himself as "witness to the century" (Bennabi [1966] 1970, 1984) and received a religious and social education in the tradition of the Qurʾān and the old Algerian school. His primary education was in French. As a young boy, he pursued his talents, indulging his illusions and naivete, by reading the work of Western intellectuals like Pierre Loti[1] and especially Claude Farrère.[2] This led him to look to the teachings of thinkers like Sheikh El-Mouloud Ben Mihoub, engaging with theological writings on monotheism that, by Bennabi's own account, strengthened his enthusiasm (Bennabi 1984, 90).

Bennabi travelled to Paris in September 1930 and took an exam to gain admission to the Oriental Studies Institute, but he was rejected for political reasons. While in Paris, he began to gradually familiarize himself with many of the practical aspects of European life, especially of the French community. As he reminisced,

> in my wanderings, my interests took me to the Arts and Industry Museum near Saint Donice, where I stayed up at night reflecting for the first time on the technological aspects of civilization. Among the museum's

1 Pierre Loti (1850–1923), né Louis Marie-Julien Viaud, was a French writer and naval officer.
2 Claude Farrère (1876–1957), né Frédéric-Charles Bargone, was a French essayist, historian, and novelist.

> masterpieces, which I stood there observing, were the first steam locomotive and the plane that flew Louis Blériot across the English Channel.
>
> (Bennabi 1984, my translation)

He was not an introverted scholar. He would exchange thoughts with some French bourgeois families, commenting that this enabled him to glimpse European life from within a family environment, and this was unlike what he could witness from Algeria.

In Paris, Bennabi joined a French Christian youth organization run by young students and working people in response to their needs, and this is how he became a Muslim advocating for his religious vision directly in this organization, contributing to what he saw as a mutually enriching exchange of views and opinions.

He could not join the Oriental Studies Institute, because the entrance exam contained a liberal arts module that as an Algerian Muslim he would not be allowed to pass. He would later recollect that

> the exams were not difficult, so I was disappointed that I did not pass, and that was all. Even the director summoned me to persuade me that it is hopeless to gain admission to the Oriental Studies Institute, especially for an Algerian Muslim, who, for political reasons, will not be able to pass a liberal arts module.
>
> (Ibid., my translation)

Afterward, he studied engineering at the École Spéciale de Mécanique et d'Électricité (ESME Sudria) in Paris. He revealed that here, after his experience with the religious youth group l'Union Chrétienne des Jeunes Gens de Paris de la Rue Trévise, he found a different angle from which to access Western civilization, and he could pursue his passion for investigating methods with which to develop his society along a civilizational path. While studying, he would exchange ideas with his peers in the Latin Quarter, engaging in discussions on thinkers such as Nietzsche and Spinoza. He earned a degree in electrical engineering in 1935.

In 1931 he married a French woman. She was persuaded by him to convert to Islam. Through her influence he developed an aesthetic sense, and she also introduced him to a larger intellectual and cultural milieu in Paris, where he met Shakib Arslan,[3] as well as Gandhi. Bennabi lived in Europe for more than thirty years. This enabled him to gain a deeper self-understanding and to free himself from the Western cultural enterprise in developing his own

3 Shakib Arslan was an Arab historian and an emir in Lebanon. He was a leader in the national Arab movement and had an important role in promoting the Arab unit. Arslan also advanced progressive causes for the benefit of social justice. He founded the Syrian National Party in 1932. He created a system for protecting Arab children. His legacy includes his role in shaping the political history of the Middle East.

ideology, even if his engagement with Western civilization was deep-rooted and from it he drew inspiration. This is an engagement he developed through his humanistic study as well as through his exchanges with public figures and intellectuals.

3. Who Is ʿAli Shariʿati?

ʿAli Shariʿati is a famous Iranian Shīʿa thinker. His full name is Ali Muhammad Takī Shariʿati. He was born near Mashhad, Iran, in 1933 and earned a degree in literature in 1955. In 1959, he was selected as part of a delegation to Paris, France, where he pursued a PhD in Islamic history and sociology. In his youth, in 1953, he joined the National Front of Iran, founded by Mohammad Mosaddegh. He worked as a teacher and was arrested twice in college. In 1969, on his return from France, he founded the Husseiniyat Al-Irshad youth association, which would later be shut down by the authorities.

Shariʿati ranks among the most important thinkers in the Iranian Islamic movement. His thinking and action played a significant role in the intellectual and political mobilization that preceded the Iranian Revolution of 1979, so much so that he came to be known as the "Ideologue of the Iranian Revolution." While still in his youth, in the late 1940s, he joined with his father a political movement led by a group of left-wing Iranian intellectuals who called themselves "Allah-Worshipping Socialists." It was with his father that, while still in high school, he joined the National Front. After Mosaddegh's overthrow, he joined the National Resistance Movement founded by Ayatollah Zanjani, Ayatollah Taleghani, and Mehdi Bazargan, a movement that would later be violently suppressed. In 1964, while a member of the movement, Shariʿati was imprisoned for six months on his return from Paris. He died in 1977 in London at the age of 43, two years before the Iranian Revolution.

Shariʿati's oeuvre is highly regarded by researchers and intellectuals, with an output of more than a hundred works (including the lectures posthumously published as books by his students), ranging across a broad spectrum of genres: philosophical, literary, political, and revolutionary.

4. The Concept of Civilization According to Malek Bennabi and ʿAli Shariʿati

Both Bennabi and Shariʿati had lives full of experiences and were patient, courageous, and skilful in carrying forward a powerful intellectual project. Their ideologies were formed in response to the issues that confronted their home countries—Algeria and Iran—taking a civilizational approach applicable to all Islamic countries. For a long time, Bennabi lived in France, where he studied electrical engineering; as mentioned, Shariʿati also studied in France, majoring in sociology, and through these experiences they both acquainted themselves with Western thought and with Oriental civilizations, particularly those of China and Japan.

The intellectual legacy they passed down is varied. Bennabi wrote his works in Algeria, France, and Egypt; some of them were in French; others were translated into Arabic. Shariʿati's works have come down to us mostly through their translations from the Persian. And, as mentioned, they covered a lot of ground. Our focus here, however, is on their concept of civilization—or what it is to be "civilized," looking at the way they critically understood this concept in addressing the civilizational question. In fact, this idea was central to their inquiries, so much so that Bennabi came to be known as the philosopher or doctor of civilization, and the major works by Shariʿati that were translated into Arabic dealt with the history of civilization.

They take a coordinated objective approach to civilization, understanding it as a concept at once descriptive and prescriptive. On the one hand, it is a concept used in the practical discourse through which we refer to civilizations and address civilizational issues; on the other hand, it acts as an ideology and normative standard through which to critique the idea of people as humans and as part of an international human community with a collective history.

But now we have to ask whether Bennabi and Shariʿati are talking about two different concepts of civilization or a single one. We also want to know how they consequently viewed the relation between a civilization and its intellectuals and their views about religion, politics, society, and the economy, as well as between civilization and the human dimension broadly. Once we answer those questions, we can discuss the features of the civilizational perspective.

As mentioned, the concept of civilization is central to Bennabi's intellectual project, for he came to see that the issues faced by any group of individuals cannot be divorced from their civilization. He accordingly sought to identify the main questions revolving around the concept of civilization and to understand how civilizations rise and fall: "Civilization is the main question for any people, which means that they cannot make sense of human events outside a civilizational frame, making it essential to understand the factors contributing to the establishment or collapse of civilizations" (Bennabi [1948] 2016, 20, my translation). And in identifying these factors—or what the components of civilization are—he came up with an equation that we might call the equation of civilization:

Civilization = man + land + time (Bennabi [1962] 2017, 33)

What this equation means is that there are three main questions: the question of man (the human being), the question of land (place), and the question of time (how civilizations change over time).

Bennabi also offered a functional definition of civilization as "the overall outcome of the moral and material conditions necessary for individuals to grow at each stage in life, from childhood to old age, within a society capable of securing those conditions" (Bennabi 1991d, 43, my translation).

Importantly as well, civilization, as Malek understands it, is not just a concept that describes this or that society: it is an overarching idea that links all human civilizations, from the earliest ones to those that will emerge in the future, in a single chain that makes up the human epic. And in this chain we each play our own role, forming our own civilizational link. But this also means that every civilization rises out of the collapse of the previous one.

Shariʿati, for his part, defines the civilization as a fertile and productive land where anyone is enabled to come and be free. We are civilized to the extent that (a) we have a land that we can claim as our own and (b) we can develop our own abilities (cf. Miri 2016).

Shariʿati argued that civilization arises out individual and societal components that complement one another: on the individual level, we have the ability to think critically, with a sense of personal independence and a correlative right to self-determination and depth and kindness of spirit; on the societal level, we have the sense of responsibility, the idea of culture as a treasure, and the ability open up to new visions, find a historical and social conscience, and commit to the future, achieving intellectual and doctrinal progress (ibid.).

A concept that Shariʿati views as connected with civilization is that of urbanism, arguing that this is ultimately a state of mind: it is moral and spiritual, not material. Urbanism, in other words, is not measured in technological progress and material well-being. For we may lack these conditions and still call ourselves "urban" if our culture, ideology, sensitivity, conscience, scholarship, and way of thinking make us urban.

5. Malek Bennabi and ʿAli Shariʿati in Comparison

Let us now compare Bennabi's and Shariʿati's understandings of civilization from six perspectives: (a) cultural, (b) societal, (c) religious, (d) political, (e) economic, and (f) humanistic.

5.1. The Cultural Perspective

Bennabi defines the culture as

> a set of moral qualities and social values which shape us from birth and which unconsciously become the relation that links our behaviour to the form of life distinctive to the place where we are born, an environment through which we are enabled to develop our personality.
>
> (Bennabi 1991c, 75, my translation)

This is a truly global understanding of culture: it is what a civilization reflects itself in, and it is the space in which civilized individuals move. So, there are two indispensable components to this definition: that of individual philosophy and that of collective philosophy, and the two interact, lighting the spark from which a new civilization is born. Likewise, there is an interaction between individual behaviour and the form of life distinctive to each society: it is partly through this interaction that individuals flourish in different roles—the artist, the shepherd, the scientist, the imam—and this is what makes civilization special.

Culture, as Bennabi understands it, is not specific to any particular social class: it is the foundation that an entire society needs to achieve diversity and enable people to develop. It is what prevents us from falling from the bridge. It offers a broad base of meaning that the shepherd and the scientist alike can rely on. It therefore belongs to all social classes and shapes the social structure. It is in this sense public as a source of guidance that enables all social classes to achieve an equilibrium. This is the equilibrium of civilization that culture is historically entrusted with ensuring (ibid., 78).

Shariʿati likewise drew a distinction between civilization and culture. Civilization is the moral and material structure that sustains peoples, ethnicities, and nations and, like Bennabi, he understood civilization as a broad, inclusive concept rather than as a concept specific to any particular people, ethnicity, or nation: it takes in the whole of humanity. This means that, in his view, we cannot speak of an Islamic, Christian, Oriental, or Western civilization but only of civilization in this or that century. And in contrast to civilization, with its broad sweep, stands culture, which is place- and people-specific and therefore particular.

But this understanding of civilization as a general concept of universal reach that encompasses the whole of humanity should not be taken to mean that there is a single model of civilization that everyone across the world is to recognize and follow. In fact, as Bennabi points out, this has been the Western conceit since the 8th century, with intellectuals of all sorts (writers, artists, historians, sociologists), as well as officials and revolutionaries, working to impose just such a model on the rest of the world, on the premise that "everyone who wants to be civilized must follow the civilization that we in the West created: if they refuse, they will continue to be primitive and barbaric, because there is one and only one culture—the Western one" (Bennabi 2012, my translation).

5.2. The Societal Perspective

Bennabi has a dynamic conception of modern society, understood not just as a group of people but as an organization with a human character based on a structure that stands on three pillars: "persons, ideas, and objects, where ideas are regarded as more significant than objects" (Dangor 2000, 126), and it is through this force (the third pillar) that societies become dynamic, always in flux—because ideas change, and with them so does society—but always cyclically, going through stages of "birth and ascendancy, expansion, and disintegration" (ibid.).

In the same way, Shariʿati sees society not as a simple collection of individuals but as a structured whole. Even if his analysis is not Marxist, he does distinguish a base structure of society from its superstructure: the base structure consists of society's material composition, which combines with the spiritual factors that make each society unique in giving expression to the individual, in whom these factors are reflected.

5.3. *The Religious Perspective*

For Bennabi, religion plays a significant role in the making of civilizations, for it is through the religious experience that we gain the ability to build the three basic components in the equation of civilization: man, land, and time. Whether directly or through any alternative set of atheist ideas, religion shapes these three structural components.

For Shariʿati, religion plays a comparable role in society, but he views it as a revolutionary force, through which people can develop a critical understanding of their material and moral environment. Through this understanding, they in turn gain a sense of responsibility in relation to the current state of affairs, and by acting on this sense of responsibility they are prompted to think about changing this state of affairs for the better in the process building their civilization.

5.4. *The Political Perspective*

Bennabi distinguishes between politics and *bolitik*. The latter term is used by the Algerian people to refer to a political system based on nepotism and disinformation, which is used to manipulate the people (Bennabi 1979, 81–83). Politics, by contrast, is a genuine effort to serve the people, and it involves organizing a group of people, where the group, in its political context, is defined by a common place and history—it is in effect a nation, one that builds on those common roots to achieve self-determination. The political work of organizing a group of people to that end also means protecting that work itself, so that people recognize its importance; it consequently also means protecting people and citizens from abuse. But it further means that people and the state need to work together in addressing the social, economic, and cultural issues that confront them, otherwise politics won't be able to direct social resources toward the aim of bringing benefit to the majority of people. It also follows from this conception that politics, properly understood, is less about claiming rights than about doing one's duty to promote the common good.

In much the same vein, Shariʿati draws a distinction between politics and *politique*. Both terms originate from the idea of the *polis*, but whereas *politique* is about the responsibilities of the state in relation to a nation and society as a whole, protecting people and running government, politics, as Shariʿati understands this term, especially in an Oriental context, is about "taming the wild horse," which means elevating people to a higher spiritual, ethical, and intellectual plane so as to promote a better society. But both politics and *politique* have a role to play in society: one is to run government and protect people (*politique*); the other is to lead, providing the guidance needed to achieve that end (Shariʿati 2007b, 52–53).

5.5. *The Economic Perspective*

For Malek, the economy is the backbone of civilization, for he understands the economy not just in a material sense but also in a moral one: it is the set of conditions that sustains society and its material and moral welfare. So, the economy is not just about the total output of goods and services but is also about forming people to acquire the discipline needed to face the problems of society. As a moral force, economics expresses the will of modernity and the ability to pursue the aims of society and indeed of civilization as a whole and the urban structure as one of its pillars (Bennabi [1973] 2022, 1987, 61). On this conception, then, there can be no material progress without the moral civilizational conditions that reveal how that progress can be achieved. Muslim society can in this sense be understood as a "civilizational factory," one through which to discover the moral conditions for the feasibility of material welfare.

For Shariʿati, the economy is likewise a basic element of any civilization. This is why there is a lot research that goes into making the economy more productive and into promoting consumer welfare, but this also means that the economy is inextricably bound up with politics (Miri 2016).

5.6. *The Humanistic Perspective*

The humanistic perspective is about the human being in relation to other human beings engaging with one another for the advancement of humanity. Bennabi approaches this idea from the standpoint of the Muslim and in the context of a Marxist conception, arguing that Muslims have a cultural role to play within an international framework, a role that requires them to embrace a liberal and humanistic vision of wide scope.

Shariʿati similarly stresses the need for Muslims to act in the world from the humanistic perspective of the relationship between human beings, and he is emphatic that this does not mean rejecting Western culture but rather understanding and engaging with it, for, through this interchange, involving as well a comparative study between East and West, we can gain a deeper understanding of ourselves and of civilization as a whole.

6. Two Different but Complementary Conceptions of Civilization

As discussed, Bennabi understands civilization as a dynamic entity that goes through cyclical phases of birth, development, and demise. Shariʿati similarly investigates civilization as a historical process, one that can be predicted. So their two conceptions can be seen as different but complementary. This can be appreciated in their discussion of social, political, religious, and economic questions, with one's discussion of these questions completing the other's and vice versa. And, more broadly, while Bennabi uses these themes to addresses civilization from a cultural angle, Shariʿati does so from a historical angle, outlining a history of civilizations.[4]

The complementarity can also be observed between disciplines as discussed by each author regardless of the other. That is the case with *The Qur'anic Phenomenon* (Bennabi [1946] 2021), which underscores the need for economic theory to work in tandem with political theory, each completing the other.

7. Economics, Religion, Society, and Criticism of the West

Bennabi takes issue with religious men who object to economics as a basis on which to organize society. He argues that economics fall outside the purview of religion. At the same time, however, he argues that while economists cannot be regarded as backward for considering how economics interacts with society, this is not an interaction that can be worked out simply by pointing to the Qur'ān. There is a similar line of criticism which he addresses at Marxism, arguing that the theory collapses all social and human phenomena into economic phenomena, seeking to explain the former in terms of the latter, and this amounts to altogether ignoring society. Nor, in his view, can this relation between economics and society be worked out by turning for help to the Muslim intellectual (Bennabi [1973] 2022, 50).

Shariʿati is similarly critical of religious men, arguing that they were backward in their orientalist criticism of the West and of Western society. But he also thinks that neither sociology not Marxist theory are self-sufficient sciences; neither do they concern themselves with or explain the Third World. He sought to make up for this inadequacy by looking for an unchanging sociological model that would make sense of society without relying on the theory of the Marxist base and superstructure.

8. Culture as a Global Phenomenon

Bennabi predicted early on that globalization would transform culture. He recognized that people do connect to their homeland, establishing deep roots in that way. In the 20th century, however, this bond is no longer as strong as it traditionally has been, so much so that the human conscience—and he thought that this was quite obvious—no longer has a sense of place: it no longer bears any connection with any single land but rather is tied to humanity as a whole and shaped by international events and foreign influences. He even argued that in order to understand culture, we have to look at the long arc of international history, whose course exerts a greater force on the moral and cultural conscience than any local context (Bennabi 1991c, 121).

4 It is worth noting here that even though Shariʿati wrote for an audience intellectuals, his prose was plain, and so his readership was much wider than that: it could even appeal to kids, owing to the simplicity with which he could explain moral concepts and make them concrete.

9. The Role of Sociology: Concrete and Purpose-driven, Not Merely Abstract and Intellectual

As mentioned, Shari'ati studied sociology in Paris, earning a PhD in that discipline in 1963, and in working toward that degree in that context he came to see sociology as a science in which it is essential to merge the theoretical with the practical. He accordingly developed a view of the sociologist as a human scientist, one who is not just versed in theory—trying to fit social facts into a theoretical framework—but who embraces an active role in the very society whose behaviour he or she is investigating. This is a socially responsible role that consists in making sociology useful in responding to the needs of modern society and in working for the people, charting for them a path that would enable them to achieve civilizational maturity.

But it is quite a peculiar conceit that the sociologist should bear a social responsibility and that this responsibility should involve pointing out a path to be followed or a destiny toward which we should work. And, in fact, the editor of *Le chiisme est une responsabilité* (Shari'ati 2007a, 7) observes how this idea of a social responsibility is not unconnected to the ideas developed in that book, with its Shi'ite framing. We can see this not only in his discussion of religious or Islamic ideas such as the imamate, the Hajj (the Pilgrimage), fear of God, and polytheism and monotheism but also in his discussion of justice, patience, tradition, the act of bearing witness, ideology, testimony, and immigration, among other topics and questions. This meant that these ideas, so framed, were bound to have a greater hold on Iranian society than in Europe. In addition, there is trouble that arises in translation with these terms and concepts: they were developed in Western sociology and specifically in the European context of 19th-century industrial society and of the capitalist society of the first quarter of the 20th century, so it is difficult to translate them in such a way that they make sense in contemporary society or outside the European context. And this is a point of criticism for Shari'ati, who argues that these sociological concepts lack the neutrality that sociology claims for them as a purportedly descriptive science. Even sociology has an agenda, no matter how scientific it seeks to be, and this is how Shari'ati justified his conception of the sociologist as someone whose responsibility it is to work for people and help them achieve their civilizational destiny.

10. Conclusion

We have seen that central to the work of both Malek Bennabi and 'Ali Shari'ati is the effort to understand society through a civilizational lens. We have also seen that their approaches differ but in such a way that they can be taken to complement each other. But there is also an overarching unifying statement that can be made about their two approaches, and it is that they are both methodically critical and structural, in that they both weave sociology, political science, and economics together in offering an analysis of society in connection with the question of what *civilization* means and what the path to civilization is. They accordingly both see this concept in historical terms in the context of colonialism. It is in the effort to make sense of that experience that Bennabi developed his civilizational equation and Shariʿati identified the need for a nation to rediscover its roots in order to confront the arrogance behind the colonial enterprise.

This led both Bennabi and Shariʿati to think about the role of religion in society—the former in *The Qur'anic Phenomenon* (Bennabi [1946] 2021), the latter in *The History of Civilization* (Shariʿati 1982b)—and even though they differed in their assessment of that role, they did agree that neither can be understood separately from the other.

I conclude by drawing attention to a little-known African thinker named Sheikh Hamidou Kan who argued that civilization is an art (Yacoub 2004, 152): it is the art through which humans establish and consolidate rules and principles on which basis, in any historical phase, we strive to solve society's problems. In this sense, civilization can be understood as both a vision of what we want to achieve and a structure that constrains our action in view of its consequences, which we have to be aware of in looking for opportunities. And it is in striving to develop such a vision and make it concrete as a basis on which to solve the problems of society that Bennabi and Shariʿati both innovated and complemented each other.

Malek Bennabi and ʿAli Shariʿati: A Combined Annotated Bibliography

Following is a selection of works by Malek Bennabi and ʿAli Shariʿati arranged in chronological order. Where a work has more than one edition or has a translated edition, those editions are linked by cross-references. The list has been compiled drawing in part on research contained in Jamsari et al. 2023, specifically as concerns some of the entries referring to Bennabi.

Bennabi, Malek. (1946) 2021. *Le phénomène coranique: Essai d'une théorie sur le Coran.* Héritage Éditions. Orig. pub. Algiers: Sharikat al-Nahda li ʾl-tibaʿa wa ʾl-Nashr, 1946. Trans. Bennabi (1983) 2001.
Bennabi, Malek. 1947. *Lebbeik: Pèlerinage de pauvres.* Algériennes en Nahdha. This is a novel—his only one.
Bennabi, Malek. (1948) 2016. *Les conditions de la renaissance.* Éditions Tawhid.
Bennabi, Malek. (1954) 1991. *Vocation de l'Islam.* Translated by Malek Bennabi. Paris: Seuil.
Bennabi, Malek. 1956. *L'Afro-asiatique: Conclusion sur la conférence de Bandoeng.* Algiers: Société d'Édition et de Communication. This work was written on the occasion of the 1955 Bandung Conference of nonaligned countries.
Bennabi, Malek. 1957a. *Mushkilat al-Thaqafah* (The Problem of Culture). Islamic Book Trust. Trans. Bennabi (1971) 1991c.
Bennabi, Malek. 1957b. *Mushkilat al-Afkar fi al-ʿAlam al-Islami* (The Problem of Ideas in the Muslim World). Cairo: Islamic Book Trust. Trans. Bennabi (2003) 2012.
Bennabi, Malek. 1957c. *al-Siraʾ al-Fikri fi al-Bilad al-Mustaʿmarah* (The Ideological Struggle in Colonised Countries). Islamic Book Trust. Orig. pub. in Cairo in Arabic in 1957.

Bennabi, Malek. 1957d. *S.O.S. Algérie (al-Najdah li al-Jaza'ir)*. Islamic Book Trust. In French, published in Cairo in 1957.
Bennabi, Malek. 1958. *Hadith fi al-Bina' al-Jadid* (The New Islamic Edification). Islamic Book Trust. In Arabic, published in Beirut in 1958.
Bennabi, Malek. 1959. *A Talk Given in Beirut About a New Reform*. Cairo: Islamic Book Trust.
Bennabi, Malek. 1960a. *Colonization Resorts to Assassination Using Knowledge Methods*. Cairo: Islamic Book Trust.
Bennabi, Malek. 1960b. *Ta'ammulat fi al-Mujtama' al-'Arabi* (Reflections on Arab Society). Cairo: Islamic Book Trust. In Arabic, published in Cairo in 1960.
Bennabi, Malek. 1960c. *The Difficulties of a Sign of Development in Arab Society*. Cairo: Islamic Book Trust.
Bennabi, Malek. 1960d. *In the Battle*. Cairo: Islamic Book Trust.
Bennabi, Malek. (1960e) 2023. *Idée d'un commonwealth islamique*. Héritage Éditions.
Bennabi, Malek. (1962) 2017. *Naissance d'une société: Le réseau des relations sociales*. Éditions Benmerabet.
Bennabi, Malek. 1963a. *Bayn al-Rashad wa al-Tih* (Between Clear Direction and Aimless Wandering). This is an anthology of articles posthumously collected and edited by Umar Masqawi. Some of these articles were originally in French, in which language they were published in newspapers such as *La Revolution Africaine Algeria* and *al-Mujahid*. They were subsequently translated into Arabic and published in this anthology in 1963.
Bennabi, Malek. (1963b). 1993. "Perspectives Algériennes. The Algerian Perspectives: Islam and Democracy." *Islamic Studies* 32 (2): 149–68. www.jstor.org/stable/20840119.
Bennabi, Malek. 1964. *Discours sur la culture, l'idéologie, et la civilisation (Afaq Jaza'iriyyah / Algerian Horizon)*. Cairo: Islamic Book Trust. This book was originally published in French in Algeria as a collection of three lectures that Bennabi delivered in Algeria looking at the country's role as an independent territory.
Bennabi, Malek. (1966) 1970. *Mémoires d'un témoin du siècle / Mudhakkirat Shahid li al-Qarn* (Memoirs of a Witness to the Century). Cairo: Islamic Book Trust. The first part of this memoir (*al-tifl*) was published in French in Algeria in 1966; the second part (*al-talib*) was published in Arabic in Beirut in 1970. Cf. Bennabi 1984.
Bennabi, Malek. 1967. *Antaj al-Mustashriqin* (The Work of the Orientalists). Cairo: Islamic Book Trust. In French. Published in Algeria in 1967.
Bennabi, Malek. 1971. *Mushkilat al-Thaqafah* (The Problem of Culture). Translated by 'Abd al-Sabūr Shāhīn. Damascus: Dār al-Fikr. Cf. Bennabi 1957a; trans. Bennabi 1991c.
Bennabi, Malek. 1972. *The Ideology of the Islamic World*. Cairo: Islamic Book Trust.
Bennabi, Malek. 1973a. *Dawr al-Muslim wa Risalatuh fi al-Thuluth al-Akhir min al-Qarn al-'Ishrin* (The Role of the Muslim in the Last Third of the 20th Century). Héritage Éditions. Published in Arabic in Damascus in 1973. Cf. Bennabi 1974a.
Bennabi, Malek. (1973b) 2022. *Le musulman dans le monde de l'économie* (The Muslim in the Economic World). Héritage Éditions. داصتقالا ملاع يف ملسملا ،يبن نب كلام (Beirut: Dār al-Fikr, 1987).
Bennabi, Malek. 1974a. *Dawr al-Muslim wa Risalatuh*. Beirut: Dar al-'Ilmiyyah.
Bennabi, Malek. 1974b. *Milad Mujtama', Shabkat al-'Alaqat al-Ijtima'iyyah*. Translated by 'Abd al-Sabūr Shāhīn. Damascus: Dār al-Fikr.
Bennabi, Malek. 1979. *Entre la rectitude et l'égarement*. Beirut: Dār al-Fikr. In French and Arabic.
Bennabi, Malek. 1981. *Wijhat al-'Alam al-Islami* (The Path of the Islamic World). Translated by 'Abd al-Sabūr Shāhīn. Damascus: Dār al-Fikr.
Bennabi, Malek. 1983. *The Qur'anic Phenomenon: An Attempt at a Theory of Understanding the Holy Qur'an*. Translated by Abu Bilal Kirkari. Indianapolis, IN: American Trust Publications. Originally Bennabi (1946) 2021; cf. Bennabi 2001.

Bennabi, Malek. 1984. *Mudhakkirat Shahid li al-Qarn* (Memoirs of a Witness to the Century). 2nd ed. Damascus: Dār al-Fikr. This book is divided into two parts. The first one, covering the years from 1905 to 1930, deals with Bennabi's childhood; the second one, 1930–1939, covers his studies in Paris. Here he gives us a glimpse of events as witnessed by an Algerian observing the scene from backstage, in the process laying out his intellectual vision, giving an account of Islamic civilization up to the edge of modern Western civilization. Cf. Bennabi 1966/1970.

Bennabi, Malek. 1991a. *Islam dalam Sejarah dan Masyarakat.* Translated by Ismail Ahmad. Kuala Lumpur: Dewan Bahasa dan Pustaka.

Bennabi, Malek. 1991b. *Islam in History and Society.* A translation, by Asma Rashid, of *Vocation de l'Islam* (Bennabi 1954). Kuala Lumpur: Berita Publishing.

Bennabi, Malek. 1991c. *Le problème de la culture.* 4th ed. Damas: Dār al-Fikr. Originally Bennabi 1957a; 1971.

Bennabi, Malek. 1991d. *Qaḍāyā Kubrā (Big Questions).* Damascus: Dār al-Fikr.

Bennabi, Malek. 1993. From an anthology collected by Youcef Huseen in the Saudi magazine *El Faysal* (issue no. 196, April 1993, page 7), we gain a sense of the criticism that Malek Bennabi levelled at the modern Western political ideology. The anthology contains the following nine works: Khrushchev and Eisenhower's Open Speech; The State of Islamic Society; Bennabi 1984, Chap. 3 (cf. Bennabi 1966/1970); Social Relationships and Religion's Impact on Them; The Jewish Question; The Mould; Judaism or Christianity; A Study of Christianity; Ideology of the Councils (about the home councils established in Algeria After Independence; some of these writings are in French).

Bennabi, Malek. 1997a. "The Conditions of the Renaissance." Translated by Asma Rashid. *Islamic Studies* 36 (1): 89–95. www.jstor.org/stable/23076084.

Bennabi, Malek. 1997b. "The Conditions of the Renaissance." Translated by Asma Rashid. *Islamic Studies* 36 (4): 643–55. www.jstor.org/stable/23076034.

Bennabi, Malek. 2000. "The Conditions of Renaissance." Translated by Asma Rashid. *Islamic Studies* 39 (3): 463–70. www.jstor.org/stable/23076063.

Bennabi, Malek. 2001. *The Qur'anic Phenomenon: An Essay of a Theory on the Qur'an.* Translated by Mohamed Tahir El-Mesawi. Kuala Lumpur: Islamic Book Trust. Originally Bennabi (1946) 2021; cf. Bennabi 1983.

Bennabi, Malek. 2003. *The Question of Ideas in the Muslim World.* Kuala Lumpur: Islamic Book Trust. Originally Bennabi 1957b; cf. Bennabi 2012.

Bennabi, Malek. 2012. *Le problème des idées dans le monde musulman.* Ozoir-la-Ferrière: Éditions Albourak. Originally Bennabi 1957b; cf. Bennabi 2003.

Bennabi, Malek. 2021. *Textes sur la lutte idéologique: Pour mieux comprendre la guerre invisible.* Foreword by Sadek Sellam. Éditions Héritage.

Bennabi, Malek. n.d. "Damascus Council." This was a series of conferences in Arabic, n.p.

Shariʿati, ʿAli. 1974. *An approach to Understanding Islam.* Houston, TX: Free Islamic Literatures.

Shariʿati, ʿAli. 1978. *Al-Hajj the Fifth Religious Obligation.* Jubilee Press.

Shariʿati, ʿAli. 1979a. *On the Sociology of Islam.* Translated by Hamid Algar. Berkeley, CA: Mizan Press.

Shariʿati, ʿAli. 1979b. *Philosophy of Education.* Tehran: Beʾsat.

Shariʿati, ʿAli. 1980. *Marxism and Other Western Fallacies: An Islamic Critique.* Translated by A. Campbell. Mizan Press.

Shariʿati, ʿAli. 1981. *Man and Islam.* Houston, TX: Free Islamic Literatures.

Shariʿati, ʿAli. 1982a. *Histoire et Destinée.* Paris: Sindbad.

Shariʿati, ʿAli. 1982b. *The History of Civilization.* Vols. 11 and 12 of *Collected Works.* Tehran: Entesharat-e Agah. The two volumes are based on university lectures delivered from 1968 to 1970.

Shariʿati, ʿAli. 1986a. "Shahādat." In *Jihād and Shahādat: Struggle and Martyrdom in Islam*, edited by Maḥmūd Ṭāliqānī, Murtaẓá Muṭahharī, and ʿAli Shariʿati, edited by Mehdi Abedi and Gary Legenhausen. Houston, TX: Institute for Research and Islamic Studies (IRIS).

Shariʿati, ʿAli. 1986b. *What Is to Be Done: The Enlightened Thinkers and an Islamic Renaissance.* Edited by Farhang Rajaee. Houston, TX: Institute for Research and Islamic Studies (IRIS).

Shariʿati, ʿAli. 1993. *Religion Against Religion.* Translated from the Persian by Laleh Bakhtiar. Kazi Publications.

Shariʿati, ʿAli. 2007a. *Le chiisme est une responsabilité.* Translated by Ibrahim Desouki Chita. Beirut: Dar Al-Amir.

Shariʿati, ʿAli. 2007b. *L'enseignement et l'imamat.* 2nd ed. Edited by Hussein Ali Shuaib. Beirut: Dar Al-Amir.

Other Works Cited

Dangor, Suleman. 2000. "Review of a Muslim Theory of Human Society: An Investigation into the Sociological Thought of Malik Bennabi, by Mohamed Tahir El-Mesawi (Kuala Lumpur: Thinker's Library, 1998)." *American Journal of Islam and Society* 17 (2): 126–30. https://doi.org/10.35632/ajis.v17i2.2066.

Jamsari, Ezad Azraai, Jaffary Awang, Mohamad Zulfazdlee Abul Hassan Ashari, Mohd Hafiz Safiai, Anwar Muttaqin, and Md Yazid Ahmad. 2023. "Malek Bennabi and the Development of Human Civilization." *International Journal of Advanced Research (IJAR)* 11 (1): 1746–54. https://doi.org/10.21474/IJAR01/16201.

Miri, Seyed Javad. 2016. "Revisiting Shariati: Probing into Issues of Society and Religion." Chap. 8 in *Debates on Civilization in the Muslim World: Critical Perspectives on Islam and Modernity*, edited by Lutfi Sunar, 226–62. Oxford: Oxford Academic. https://doi.org/10.1093/acprof:oso/9780199466887.003.0009.

Yacoub, Joseph. 2004. *Après les minorités: Une alternative à l'état-nation.* Translated into Arabic by Hussein Omar. Casablanca: Centre Culturel Arabe.

3 Islamic Feminism

The Politics of Representation in Germany

Lana Sirri

Background and Overview

Islamic feminism has gained increasing attention in Germany, with Berlin hosting over a dozen events on the topic in 2016 alone. This chapter focuses on a conference series by the Friedrich Ebert Foundation (Friedrich-Ebert-Stiftung, or FES), which I view as representative of mainstream Western feminism, offering insights into its broader dynamics and implications.[1] The series included three key conferences: (a) *Islamic Feminism: International Approaches*; (b) *Islamic Feminism: A Glance toward Germany—an Exchange of Feminist Concepts and Strategies*; and (c) *Feminism in the Islamic World: An Exploration*.[2] These events must be understood within the broader German context, where media coverage has often emphasized the negative aspects of Muslim life, frequently linking them to gender-based violence. This narrative has contributed to a one-dimensional portrayal of Muslims as a singular, homogenous community (Schiffauer 2014). Additionally, anti-Muslim racism in Germany has taken on a gendered dimension, with feminist rhetoric being used to reinforce stereotypes of Muslims as inherently gender-unequal (Shooman 2014). Public discourse surrounding gender inequality in Muslim communities has further depicted Islam as fundamentally patriarchal and in conflict with German values on gender and sexuality (Amir-Moazami, Jacobsen, and Malik 2011).

1 The FES conferences forming the object of the analysis undertaken in this contribution were held in 2016. Eight years have therefore elapsed—such is the process of academic publication—and yet the material that is being analysed does not appear to be outdated. Indeed, even from a cursory examination of more recent events—one example being the TV show *Lass Uns Reden*, which aired in 2019 on ZDF, one of Germany's main public-service television broadcasters, where journalist Necla Kelek and rapper Reyhan Sahin discussed Islam and feminism—we can appreciate that the main arguments presented in this chapter remain pertinent.

2 This conference series, titled *Islamischer Feminismus*, was organized by the Friedrich Ebert Foundation (FES) in collaboration with the Muslim Women's Alliance for Action (*Aktionsbündnis muslimischer Frauen in Deutschland*, or AmF). It can be accessed via the FES website at www.fes.de/e/islamischer-feminismus-1 (last updated 24 May 2016).

DOI: 10.4324/9781003431206-6

FES is a political foundation affiliated with the Social Democratic Party in Germany, though it operates independently. Its mission is to promote political education and facilitate access to political discourse. However, as my analysis will reveal, it inadvertently reproduces exclusions. I view FES as an agency that seeks to control and normalize Muslims, effectively materializing anti-Muslim racism in Germany. This stems from the FES's approach, which represents Islam and Muslim women's rights as problems to be solved through governmental and biopolitical power techniques. This representation hinges on widely accepted perceptions of an ontological difference between Muslims and Germans: it is a representation rooted in distinctions related to values, norms, historical development, and racial characterizations (Hernandez Aguilar 2017).

Drawing inspiration from Stampnitzky's work on the idea of terrorism, I examine conferences as sites where expert-actors shape the object of knowledge. Stampnitzky (2013) analysed the emergence of "terrorism" as a problem subject to certain forms of knowledge and governance. She refers to Foucault's concept of eventalization, seen as a

> historical process resulting in the diagnosis of a new problem subject to certain forms of knowledge. This is not simply the relabeling of a prior phenomenon but a concrete historical development that makes a problem "subject to thought," and requiring action.
>
> (Ibid., 6)

In other words, conferences such as the FES series are sites where knowledge about Islam and feminism is produced, legitimized, and disseminated. Presentations, discussions, and collaborations at these events contribute to the creation of expertise and the establishment of certain narratives and discourses surrounding Islamic feminism. Building on this, I apply this lens to the study of Islamic feminism, asserting that the emergence of "Islamic feminism" is diagnosed as a new problem subject, and conferences serve as spaces where it is shaped through the production of knowledge.

The programmes and statements of the conference series raise three main critical questions that I aim to address: (a) How is Islamic feminism constructed? (b) How is knowledge on the topic produced and by whom? And (c) who is included or excluded in the process? To answer these questions, I examine event statements on the FES website and the guest speakers' list. My analysis will offer a critical examination of the events, their aims, and their objectives, highlighting the issue of marginalized and underrepresented communities in such international gatherings. Through this exploration, I aim to highlight the significance of comprehending the complexity and diversity of "Islamic feminism." The subsequent three sections delve into each of the FES events, unpacking the issues raised by their respective statements and guest speakers' lists.

The journey into the interplay of Islam and feminism commences with an act of humility, as elucidated by Mahmood (2005), wherein one recognizes the fluidity of cultural translation and acknowledges the potential instability of one's own perceptions when encountering diverse life-worlds. This attitude of humility becomes paramount when discussing "Women in Islam" and the "Muslim Woman," topics that have fascinated Western societies for centuries. Over this time span, Muslim women have been subject to the European colonial imagination and its myriad fantasies (Lazreg 1990). As part of their justification for colonization, European colonizers positioned themselves as liberators of women in Muslim-majority societies through the discourse of women's rights (Ahmed 1992). This discourse, rooted in European colonial history, continues to influence contemporary neo-Orientalist feminist discussions, particularly among Western feminists (Abu-Lughod 2002; Mahmood 2001). Recently, we have witnessed a growing interest in Islamic feminism, an interest often built on the premise that Islam and feminism are fundamentally incompatible. Yet, these discussions persistently revolve around the Muslim woman, her body, and her rights, overshadowing a holistic exploration of both Islam's and Muslim women's complexities.

1. Islamic Feminism: International Approaches

> Islamic feminism—are you stumbling over these words? In the media debate on Islam-related issues, religion comes through mostly as misogynist, most recently in the reports of the [2015–2016] New Year's Eve mass attacks against women in several German cities. The headscarf is and remains controversial in its significance for women, and many critics of Islam cite women's rights as a reason for their criticism of Islam. But, as is so often the case, the reality is more complex. Just as "Islam" does not exist, there can't be any talk of uniform Islamic gender images. And there is both an Islamic tradition in the fight for women's rights and a contemporary landscape of Muslim women today who see themselves as feminists. What exactly is meant by Islamic feminism? What current debates on women's and men's images and gender roles are being discussed in Islamic communities? What ideas of women's rights and equal rights are driving Islamic feminists? These and other questions are the subject of an international symposium organized by the Muslim Women's Alliance for Action (AmF) and the Friedrich Ebert Foundation (FES) We look at different countries of immigration and seek input on similarities and differences in gender images, sociopolitical debates, and concrete everyday issues of coexistence in diversity. You are cordially invited to this symposium.[3]

3 From the poster announcing the first of the three conferences in the AmF/FES series. The conference, held in Berlin on 3 February 2016, was titled *Islamischer Feminismus: Internationale Annäherungen*, and the poster itself (with the conference programme) can be found at https://bit.ly/FES-islamfem-03-02-2016 (opens a PDF file). All poster and FES website translations (from the German original) are my own.

The first conference in this series was focused on international approaches to Islamic feminism. Notably, the event featured speakers from Belgium, France, and the United States. However, it is essential to critically assess the extent of international representation when the primary speakers hail exclusively from Western countries. This phenomenon is not unique to this conference; it reflects a broader trend in academia. Many so-called international events often feature predominantly Western voices. This tendency can be attributed to an Americo-Eurocentric perspective that perceives Western representatives as qualified to speak on behalf of others—a perspective that aligns with Said's (1978) critique of orientalism. This critique emphasizes how Western epistemological traditions produce supposedly objective knowledge about the world, often detached from the context. Said begins his discourse by invoking the renowned remark by Karl Marx which posits that Orientals are incapable of representing themselves and thus rely on external representation.[4] This premise was subsequently dissected by Spivak in her seminal 1988 article "Can the Subaltern Speak?" (Spivak 1988). Building on this critical foundation, Achille Mbembe further extends the scrutiny thus:

> Western epistemic traditions . . . are traditions in which the knowing subject is enclosed in itself and peeks out at a world of objects and produces supposedly objective knowledge of those objects. The knowing subject is thus able, we are told, to know the world without being part of that world and he or she is by all accounts able to produce knowledge that is supposed to be universal and independent of context.
>
> (Mbembe 2015)

In this instance, the presumption is that speakers hailing from Belgium, France, and the United States are tasked with representing the so-called international perspective on Islamic feminism.[5] The act of speaking about, speaking for, and speaking on behalf of the Other, often in their presence, evokes what Barlas (2008, 17) terms the "racial politics of speaking for women of color," a concept rooted in her personal interactions with white feminists. Barlas's expression reflects her profound frustration with feminists who, under the banner of "sisterhood," inadvertently silence women of color. Echoing this sentiment, Lorde ([1984] 2007) sharply criticized an event that was ostensibly designed to address the role of difference in the lives of American women and yet glaringly omitted the inclusion of Black women. She characterized this form of representation as "a particular academic arrogance" (ibid., 110). Drawing here on Lorde's example serves to underscore the enduring decades-long stance of white feminists toward their marginalized counterparts, encapsulating a

4 "They cannot represent themselves; they must be represented" (Marx 1979, 187).

5 My reference to speakers here does not pertain to their nationality or ethnicity but rather to their geopolitical positioning within, and their discourse emanating from, Western societies.

historical perspective on the dynamics of solidarity and representation within the feminist movement.

The label "international" can be seen as a pseudo-international Euro-American concept. Moallem's (2006) critique of feminist scholarship underscores the intertwining of knowledge production with a global system defined by colonial modernity and neocolonial alignment. Within this framework, Western institutions operate, and Mohanty (2003, 172) argues that they are bound by it, fostering what she terms "academic capitalism." This global system, where the West often assumes a central role, shapes the politics of feminist exchange and cross-cultural dialogue. Consequently, it may appear sufficient to organizers to invite speakers from Western countries to represent "international approaches." However, Moallem warns that such internationalization of feminism is rooted in colonial modernity and may overlook power relations and feminist complicity with oppressive regimes:

> [I]nternationalization has never been about any kind of exchange or flow of ideas or the politics of translation, the articulation of transactional moments as moments exposing the inequality of power relations, or even an interrogation of particular forms of cultural exchange, but has rather been a reference to an imagined community of women who are victimized by the universal regime of patriarchy.
>
> (Moallem 2006, 333)

Many conferences adopt a "postcolonial" perspective that can perpetuate the notion that we have moved beyond colonialism and anticolonial struggles. Shohat (1992) highlights how this universalization masks geopolitical differences between colonizing and colonized nations, potentially side-lining non-Western viewpoints. This global system reinforces unequal power relations between geopolitical regions, such as the West and the Rest (Hall 1992). The event organized by FES is an example of how imperialism extends beyond economic control; it also encompasses knowledge production and the valuation of specific types of knowledge. When conferences like this one claim to explore the intricate reality of Islamic feminism from an "international" standpoint but primarily feature voices from Western countries, they inadvertently marginalize and ignore non-Western perspectives. This practice represents a form of colonial representation, perpetuating unequal power dynamics and silencing the voices of the global majority. In this context, one must recognize that the term *international* often carries a Western bias. It's crucial to question representation and knowledge production within such events, particularly in promoting a specific discourse on Islam and feminism, including Islamic feminism. In looking at the next conferences in this series, I will continue to examine the implications of these practices and their influence on our understanding of Muslim women's rights.

2. Islamic Feminism: A Glance Toward Germany—an Exchange of Feminist Concepts and Strategies

> Feminists are fighting for the self-determination of women, for equal rights, and against sexism. Islam, too, knows feminism, and its advocates are as present today as they have been in the past, giving their voice to the movement. In February 2016, the Friedrich Ebert Foundation (FES) hosted a symposium titled *Islamic feminism: International Approaches*, offering a wide audience an opportunity to exchange and discuss Islamic gender images, women's rights and equal rights, and the self-image of Islamic feminists, and bringing the international perspective into view with contributions from Belgium, France, and the United States. On 25 May 2016, we would like to build on this experience and cast our gaze to Germany. What kinds of theoretical discourse are being engaged in on Islamic feminism in Germany? What are the practical strategies for empowering Muslim women? And what kind of scenario does Islamic feminism face in Germany? We cordially invite you to an evening event that discusses Islamic feminism in Germany and dares to look ahead to the future. We look forward to your registration and participation.[6]

The second conference of the 2016 series sought to examine Islamic feminism within the German context. It is indicative that all guest speakers at this event were selected from Germany. Not unlike mainstream Western feminist discourse, the unspoken premise of the discussions at this event—or the backdrop against which they unfolded—was often the perception that religion, particularly Islam, inherently oppresses and marginalizes women. This perspective positions secularism as a counterforce to religious patriarchy. Asad's exploration of secularism in *Formation of the Secular* (Asad's 2003) reveals how secularism operates as a political doctrine in discussions about Muslims as religious minorities, human rights, and the modern nation-state. In this work, he highlights the complexities hidden beneath the seemingly neutral facade of the term "secular." In this secularist discourse that rejects religion as a social construct that shapes people's lives, a tension exists between the feminist project and the religious subject.

The same problem is similarly highlighted by Salem (2013): "Arguing whether religions are patriarchal based on the types of 'rights' women have, reproduces an approach to feminism that assumes an individualistic premise,

6 The poster announcing the second of three conferences in the AmF/FES series promoted *Islamischer Feminismus: Der Blick nach Deutschland; Ein Austausch zu feministischen Konzepten und Strategien*, held in Berlin on 25 May 2016. The poster, along with the full conference programme, is available on the FES website at https://bit.ly/FES-islamfem-25-05-2016 (PDF). The conference can also be viewed on YouTube at https://bit.ly/FES-islamfem-deutschland-25-05-2016.

which is a key part of the secular meta-narrative that informs feminist scholarship today."

In effect, this discourse assumes that religions, none more so than Islam, inherently disempower women. However, this viewpoint ignores the potential of religious practices and beliefs to foster new knowledge and agency. Religion should not solely be seen as a source of oppression; it is also a site where new perspectives can emerge. Religion provides a space for the emergence of new knowledge, one that is often overlooked within secular feminist narratives. Ulrike Auga holds that secular Western feminism omits this fact, namely, that "religion" and religious practices are a place where new knowledge can emerge and that religion can indeed "enable agency or the creation of new knowledge and is a location of the projection of social imaginary" (Auga 2015, 59). However, this is just one facet of the broader issue at hand. In discussions of Islam and gender, women, particularly Muslim women, play a pivotal role in constructing religious boundaries. Roald (2006) argues that Muslim women's bodies become central in delineating communal boundaries, especially where Islam is concerned. In this context, the Muslim woman or, more specifically, the Islamic feminist becomes a symbol defining the boundaries between German society and the Muslim community. And "feminism" serves as a common ground bridging these two groups. The FES conference effectively acts as a facilitator, connecting German and Muslim communities through a shared focus on feminism. This approach has political implications.

It is essential to recognize that such events often receive governmental support, which can influence the sexual politics and the formulation of policies regarding Islam and women's rights. Amir-Moazami, Jacobsen, and Malik (2011) analyse the emergence of the sexual politics that take place within specific national platforms as expressions of "governmentalizing" gendered Islam. They look at its forms of subject production via a rhetoric that endorses Muslims, all the while aiming to rewrite Muslim gender norms according to a particular liberal-secular script. In resonance with that analysis, Zakaria (2015) raises a pertinent concern within the sphere of feminist global knowledge production. Specifically, Zakaria scrutinizes instances where this knowledge production blurs the distinction between sexual liberation and gender equality. Her critique underscores how American feminists employed such discourse to rationalize the intervention in Afghanistan, ostensibly in the name of liberating Afghan women, while overlooking the complexities of cultural norms and values. The claims made by Roald (2006); Amir-Moazami, Jacobsen, and Malik (2011); and Zakaria (2015) underscore that most events that address Islam tend to focus exclusively on women and feminism, narrowing the lens through which Islam and Muslim societies are viewed. This oversimplified perspective overlooks the multifaceted nature of Muslim societies, relegating them to discussions solely concerned with gender relations. Therefore, many Muslims perceive Western feminist approaches as reinforcing a reductionist view of Islam as intrinsically sexist. For these individuals, this misrepresents Islam and imposes the label "feminist" on them without their consent. This flattening stereotype that reduces Islam and Muslims to their gender relations leads to the oversimplification of complex societies with diverse cultural, political, and economic aspects (Tibi 2000).

I reference the FES conference as a proponent and embodiment of mainstream Western feminism. This specific strain of feminism, rooted predominantly in the early waves of feminism in the Western world and exhibiting minimal evolution or inclusivity over time, not only establishes but also imposes its definitions of "emancipatory" and "oppressive" practices on others. In the process, Third World and Muslim feminisms find themselves relegated to the margins, subjected to exclusion. In her seminal work, "Mapping the Margins: Intersectionality, Identity Politics, and Violence against Women of Color," Crenshaw (1991) illuminates the intricate dynamics of power and the ensuing conflicts that unfold in the struggle over the question of determining which differences hold significance:

> The problem is not simply that women who dominate the anti-violence movement are different from women of color, but that they frequently have the power to determine, either through material or rhetorical resources, whether the intersectional differences of women of color will be incorporated at all into the basic formulation of policy.
>
> (Crenshaw 1991, 1265)

Numerous Muslims perceive contemporary Western feminist approaches as reinforcing a reductionist perspective on Islam as an inherently sexist religion. They view this as a misrepresentation of Islam and assert that their understanding of gender equality and women's rights derives from the Qur'ān and not from feminism (Barlas 2008, 16). The imposition of the feminist discourse on Muslim women has led many to reject the "feminist" label, arguing that it is an externally constructed identity forced upon them. Despite increased awareness among Western feminists regarding diversity issues, it appears that, when it comes to Islam and Muslim women, negative stereotypes continue to be perpetuated without delving into the nuanced complexities of Muslim women's experiences. This raises the question of whether the organizers of such events aim to reshape Muslim gender norms by promoting a particular Western form of Muslim feminism.

In her article "Feminist Scholarship and the Internationalization of Women's Studies," Moallem (2006) raises concerns about the terms and conditions of the politics of translation and the conceptual spaces beyond Western imaginings. It seems that the prerequisite for involving Muslim scholars and activists, both from Western and non-Western contexts, is that they must comply with Western feminist discourse.[7] Is it possible, then, for the FES to

7 While certain Muslim scholars and activists offer criticism of Western feminist discourse and actively distance themselves from the "feminist" label, others adopt it strategically, in a manner

host events that engage with Muslim women's rights outside the framework of feminism? Or is it the case that understanding the subject and generating knowledge about it can only be achieved through a familiar, accessible, and relatable lens? Does the struggle for justice on behalf of Muslim women gain legitimacy only when framed as feminist? Are these the conditions imposed by FES for discussing Muslim women's rights? Mbembe (2015) contends that the Western epistemic tradition not only wields hegemony but also generates discursive scientific practices and constructs interpretive frameworks that restrict thinking beyond these boundaries. It suppresses any discourse articulated, contemplated, or envisioned from perspectives external to its own. In this context, I argue that "feminism," viewed as a Western epistemic tradition, gains hegemony in any discourse pertaining to women's rights, even for those who derive their understanding of women's rights from religious sources such as Islam rather than "feminism." Within this context, feminism becomes the interpretative framework for discussing the rights of Muslim women.

3. Feminism in the Islamic World: An Exploration

> Feminism and Islam—do they go together? In view of the recurring conflicts over headscarves, burkinis, or forced marriages, this question comes up over and again in discussion. On the other hand, especially in Germany, we see self-confident, self-determined, and motivated young Muslim women advocating equality and women's rights, in their Muslim communities and in society as a whole. In a series of events this year, the Friedrich Ebert Foundation (FES) is addressing the relationship between equality, feminism, and Islam, in Germany and internationally. In the third conference in this series we looked at the Islamic world, and with female experts from the Arab world we discussed women's movements, feminist demands, and what—if anything—that has to do with religion.[8]

akin to Spivak's concept of "strategic essentialism" (from a 1984 interview with Elisabeth Grosz, published in Spivak 1990). They perceive it as an analytical instrument with the potential to facilitate engagement in global politics, forging connections with other marginalized groups and fostering coalitions. It is conceivable that Muslim women participating in this conference are employing strategic essentialism as a means of resistance—resistance against the prevailing Islamophobic discourse in Germany. However, a comprehensive exploration of this aspect, including interviews with conference speakers and attendees, falls beyond the purview of this chapter and warrants further investigation.

8 From the FES webpage announcing the final of the three conferences in the AmF/FES series at https://bit.ly/feminismus-islamischen-welt-05-10-2016. The conference, held in Berlin on 5 October 2016, was titled *Feminismus in der islamischen Welt*, and the conference poster (with the conference programme) can be found at https://bit.ly/feminismus-islamischen-welt-programm (opens a PDF file).

The final conference in the AmF/FES series centred on the Islamic world. However, while the "international perspective" event featured speakers exclusively from Western contexts, and the second event focused on Germany, the third event included four guest speakers hailing from Egypt, Tunisia, Jordan, and Palestine. Although these speakers represented Muslim-majority countries or regions, these are exclusively Arab.

It bears noting here that in 2021 the Pew Research Center estimated the global Muslim population at 1.9 billion. Arab Muslims constituted merely 20 percent of this global population. This raises a critical question: Did the organizers of these conferences perceive Muslims solely as Arabs, or, more specifically, did they perceive Arabs as the exclusive representatives of Islam? Considering that Arabs constitute a relatively small minority within the broader "Islamic world," it becomes evident that these conferences, despite their claims to delve into the complex reality of Muslim feminists within Muslim-majority countries or regions, inadvertently marginalized more than 70 percent of the global Muslim population. These events seemed to ignore the voices and perspectives of Muslims residing in non-Arab and non-European regions. In an era marked by mass social media and global connectivity, it seems implausible that the FES organizers didn't know whom to invite or were unaware in making the choices they made. One is therefore led to ask whether the FES organizers took it upon themselves to define who qualifies as a Muslim and a feminist.

Defining who qualifies as a Muslim and what constitutes feminism involves a problematic process of essentialization and homogenization. In this power dynamic, knowledge about Islam, feminism, and Islamic feminism is produced, while the diversity of the lived experiences of non-Western women is marginalized. This perspective fails to acknowledge the rich tapestry of women's lives and their self-identifications, neglecting the potential strength that diversity offers. Shaikh (2003) makes the following observation:

> Within the diverse worlds of Islam gender issues have been indigenously engaged with, argued about, harmonized, problematized, synthesized, negotiated, and re-negotiated in varying ways throughout history . . . different groups of Muslim women come from varying cultural and geographical backgrounds, so that Jordanian Muslim women are often grappling with very different realities from Indonesian or Senegalese Muslim women.
>
> (Shaikh 2003, 148)

By homogenizing Muslim women as a singular category—or a "Muslimwoman," to borrow from Cooke (2008)[9]—one ignores this diversity and

9 In coining ***Muslimwoman*** as a label referring to a singular identity, Miriam Cooke (2008, 91) argues that "[t]he neologism Muslimwoman draws attention to the emergence of a new

inadvertently contributes to the problem of speaking for and on behalf of other women. This homogenization fails to capture the complex and specific experiences of Muslim women, further perpetuating stereotypes and reducing their agency. By focusing on the "Arab world" as a representative of the "Muslim world," the FES ignores the plurality and diversity within the world of Islam, which encompasses the realities of people from varying sociocultural backgrounds and political traditions and persuasions. Furthermore, by confining the Islamic world to the Arab domain, the FES inadvertently neglects the intricate power dynamics within the Muslim community. These dynamics encompass issues of Arab supremacy, the presence of anti-Black and non-Arab discrimination, the divisions between Sunni and Shīʿa Muslims, and a multitude of other complexities. While delving into these matters lies outside the immediate purview of this discussion, it is absolutely essential to acknowledge their significance.

An unsettling assumption underlies these conferences, particularly when viewed as a connected series. The first event, the "international perspective," focuses on the global stage, with speakers primarily from Western countries. The second event zooms in on Germany, while the third event turns to the "Islamic world" as represented by Arab countries or regions. This binary division appears to reiterate the Western versus Islamic binary, creating a clear and imaginative geographic distinction between the West and Islam. This binary construction perpetuates the Orientalist discourse originally outlined by Said (1978). It divides the world into distinct geographic spheres and, by extension, cultural and religious categories. Such a construction is instrumental in maintaining power imbalances and reinforcing stereotypes. As I conclude my analysis of this conference series, it is imperative to reflect on the broader implications of these representational practices and their influence on our understanding of Islamic feminism.

4. Conclusion

This chapter analysed a 2016 conference series organized by the Friedrich Ebert Foundation in Berlin, focusing on the intersection of Islam and feminism. My critique centered on the event's statements and the organizers' choice of guest speakers, raising questions about accessibility, inclusion, exclusion, and diversity within these discussions. To be clear, the Friedrich Ebert Foundation's 2016 series on Islam and feminism commendably acknowledges the subject's inherent complexity, recognizing that any singular discourse on Islamic gender roles is untenable. Yet, paradoxically, the way these events were structured inadvertently reinforced the very ideas

singular religious and gendered identification that overlays national, ethnic, cultural, historical, and even philosophical diversity."

the organizers aimed to challenge. I will make four key observations in this regard.

First, the "international" perspective was predominantly represented by speakers from Western societies such as France, Belgium, and the United States. This choice inadvertently reinforces the problematic dynamics of Western voices speaking on behalf of others, particularly those from the non-Western periphery. Second, the conferences juxtaposed the first event, claiming to offer an "international" perspective, with the third event, which purported to bring voices from the "Islamic world." This juxtaposition inadvertently reinforces the binary between the West and Islam, implying an inherent and divisive separation between these two spheres. Third, by featuring speakers solely from Arab countries when addressing the Islamic world, a narrow construct of Islam and Islamic feminism is projected. In reality, Arab voices represent a minority within the broader Islamic world, accounting for merely 20 percent. This selective focus results in a homogenization of the Muslim woman and a disregard for the rich tapestry of experiences and diverse voices among Muslim women. Fourth, the event centred on Germany frames discussions of Muslim women's rights predominantly through the lens of feminism. Western feminism's engagement with Muslim women's rights and gender equality in Islam is portrayed as conditional on adherence to a feminist discourse. This approach, exemplified by the Friedrich Ebert Foundation, taken here as emblematic of mainstream Western feminism, yields two concerning outcomes. First, it perpetuates the notion that feminism proceeds in linear progression and that all discussions of women's rights and liberation must be channelled through the feminist discourse, especially through the Western feminist lens. Second, it reduces an entire religion, which encompasses multifaceted aspects of life, to the narrow question of women's rights and the emancipation of the Muslim woman.

What becomes apparent is the manner in which the Friedrich Ebert Foundation employs Muslim women to fulfil this role. Although these women are presented as analysts, the terms of the discussion are tightly framed by the foundation, positioning these participants more as native informants. They are prompted to speak only as feminists, which neglects their multifaceted identities and perspectives. Taking our cue from Stampnitzky's (2013) concept of expert knowledge—under which the "problem" and the "solution" align and remain static long enough to be comprehensible—we can see that the organizers of the conference series appear to have defined Islam as the "problem" and feminism as its prescribed "solution." The Friedrich Ebert Foundation not only describes the field of Islamic feminism but actively shapes it, establishing claims to authority and credible positions from which to speak.

This analysis underscores the persistence of neo-Orientalist discourse within mainstream Western feminism, particularly with regard to religion and Islam. To comprehensively understand the category of the Muslim woman and its significance across diverse geopolitical contexts, it is imperative to meticulously examine the circulation of academic representational practices and their intricate local variations. The production, publication, and consumption of information and ideas relating to the Muslim woman or to Islam and feminism should be contextualized within the overarching global dominance of Western scholarship. By homogenizing these categories, we inadvertently strip women of their historical and political agency.

It is worth noting that this analysis is based exclusively on the materials published on the Friedrich Ebert Foundation's website. A more comprehensive analysis would necessitate engaging with the organizers to gain insights into their decision-making processes, including considerations about how and why certain individuals were invited. Exploring the composition of the Friedrich Ebert Foundation itself, and speculatively contemplating whether Muslim women within the organization would have organized the conference differently, is also a pertinent avenue for future inquiry.

The essays in *Cognitive Justice in a Global World* (Santos 2007) challenge the dominance of Western knowledge systems and highlight the need to recognize and value alternative forms of knowledge from non-Western, indigenous, and marginalized communities. Santos emphasizes the need for a more inclusive and equitable approach of knowledge production, dissemination, and validation. In the context of the FES events in question, true inclusion and diversity require genuinely listening to a wide range of experiences, recognizing that each individual's encounter with privilege and oppression is unique and cannot be generalized. Abu-Lughod urges us "to develop a serious appreciation of differences among women in the world—as products of different histories, expressions of different circumstances, and manifestations of different structured desires" (Abu-Lughod 2002, 783). Only through such a deep understanding can we facilitate an authentic exchange among disparate groups and attain a deeper understanding of the intricate realities that people navigate.

Works Cited

Abu-Lughod, Lila. 2002. "Do Muslim Women Really Need Saving? Anthropological Reflections on Cultural Relativism and Its Others." *American Anthropologist* 104 (3): 783–90. https://doi.org/10.1525/aa.2002.104.3.783.

Ahmed, Leila. 1992. *Women and Gender in Islam: Historical Roots of a Modern Debate.* New Haven and London: Yale University Press.

Amir-Moazami, Schirin, Christine M. Jacobsen, and Maleiha Malik. 2011. "Islam and Gender in Europe: Subjectivities, Politics and Piety." *Feminist Review* 98 (1): 1–8. https://doi.org/10.1057/fr.2011.9.

Asad, Talal. 2003. *Formation of the Secular: Christianity, Islam, Modernity.* Stanford, CA: Stanford University Press.

Auga, Ulrike. 2015. "Decolonizing Public Space: A Challenge of Bonhoeffer's and Spivak's Concepts of 'Resistance,' 'Religion,' and 'Gender.'" *Feminist Theology* 24 (1): 49–68. https://doi.org/10.1177/0966735015593859.

Barlas, Asma. 2008. "Engaging Islamic Feminism: Provincializing Feminism as a Master Narrative." In *Islamic Feminism: Current Perspectives*, edited by Anitta Kynsilehto, 15–24. Tampere: Tampere Peace Research Institute.

Cooke, Miriam. 2008. "Deploying the Muslimwoman." In "Roundtable Discussion: Religion, Gender, and the Muslimwoman." With Miriam Cooke, Fawzia Ahmad,

Margot Badran, Minoo Moallem, and Jasmin Zine. *Journal of Feminist Studies in Religion* 24 (1): 91–99. https://doi.org/10.2979/fsr.2008.24.1.91.

Crenshaw, Kimberlé. 1991. "Mapping the Margins: Intersectionality, Identity Politics, and Violence Against Women of Color." *Stanford Law Review* 43 (6): 1241–99. https://doi.org/10.2307/1229039.

Hall, Stuart. 1992. "The West and the Rest: Discourse and Power." *Formations of Modernity*, edited by Stuart Hall and Bram Gieben, 275–331. Cambridge: Polity Press, in Association with Blackwell Publishers and the Open University.

Hernandez Aguilar, Luis Manuel. 2017. "Workstream 1: Dominant Islamophobic Narratives—Germany." CIK Working Paper 2. Centre for Ethnicity & Racism Studies.

Lazreg, Marnia. 1990. "Gender and Politics in Algeria: Unraveling the Religious Paradigm." *Signs: Journal of Women in Culture and Society* 15 (4): 755–80. https://doi.org/10.1086/494627.

Lorde, Audre. (1984) 2007. *Sister Outsider: Essays and Speeches.* Berkeley: The Crossing Press.

Mahmood, Saba. 2001. "Feminist Theory, Embodiment, and the Docile Agent: Some Reflections on the Egyptian Islamic Revival." *Cultural Anthropology* 16 (2): 202–36. https://doi.org/10.1525/can.2001.16.2.202.

Mahmood, Saba. 2005. *Politics of Piety: The Islamic Revival and the Feminist Subject.* Princeton, NJ: Princeton University Press.

Marx, Karl. (1851–1853) 1979. "The Eighteenth Brumaire of Louis Bonaparte." In *Marx/Engels Collected Works*, Vol. 11, Chap. 3, 99–197. Moscow: Progress Publishers; London: Lawrence and Wishart.

Mbembe, Achille. 2015. "Decolonizing Knowledge and the Question of the Archive." *TRAFO: Blog for Transregional Research* (December 9, 2022). Lecture transcript. https://doi.org/10.58079/usgu.

Moallem, Minoo. 2006. "Feminist Scholarship and the Internationalization of Women's Studies." *Feminist Studies* 32 (2): 332–51. https://doi.org/10.2307/20459089.

Mohanty, Chandra Talpade. 2003. *Feminism Without Borders: Decolonizing Theory, Practicing Solidarity.* Durham, NC: Duke University Press.

Roald, Anne Sofie. 2006. "The Shaping of a Scandinavian 'Islam': Converts and Gender Equal Opportunity." *Women Embracing Islam: Gender and Conversion in the West*, edited by Karin van Nieuwkerk, 48–70. Austin, TX: University of Texas Press.

Said, Edward W. 1978. *Orientalism.* New York: Pantheon Books.

Salem, Sara. 2013. "Feminist Critique and Islamic Feminism: The Question of Intersectionality." *The Postcolonialist* 1, no. 1 (November 18). http://postcolonialist.com/civil-discourse/feminist-critique-and-islamic-feminism-the-question-of-intersectionality/.

Santos, Boaventura de Sousa, ed. 2007. *Cognitive Justice in a Global World: Prudent Knowledges for a Decent Life.* Lanham, MD: Lexington Books.

Schiffauer, Werner. 2014. "The Irresponsible Muslim: Islam in German Public Culture." In *Islamic Movements of Europe: Public Religion and Islamophobia in the Modern World*, edited by Frank Peter and Rafael Ortega, 344–51. London and New York: I. B. Tauris.

Shaikh, Sa'diyya. 2003. "Transforming Feminisms: Islam, Women, and Gender Justice." In *Progressive Muslims: On Justice, Gender, and Pluralism*, edited by Omid Safi, 147–62. Oxford: Oneworld Publications.

Shohat, Ella. 1992. "Notes on the 'Post-Colonial.'" In "Third World and Post-Colonial Issues." Edited by John McClure and Aamir Mufti, special section. *Social Text* 31–32: 99–113. https://doi.org/10.2307/466220.

Shooman, Yasemin. 2014. *". . . weil ihre Kultur so ist": Narrative des antimuslimischen Rassismus.* Bielefeld: Transcript Verlag.

Spivak, Gayatri Chakravorty. 1988. "Can the Subaltern Speak?" In *Marxism and the Interpretation of Culture*, edited by Cary Nelson and Lawrence Grossberg, 271–313. Basingstoke, UK: Macmillan Education.

Spivak, Gayatri Chakravorty. 1990. "Criticism, Feminism, and the Institution." Interview with Elisabeth Grosz, June 1984. In *The Post-Colonial Critic: Interviews, Strategies, Dialogues*, edited by Sarah Harasym, 1–16. New York and London: Routledge.

Stampnitzky, Lisa. 2013. *Disciplining Terror: How Experts Invented "Terrorism".* Cambridge: Cambridge University Press. https://doi.org/10.1017/CBO9781139208161.

Tibi, Bassam. 2000. *Der Islam und Deutschland: Muslime in Deutschland.* Stuttgart: Deutsche Verlagsanstalt.

Zakaria, Rafia. 2015. "Sex and the Muslim Feminist: On Refusing to Equate Sexual Pleasure with Freedom." *The New Republic*, November 13, 2015. https://newrepublic.com/article/123590/sex-and-the-muslim-feminist.

Part II

Islam, Colonialism, and Decolonization

4 Colonial Law and Muslim Law

Gustavo Gozzi

1. Colonial Law

In this chapter, we turn to the relation between colonial law and Muslim law, analysing the processes of contamination between these two different systems of law. In so doing, we will also consider the institutional aspects of colonial rule in order to understand in what way the organizational structure of colonialism, specifically its administrative structure, was imposed on the colonies and what its legacy has been and continues to be.

The premise for this discussion is that of colonial domination, with its aim to economically exploit the native population, ostensibly to "civilize" it, and in this regard it is worth noting that this two-pronged aim—one economic, the other "principled" and justificatory—informed the science of colonial law, explaining its appropriation of local customs and law.

In light of this background, Jean-Philippe Bras (2015, 18) has offered an analysis of colonial law that breaks it down into three elements: there was (a) a *metropolitan law*, meaning French law, which was partly applied in the colonies; (b) a *special law* for the colony established by the metropolitan authorities and by the colonial ones; and finally (c) a *local law*, which would typically have been the Muslim law of the country under colonial rule.

2. Muslim Law and Metropolitan Law

Muslim law consisted of all the nonmetropolitan, *local* law that governed the native population. Particularly significant in clarifying the relation between the local Muslim law and the legal principles of metropolitan law is the analysis of the Algerian case.

Algerian Muslim law—mainly drawn up by French lawyers—was used as a tool of colonial practice to suit the political and economic needs of colonization (Henry and Balique 1979, 13). And indeed *it is a key feature of Algerian Muslim law that, in it, the concepts and categories of French law are imposed on the local Muslim law* (ibid., 16).

After an initial stage in which the French colonizers sought to gain a proper understanding of Muslim law as key to understanding Algerian society, Muslim law came to be interpreted through the distorting lens of its "Frenchification,"

DOI: 10.4324/9781003431206-8

which meant that French law became the benchmark against which to assess Muslim law (ibid., 45).

As soon as the Ottoman regency of Algiers was defeated in 1830, the entire territory was uniformly placed under French public law. But no such uniformity was to define civil or private law, which was fashioned into a hybrid system differentiated by subject matter: personal status was retained as a concept of Muslim law, whereas property was governed by French law. Colonial policy indeed pursued the twofold aim of maintaining Muslim people in their own personal status, on the one hand, while subjecting their property to French law, on the other. Jurists thus enthusiastically set about the task of reshaping Muslim law consistently with the aims of colonial rule.

The Algerian Muslim lands were classified under a threefold legal regime: (a) the beylik's lands, over which the bey exercised his own property right; (b) the lands on which this right was exercised as a *collective* property right; and (c) the institute of *waqf* or *hubus*, that is, a charitable endowment for the benefit of needy people or a religious foundation devoted to serving the general welfare. Both legal scholarship and legislation contributed to drawing up new legal rules for Muslim property, with the aim of destroying the Muslim property regime. That happened through the abolition of the inalienability of the *waqf* through a decree of 1844 and then a law enacted in 1858.[1] The beylik's lands were allotted by the colonial power to the French colonizers and the collective properties were subjected to procedures that transformed them into private property, individually owned and transferable (Henry and Balique 1979, 34). This "Frenchification" of the Algerian lands made it so that they could be purchased by the French colonizer.[2]

No such Frenchification was extended to the law of Muslim personal status in Algeria: the juristic consensus became that this was a kind of foreign law, of a spiritual or religious nature, that left no room for any intervention by the political colonial power.[3] This statement of *legal irreducibility* of the law of Muslim personal status was considered the necessary consequence of a *natural inequality* between the colonizers and the colonized population, and politically it was used to reject the notion that Muslim people should be granted French citizenship.

1 On this question see Samour 2017, 253–56.

2 This Frenchification, assimilating this branch of Muslim law to French law, was justified by some scholars on the ground that the constitution of Algerian property was continuous with Roman law, of which French law was a reproduction, making it unnecessary to acknowledge any distinctive trait of Algerian Muslim land law: "We must understand that Islamism did not create anything in the field of law"—such was the conclusion that Rodolphe Dareste came to in his foreword to Robe 1885 (my translation).

3 On the subject of Muslim personal status, Émile Larcher and Georges Rectenwald wrote: "This solution, at first sight improper, can be explained on the grounds of the deep chasm in behaviour, religion, and civilization that divides Islam and France" (Larcher and Rectenwald 1923, 433, my translation).

But clearly manifest in this stance was a blatant contradiction, for just as the French metropole was using the law of personal status to justify the condition *inequality* among persons in the colony, while asserting the supposed superiority of the colonizer over the colonized "other," at home it was celebrating the principle of *equality* under the law recognized as a bedrock of the French legal order. As Henry and Balique (1979, 41) recognized, "the whole problem faced by the French colonial legislators and lawyers was how to adapt the principle of legal equality to colonial relationships whose reality was perceived to be inegalitarian, all the while not rejecting that principle" (my translation).

Much to the same effect, Martti Koskenniemi observes that

> the legal situation in the colonies was often of great complexity and, as Lauren Benton [e.g., Benton 2002, 2010] and others have shown, often best grasped under the perspective of legal pluralism: different laws applied to *different human groups* and activities. (Koskenniemi 2016, 249, italics added.)

In order to wriggle out of this contradiction, legal scholarship took a kind of long view arguing from a legal positivist premise: in the here and now, it was necessary to recognize Algerian Muslim law as the law of Algerian Muslims currently in force in the colony, but in the long run, in a distant future far removed from the present circumstances, the contradiction between this inequality codified in colonial law and the egalitarian principle underpinning the French legal order would eventually somehow work itself out.

Algerian Muslim law was thus conceived as a *transitional law* that, *by assimilation*, would *dissolve* into French law, as had already happened with Muslim land ownership and tenure. So, on the one hand, Algerian Muslim law denied the alleged universality of French law, acknowledging the specificity of the Algerian colonized people and in this way justifying their unequal treatment. On the other hand, the idea of a future *assimilation* would be put into practice through the process of "civilizing" the colonized population by progressively denying their cultural identity, their "otherness." And this clearly reveals the most disturbing and violent aspect of the colonial enterprise, whose legacy we can still observe in current French society as well, where the ideology of assimilation explains the policy of denying the cultural identities of migrants by imposing French culture, or its acceptance, as a condition for accepting them into French society.[4]

4 Here we can see the application of the ideology of assimilation, in which regard an African scholar, Achille Mbembe, observes that, "as was the case in the age of colonialism, the model . . . in the [French] Republic is that of assimilation, under which all are to adhere to a single rule of undifferentiation, which in turn means that no group will be granted any 'special status' on the basis of its belonging to a distinct community." The paradoxical consequence of this universalism is the presence "in this country of citizens made invisible by the colour of their skin" (Mbembe 2005, 152, my translation).

Indeed, as Henry and Balique (1979, 44) commented, Algerian Muslim law was best conceived not as the law *of* a society but as law *for* a society, and this resulted in a policy aimed at destructuring both Algerian society and Algerian law.

After independence came a rejection of colonial law in its entirety, followed by a process of "Algerianization" of the law, even if this process was largely influenced by the French legal model. This enterprise, rejecting colonial law and then undertaking to make the law distinctly Algerian, did do away with the old colonial law, but it left a complex legacy. Two aspects of this legacy need to be highlighted.

The first of these is that Muslim personal status did not fall away but was "repurposed." In the colonial era, this body of law was kept in place in order to justify the *unequal condition* in which the French metropole kept the native population. And when the nationalist movements began to take hold in the 1930s, they turned Muslim personal status on its head, putting it to use *against* the colonial ruler's efforts at cultural assimilation, so much so that this status became the basic criterion for Algerian citizenship in keeping with the principle of jus sanguinis (ibid., 49).

Even more important, however, is the second aspect of the legacy of Algerian Muslim law: it consisted in the French jurists' *codification* project, an effort that produced a model code containing legal rules and principles adapted to the socioeconomic context of the Algerian colony (ibid., 47). It specifically came in the form of the *Avant-projet de Code du Droit Musulman Algérien*, drawn up by the French lawyer Marcel Morand and published in 1916. This became the essential sourcebook for Algerian Muslim law, a text that would go on to exert a lasting influence on Algerian jurisprudence, even many years after independence.

We can now briefly examine this codification effort, which proved to be of paramount importance in shaping *local* Algerian Muslim law and then the *special* law the colonial ruler introduced in the colony.

3. Muslim Law and Customary Law

Marcel Morand had been a barrister pleading cases before the Paris Court of Appeals when, in 1892, he took a position teaching public international law at the Montpellier Law School. Two years later he was at the École de Droit d'Alger, where he was entrusted with teaching civil law and French law to native students.

In researching Muslim law, Morand came to reject the thesis of its fixity, a thesis based on the religious foundation on which this body of law rests. He argued, on the contrary, that Muslim law had evolved along with the evolving course of local practices.[5] This is an argument he laid out in research published

5 Like Marcel Morand, René Maunier (1932) also rejected the notion of the immutability of Muslim law. He introduced the concept of "legal nationalism," further underscoring how the law is not absolute but relative, being dependent on the territorial context out of which it emerges.

in the *Revue Algérienne, Tunisienne et Marocaine de Législation et de Jurisprudence*, specifically with a focus on the Muslim family (Morand 1903) and on Algerian Muslim law of the Maliki School (Morand 1913). Here Morand argued, more to the point, that the thesis of the immutability of Muslim law, a thesis widely upheld among French jurists, was not without consequence, for it meant that

> we revived . . . the Muslim society of the 14th century, restoring the Muslim influences that for several centuries had been exercised on the Algerian natives; we re-Islamized them, and there is no doubt that these natives, socially as well as in their outlook, are today farther from us than they were at the time of conquest.
>
> (Morand 1913, 223, my translation)

He observed that from the moment the French conquered Algeria, what they considered to be the code of the Maliki Muslims was the Mukhtaṣar of Khalīl, a jurisprudent from the 8th century AH (corresponding to the 14th century CE). This legal compendium was translated into French as *Précis de Jurisprudence Musulmane* (Khalīl ibn-Isḥāq 1848–54), and they looked to this code because

> it was after the fashion of Khalīl, and exclusively on that basis, that this justice [the justice rendered to Maliki Muslims across the whole of Algeria] was being dispensed both by the native judges trained and appointed in France and by French judges.
>
> (Morand 1913, 221)

But, according to Morand,

> we cannot pretend that the principles set forth in this handbook could still be, at the eve of the French conquest, those that governed legal relations among natives in Algeria. . . . Indeed, the law is in constant transformation, and if the written law is not adapted to the new legal relations that establish themselves, there will inevitably come a moment when the judge will find it impossible . . . to ground . . . his decisions in that written law, and will find it necessary . . . to look to current practices and recognize *custom* among the sources of law.
>
> (Ibid., 216, italics in the original)

Morand thought that custom had indeed modified Muslim law, in particular family law. As evidence of this development, he pointed out that the weight of written testimony in Algeria had gradually overtaken that of oral testimony, reflecting the diminishing role that, in the Muslim world, was traditionally accorded to witnesses.[6] By contrast, French courts in Algeria were upholding the role of the witness even against an act by a judge. At the basis of this attitude, Morand found, were the French "habits of clarity; our need for precision, security, certainty; our fixation on uniformity," where we should "instead be inquiring into the customs, traditions, and mores specific to each region" (ibid., 222) and adapting the law accordingly. He therefore took the view that "the French intervention marked a regression in the evolution of Algerian institutions" (ibid., 223) and instead made the case for "modernizing" Muslim law by bringing it close to the rules of French general law, as opposed to applying the local law (Renucci 2015, 192).

These views formed the premise of his *Avant-projet de Code du Droit Musulman Algérien*, published in 1916 (Morand 1916b), to which we will now turn.

4. The *Avant-projet de Code du Droit Musulman Algérien*

The first task of the project to codify a body of Algerian Muslim law was to analyse the codification processes existing in other countries, beginning with Turkey and Egypt. But the Turkish Mecelle—or Ottoman Civil Code—did not comprise the whole of private law, since it was mainly a code of civil and commercial obligations, while in Egypt there were some "indigenous codes," but they had been modelled on the European codes and, in particular, on the French code, and for this reason they could not offer much guidance in drawing up an Algerian code. As for other countries with a Muslim population under European rule, such as British India or the Dutch East Indies, none had any codification of Muslim law. So Morand (1916a, 7) could proudly declare that "none of these powers, except France, had until that time undertaken to codify Muslim law in the interest of their Muslim subjects" (my translation).

Two main effects resulted from this codification process. First, as noted, the scope of Muslim law was restricted, and French law was correspondingly expanded. Indeed, on the basis of a French decree of 17 April 1889, under which "Muslims living in Algeria are subject to Muslim law only as concerns their personal status, their inheritance, and certain of their properties" (ibid., 12), the *Code du Droit Musulman Algérien* consequently established, in the Third Book, Title III, that "property can be acquired

6 Morand claimed in this regard that "in Algeria, as in all Muslim countries, it had become customary for marriages and their repudiation to be certified by a qadi [or judge], and the case law had come to accept that, absent such certification, no marriage or repudiation would be considered existent. By custom, marriage and repudiation had become official acts, and this was an extremely welcome development" (ibid., 224), for it offered married women protection against any witnesses from the husband's family who might offer testimony denying that there had been any marriage or that the marriage was still good.

only in accordance with the rules of French law" (Morand 1916b, 381, my translation).

Second, very much in keeping with the effort to restrict the scope of Muslim law, the point was to exert control over its application. In fact the code's stated purpose was to "clearly and methodically set out the *true principles of Muslim law*" (Morand 1916a, 13, italics added). This meant that the French colonizer asserted the right to choose which of the interpretations of Muslim law expressed by Muslim lawyers were to count as being "*in closest accord with morals and fairness*, and with the social condition of our natives and their true economic interests" (ibid., italics added).

On this basis, Morand concluded that, even if Algerian Muslims were mainly Malikite, the French codification of Algerian Muslim law would follow those interpretations of such law that were rooted in the Hanafite tradition—because, as he put it in the *Avant-projet*, they were often "more human" and "more tolerant" (ibid.).

However, the French attempt to legislate over the customs of the Algerian population, even to establish an "authentic" interpretation of Muslim law, met with strong resistance from the Algerian people and thus failed.[7] But even though this codification project was never enacted into law, it stood as a secondary source of legal authority that judges would look to until the passage of the Algerian Code of Family Law in 1984 (Henry 2015, 230), when the Code Morand was rejected.

There was clearly no comprehensive design behind Morand's codification project, its aim being to achieve dominance within a plural legal system. This can be appreciated by going back to the question of legal personality and property under colonial rule: although these legal regimes were recognized in accordance with local tradition under the Muslim law established in colonial Algeria through the 1830 *Convention de Capitulation* (ibid., 229),[8] their application fell under the authority of French judges. As a result, Muslim law came to be restricted in its scope, "while French law underwent a process of colonial Algerianization by which it was adapted to the Algerian context" (ibid., 226–27). So it was colonial law that set this process

7 This attempt to codify an "indigenous law" also came under criticism from some French scholars. Arthur Giraud, for instance, observed that these codification projects were carried out using Western codes as blueprints, with the result of "completely misrepresenting indigenous law." And with this modus operandi came the risk of failing to appreciate "the importance of some original institutions that had no equivalent in our codes." More importantly, however, these codifications would "delay the natural evolution that would probably have taken place on contact with European domination" (Girault 1929, 387–88, my translation).

8 The *Convention de Capitulation*, enacted on 5 July 1830, is the act through which Hussein Dey, the provincial ruler of the Regency of Algiers, surrendered to the French army. The Convention guaranteed some basic liberties for the inhabitants, including their freedom to practice the Muslim religion, as well as freedom of property, commerce, and industry.

in motion,[9] as a result of which the Muslim population was placed under a scheme of differentiated and unequal relations.

5. The *Code Tunisien des Obligation et des Contrats*

The 1916 *Code Morand*, as we saw, was an attempt to restrict the scope of Muslim law by extending and adapting French law to the Algerian cultural and legal landscape. But it was preceded in 1906 by the *Code Tunisien des Obligation et des Contrats*, and the contrast between the two could not be more clear-cut, for here was a case of *positive cross-fertilization* between Muslim law and European law, with a lasting legacy that can still be felt today.

On 6 September 1896, under the French protectorate in Tunisia, a commission was charged with drafting a code for the civil, commercial, and criminal law of Tunisia "on the model of the French Codes" (Santillana 1899, 1). The commission was given two tasks: it had to find (a) in French law the elements that could be used in codification, setting aside matters relating to personal status and land ownership and (b) in Muslim law all the rules that could be useful in this codification enterprise (Charfeddine 1996, 425).

The first draft of the code, issued in 1897, was essentially concerned with French law. The second one, issued in 1899, was instead concerned with European law—because, according to David Santillana, the rapporteur appointed to relate the codification project, "it was impossible not to consider this great movement of ideas that is encouraging Europe to embrace the unification of law" (Santillana 1899, sec. 1, my translation; cf. Charfeddine 1996, 425). And so, when the *Code Tunisien des Obligation et des Contrats* was finally enacted in 1906, it drew not only on the French *Code Napoléon* of 1804 but also on the Italian Civil Code of 1865, the Swiss Federal Code of Obligations of 1881, and the German Civil Code of 1900 (Charfeddine 1996, 430–31). The 1906 *Code Tunisien* was thus based on a plurality of sources.

But it was necessary to find some common ground for European law and Muslim law. Santillana thought this common ground lay in Roman law—for,

9 The complexity of colonial law within the frame of the legal pluralism that existed under colonial rule can be appreciated by considering two law courses introduced in the late 19th century at the École de Droit d'Alger and in 1909 at the University of Algiers—the first on Algerian legislation, the second on Algerian Muslim law. Both were influential in the training of civil servants within the colony, who were required to be proficient in Algerian law. Algerian legislation was taught until independence. Algerian Muslim law served the need to impart a deeper understanding of Algerian Muslim society, whose law was characterized as "composite," being the result of the French courts intervening in the civil law of Islam: it was Ernest Zeys who so described it in his 1885 *Traité Élémentaire de Droit Musulman Algérien* (Zeys 1885; see Henry 2015, 230). And then in 1916 came Marcel Morand's *Avant-projet*, which, as mentioned, would stand as the most important attempt at setting out an "Algerian Muslim law." But the discrimination this law imposed on the local Muslim population meant that it could not survive independence. The teaching of Muslim law was thus integrated into the private law curriculum, because at this point Muslim law had once again become the common body of law governing matters pertaining to the family.

as he argued, Roman law had influenced the great Muslim lawyers in Medina, Kufa, and Cordoba, thus making its way into Muslim civilization and imperceptibly becoming incorporated into it (Santillana 1899, 12). In this way, by way of Roman law, the comparative approach achieved its desired synthesis, combining the rules and principles of the Muslim legal civilization with those of Western legal systems. The *Code Tunisien* thus stands as an important example of wholesome legal cross-fertilization among different legal traditions. The code's significance stretches to the present day, for it is now regarded as the core of a future Maghrebin code.

As the foregoing historical reconstruction suggests, the "colonial encounter" can be described as having had different effects in different colonial contexts.

6. The *Code de l'Indigénat*

We have seen that French colonial domination was organizationally dependent on the enforcement of a *local* colonial law. But no less important in this respect was the use of a *special* colonial law, the chief example of which lay in the *Code de l'Indigénat* or Native Code—a system of repression the French introduced in Algeria (as well as in their other colonies) next to its local law.

It was also noted that, although the local Algerian population after the French conquest continued to be governed under Muslim law, the interpretation of this law was entrusted to French jurists and judges. According to some jurists commenting on colonial law, this arrangement legitimated the specificity of the legal status that attached to the Algerian population: "To be sure," Larcher and Rectenwald (1923, 408) argued, "the native is . . . French. But he has maintained his own law, and for this reason he cannot be deemed a citizen; he is merely a *French subject*" (my translation, italics added). As mere subjects, the local Muslim people were placed under a regime of *special legislation*. Here we can see the "heart of darkness" of the Western civilization of law and rights, which was held up as universal but in fact was not recognized outside the West (ibid., 410).

The repressive thrust of the *Code de l'Indigénat* can be clearly appreciated in the criminal norms it contained: these were *special* norms informed by a notion of the "inherent nature of the native people" (ibid., 474), and they accordingly stiffened the punishments imposed for the crimes set forth in the criminal code.

Moreover, even some *customs* and *folkways* were made criminal, solely on the basis that they were rooted in the local tradition. Examples were nuisance in the form of loud or disorderly conduct at a marketplace and unauthorized gatherings of more than twenty people heading on a pilgrimage or attending a public banquet. And restrictions were also placed on freedom of movement—permits being required to travel outside one's own hometown.

With these legal provisions—stiffening punishments and criminalizing customary practices on the basis of the ethnicity of those who engaged in them—one can reasonably say that what the *Code de l'Indigénat* enacted was a form of "state racism" proper, or at least this is the argument made by Olivier Le Cour Grandmaison (2005, 252).

But the "colonial encounter"—the contamination between Islam and Western civilization—concerned not only the law but also the political institutions.

7. Colonialism and Institutional Transformations

In Algeria there existed two systems of law, two logical systems (*deux systèmes logiques*): "an Algeria subjected to all the laws in force in France; an Algeria exclusively governed by special legislation" (Girault 1908, 191, my translation). However, the legislature never committed to either of these two systems, and the outcome was that the country eventually fell under a patchwork of decrees enforced by colonial rule, effectively depriving it of any semblance of autonomy.

Before the French conquest, the Ottoman Empire had left Algeria's social structure unchanged. French colonial rule, by contrast, imposed on Algeria the centralized administrative organization of the French state. Thus in 1879 the Third Republic instituted a civil governor.

Thus Alexis de Tocqueville argued that Algeria needed a strong administrative centralization under the authority of a civil governor,[10] who needed to be reasonably independent from Paris when it came to implementing general rules, appointing lower-ranking officials, and so on. He moreover thought it necessary for there to be an independent ministry for Algeria.[11] In short, Tocqueville thought it essential that the government of Algeria be centralized in Paris and its administration be in Algiers.

But the larger point of this overview is that, under the colonial system, *the French administrative state imposed its centralized structure on a social and cultural reality that was completely extraneous to it.* So, too, after independence, in 1962, during decolonization, this structure was maintained in the form of the nation-state. Let us therefore consider this post-independence nation-state: what were its characteristics?

8. Anticolonial Nationalism: The Nation and the Nation-State

The transformations that Algeria went through following the French conquest have been analysed in a posthumous essay by the Algerian sociologist Abdelmalek Sayad, who observes that even though an "anticolonialist" nationalism emerged within the colonial system, this movement never managed to shake off the dead hand of its colonial past: it "could never wrest itself from the

10 A civil governor for Algeria was instituted in 1879, at the time of the Third Republic.

11 During the Third Republic, under the prime ministership of Léon Gambetta, an undersecretary of the colonies was appointed.

constraints of colonization and develop an independent self-conception and worldview" (Sayad 2003, 42, my translation).

At the same time, however, this nationalist surge was not assimilationist, for it took hold in a Muslim country and so was necessarily "sacralized in a literal sense, collapsing the political sphere into the . . . religious one, and in this way religion became the essential element of national identity" (ibid.).

As a movement that took hold under colonial domination, Algerian anticolonialist nationalism modelled itself after the French nation-state: this model was first imposed on Algeria, which was declared a "French department," and then it provided the template for the Algerian state even after independence. In Sayad's words, France represented "the institutional point of view, the omnipresence of the state in all sectors of national life," as well as "the organizational point of view, shaping the country's territorial, administrative, social, and economic organization, and so on" (ibid., 57).

The only claim to legitimacy the independent state could make lay in its response to colonial rule, not in any independent discourse that might seize on the condition of society as the product of a colonial past. The state's *political* legitimation, in other words, could not be rooted in its *social* legitimation—for its anticolonial struggle failed to establish any connection with the sensitivities or daily needs of people in society.

As a result, the militancy and the nationalism, though certainly authentic at their inception, morphed into a patronage system of nepotism, clientelism, and servile vassalage that tarnished the state's early prestige. Likewise, the political legitimation of regimes that wrapped themselves in nationalistic ideology eventuated in forms of government where political power came increasingly to rely on the ability to exercise repressive and military power. Democracy proved in the end unattainable, then, as a result of curtailing freedoms and undermining the rule of law, both of which wound up shedding their unconditionality and universality.

This diagnosis can explain the makeup of the political system that established itself after colonialism. For a wall of separation was erected between the people on one side and an autocratic regime on the other, with its coterie of loyal followers, on whom its survival depends.

It is against the background of this colonial legacy that in many Arab states the problem of democracy needs to be framed and analysed.

9. Economic Development Planning and the Continuity of Colonial Rule

The continuity between colonial rule and the postcolonial nation-state can also be observed in the area of economic development planning. In this regard, turning once more to Algeria, we can point to the Constantine Plan, which the French government launched in October 1958, promising

> 15 billion francs in public works and urban development, the construction of housing for one million individuals, the creation of 400,000 new

> jobs, the education of two-thirds of Algerian children, the redistribution of 250,000 hectares of land to Muslim farmers, and the recruitment of one-tenth of metropolitan cadres from Muslim Algerians.
>
> (Haleh Davis 2015, 1)

This plan gave start to the industrialization of Algeria, and so, after independence, Algerians wanted the French colonial development policy to be maintained (ibid., 248). However, with the plan came the idea of forging a "new man" who would drive the envisaged economic transformation. And this meant that, before independence, the plan took on a racial tone by raising the question of whether the "Algerian type" was even fit to sustain the economic development sought to be achieved.

The director of the Constantine Plan, Jean Vibert, declared that with the introduction of this plan "*homo-economicus* has been born. He has replaced *homo-islamicus*, that man who accepted an extremely low level of [material] needs and who, as a result, did not feel the need to work more than was necessary" (quoted in Haleh Davis 2017, 76). Clearly at work here is the bias that can easily be recognized to this day in our judgment of the peoples of the southern Mediterranean.

In making this assessment, French technocrats espoused the racial idea that it would be possible to effect an anthropological transformation of Muslim people. But after independence, despite the continuity of the Constantine Plan, the first president of the Algerian Republic, Ahmed Ben Bella, sought to use Islam as the grounds on which legitimize his socialist policies. This continued until the presidency of Houari Boumédiène, who rejected Ben Bella's approach and introduced a more straightforwardly industrial development policy.

So we have to conclude that we "cannot adequately understand the genesis of the postcolonial state in Algeria [or of many other Arab states], current understandings of race and [neo-]colonialism in France, without taking seriously the economic and technical dimensions of colonial rule" (Haleh Davis 2015, 275) or its legal and political dimensions.

Works Cited

Benton, Lauren. 2002. *Law and Colonial Culture: Legal Regimes in World History, 1400–1900.* Cambridge: Cambridge University Press. https://doi.org/10.1017/CBO9780511512117.

Benton, Lauren. 2010. *A Search for Sovereignty: Law and Geography in European Empires, 1400–1900.* Cambridge: Cambridge University Press. https://doi.org/10.1017/CBO9780511988905.

Bras, Jean-Philippe. 2015. "Introduction." In Faire l'histoire du droit colonial: Cinquante ans après l'indépendance de l'Algérie, edited by Jean-Philippe Bras, 9–22. Paris: Karthala.

Charfeddine, Mohamed Kamel. 1996. "Esquisse sur la méthode normative retenue dans l'élaboration du Code tunisien des obligations et des contrats." *Revue Internationale de Droit Comparé* 48 (2): 421–42. https://doi.org/10.3406/ridc.1996.5365.

Girault, Arthur. 1908. *Principes de colonisation et de législation coloniale*. Tome III, *Algérie et Tunisie*. Paris: Librairie J.-B. Sirey.

Girault, Arthur. 1929. *Principes de colonisation et de législation coloniale*. Tome II, *Notions administratives, juridiques et financières*. Deuxième partie, *"Les colonies françaises depuis 1815."* Paris: Librairie du Recueil Sirey.

Haleh Davis, Muriam. 2015. "Producing Eurafrica: Development, Agriculture and Race in Algeria, 1958–1965." PhD diss., New York University.

Haleh Davis, Muriam. 2017. "'The Transformation of Man' in French Algeria: Economic Planning and the Postwar Social Sciences, 1958–62." *Journal of Contemporary History* 52 (1): 73–94. https://doi.org/10.1177/0022009416647117.

Henry, Jean-Robert. 2015. "Le passage du droit colonial à son histoire dans l'Algérie de l'indépendance." Chap. 9 in *Faire l'histoire du droit colonial: Cinquante ans après l'indépendance de l'Algérie*, edited by Jean-Philippe Bras, 225–39. Paris: Karthala. https://doi.org/10.3917/kart.bras.2015.01.0227.

Henry, Jean-Robert, and François Balique, eds. 1979. *La doctrine coloniale du droit musulman algérien: Bibliographie systématique et introduction critique*. Paris: Éditions du Centre National de la Recherche Scientifique.

Khalīl ibn-Isḥāq. 1848–54. *Précis de Jurisprudence Musulmane, ou Principes de Législation Musulmane Civile et Religieuse, selon le Rite Mālékite*. Translated by M. Perron. Paris: Imprimerie Nationale.

Koskenniemi, Martti. 2016. "Colonial Laws: Sources, Strategies and Lessons?" *Journal of the History of International Law* 18: 248–77. https://doi.org/10.1163/15718050-12340059.

Larcher, Émile, and Georges Rectenwald. 1923. *La Justice—Les Personnes*. Vol. 2 of *Traité Élémentaire de Législation Algérienne*. 3rd ed. Paris: Librairie Arthur Rousseau. https://gallica.bnf.fr/ark:/12148/bpt6k3764908.

Le Cour Grandmaison, Olivier. 2005. *Coloniser, exterminer: Sur la guerre et l'État colonial*. Paris: Fayard.

Maunier, René. 1932. *Loi française et coutume indigène en Algérie*. Paris: Domat-Montchrestien.

Mbembe, Achille. 2005. "La République et l'impensé de la 'race.'" Chap. 12 in *La fracture coloniale: La société française au prisme de l'héritage colonial*, edited by Nicolas Bancel, Pascal Blanchard, and Sandrine Lemaire, 137–53. Paris: La Découverte. https://doi.org/10.3917/dec.blanc.2005.01.0137.

Morand, Marcel. 1903. "La famille musulmane." *Revue Algérienne, Tunisienne et Marocaine de Législation et de Jurisprudence*, pt. 1, §§ 12–19, pp. 149–64, 197–228, 229–52, 253–64. https://revcoleurop.cnrs.fr/ark%3A/67375/2CJkbrPjSnXm.

Morand, Marcel. 1913. "Le droit musulman algérien (Rite Malékite): Ses origines." *Revue Algérienne, Tunisienne et Marocaine de Législation et de Jurisprudence*, pt. 1, § 15, pp. 205–25. https://revcoleurop.cnrs.fr/ark%3A/67375/2CJNmDhV84Sh.

Morand, Marcel. 1916a. "Rapport fait à la Commission de Codification du Droit Musulman Algérien." In *Avant-projet de Code, Présenté à la Commission de Codification du Droit Musulman Algérien*. Algiers: Typographie Adolphe Jourdan.

Morand, Marcel. 1916b. *Avant-projet de Code, Présenté à la Commission de Codification du Droit Musulman Algérien*. Livre III, *Statut réel immobilier*. Titre III, *Des modes d'acquérir les droits réels immobiliers: Observations préliminaires*. Algiers: Typographie Adolphe Jourdan.

Renucci, Florence. 2015. "La Revue algérienne, tunisienne et marocaine de législation et de jurisprudence entre 1885 et 1916: Une identité singulière?" Chap. 7 in *Faire l'histoire du droit colonial: Cinquante ans après l'indépendance de l'Algérie*, edited by Jean-Philippe Bras, 181–201. Paris: Karthala. https://doi.org/10.3917/kart.bras.2015.01.0183.

Robe, Eugène. 1885. *Origines, formation et état actuel de la propriété en Algérie*. Foreword by Rodolphe Dareste. Paris: Challamel.

Samour, Nahed. 2017. "From Imperial to Dissent: Approaches to Territory in Islamic International Law." Chap. 11 in *International Law and Religion: Historical and Contemporary Perspectives*, edited by Martti Koskenniemi, Mónica García-Salmones Rovira, and Paolo Amorosa, 239–68. Oxford: Oxford University Press. https://doi.org/10.1093/oso/9780198805878.003.0012.

Santillana, David. 1899. *Avant projet de l'Avant-Projet de Code Civil et Commercial Tunisien*. Tunis: Imprimerie Générale (J. Picard & Cie).

Sayad, Abdelmalek. 2003. *Algeria: Nazionalismo senza nazione*. Edited by Salvatore Palidda and Nino Recupero and translated by Anna Vio. Messina: Mesogea.

Zeys, Ernest. 1885. *Traité Élémentaire de Droit Musulman Algérien (École Malékite)*. Algiers: Adolphe Jourdan.

5 Religion, Democracy, and Human Rights

The Example of Islam

Raja Bahlul

1. Introducing the Main Concepts

There is an age-old understanding of democracy according to which the latter involves at least three important elements: equality, liberty, and self-government. This way of understanding democracy can be found in the writings of Plato and Aristotle. For Plato, democracy is a place where "liberty and free speech are rife everywhere" (Plato, *Republic*, VIII, 557B, quoted from Plato 1941, 276). According to the latter, "if, as is generally held, freedom is especially to be found in democracy, and also equality, this condition is best realized when all share in equal measure the whole *politeia*" (Aristotle, *Politics*, IV.4, 291b35–39, quoted from Aristotle 1962, 159).

Relating democracy to human rights is straightforward. In a democracy, the people "govern" themselves (*demos* + *kratia*). And the idea of self-government is not foreign to human rights. This is implied by Article 22(3) of the 1948 Universal Declaration of Human Rights: "The will of the people shall be the basis of the authority of government; this shall be expressed in periodic and genuine elections which shall be by universal and equal suffrage and shall be held by secret vote or by equivalent free voting procedures." This article stops short of mentioning democracy by name, but it is obvious that this is what the article implies.

Self-government is not the only idea that brings democracy and human rights together; the same can be said of the ideas of equality and liberty. Article 1 of the Universal Declaration states, "All human beings are born free and equal." Article 19, which speaks of "freedom of opinion and expression," corresponds to Plato's assertion that, in a democracy, "liberty and free speech are rife everywhere" (Plato, *Republic*, VIII, 557B, quoted from Plato 1941, 276). In sum, democracy and human rights are relevant to each other in that human rights imply that we have a right to democracy, while democracy says that political life is to be based on freedom and equality, which are primary human rights.

Religion, on the other hand, may seem to lie farther afield. But that is not the case—for implicit in the monotheistic faiths of Islam, Christianity, and Judaism (and others, to be sure) are two ideas that have significant implications

DOI: 10.4324/9781003431206-9

for the ideas of democracy and human rights. These are the ideas of *human equality* and *human dignity*. The first may be used to relate religion to democracy, while the second may be used to relate religion to human rights.

Monotheistic religions view the creation of man as a purposeful divine act that grants humans a special status in the order of creation. It is true, of course, that in several places in the divine scriptures, God addresses specific groups of people (the Arabs or the Israelites, for example), but there are many other places where God addresses all humans, regardless of gender, race, or faith. An example of this is the Qur'anic verse where it is stated, "O mankind, We have created you male and female, and appointed you races and tribes, that you may know one another. Surely the noblest among you in the sight of God is the most godfearing of you" (49:13).[1] Addressed to mankind as such, this verse implies that all human beings have the same equal standing before God. Speaking for the Christian side, Schumpeter expresses this thought by saying that

> Christianity harbors a strong equalitarian element. The Redeemer died for all; He did not differentiate between individuals of different social status. In doing so, He testified to the intrinsic value of the individual soul, a value that admits of no gradation. Is not this a sanction—and as it seems to me, the only possible sanction—of "everyone to count for one, no one to count for more than one"—a sanction that pours super-mundane meaning into articles of the democratic creed for which it is not easy to find any other?
>
> (Schumpeter 1976, 265–66)

This is not an insignificant matter, given that democratic thought, which began its long journey of evolution outside the context of religion, took many centuries before it could accommodate the notion of equal and inclusive humanity. In fact, it was not until fairly recently that differences in gender, wealth, race, and religion ceased to matter for democratic theory. In this respect, it could be said that religion was centuries ahead of democracy.

The other idea which relates religion to human rights is the idea of human dignity, which provides a foundation for human rights—at least for those who believe that human rights need a foundation. The Universal Declaration, not being a philosophical tract, does not attempt to answer the question of what it is about human beings that entitles them to claim the numerous rights mentioned in the Declaration itself, but it does speak, in the Preamble, of the need to recognize "the inherent dignity and . . . the equal and inalienable rights of all members of the human family." There are no religious tones here, in contrast with the American Declaration of Independence, which in the second paragraph speaks of a Creator who endowed human beings with inalienable

1 All of the translations of the Qur'an are from Arberry 1964.

rights. Nevertheless, just as in the case of equality, it can be argued here, too, that religion has something to say about human dignity. For example, it is stated in the Qur'an that "We have honoured the Children of Adam and carried them on land and sea, and provided them with good things, and preferred them greatly over many of those We created" (17:70). The Hebrew Bible expresses man's dignified status by saying that "God created man in His own image, in the image of God He created him; male and female He created them" (Genesis 1:27). Regardless of the imagery or lack thereof, it is obvious that man has a very special status in the sight of God; he is somehow godlike or has an elevated status, unlike that of other creatures. This can serve as grounds (religious grounds, to be sure) for the idea that human beings have human rights.[2]

With these ideas in place, we can confidently assert that the concepts of democracy, human rights, and religion are mutually relevant to each other. But the relations between them prove to be less harmonious than what our attempt to show mutual relevance may have suggested. In Section 2 of this chapter I shall present an abstract, value-neutral, and purely procedural conception of democracy with reference to the classic work of Joseph Schumpeter. Owing to its simplicity, clarity, and relatively rigorous formulation, this conception will serve as a convenient starting point for the discussion of democracy, religion, and human rights. In this section we shall also raise the question of how membership (inclusion and exclusion) in the political community is to be determined.[3] Not only does this question create problems for Schumpeter's view of democracy, but it also problematizes the relationship among religion, democracy, and human rights.

In Section 3, I shall explain how the abstract and value-neutral conception of democracy discussed in Section 2 is enacted in two possible models of Islamic democracy, one to be found in the writings of the moderate Islamists, the other in the writings of the liberal Islamists. I also discuss how these two views position themselves in relation to the problem of membership raised in the previous section and the consequences this has for their position on human rights.

In Section 4, I argue that the problem of membership arises for Schumpeter's conception of democracy at least in part because of his sharp distinction between the question of procedure and the question of value and that this problem becomes possible to conceive of only in light of our modern notion of universal human rights. We conclude that a dilemma with no obvious solution begins to take shape here—between taking seriously the notion

2 Admittedly, many thinkers have sought grounds for human rights elsewhere—in reason, nature, or convention—so it is by no means the case that the justification of human rights has to invoke religion. Still, the existence of religious grounds (even if only in the minds of those who believe in religion) suffices to make religion a legitimate party in the conversation about human rights and democracy.

3 More familiarly, we can simply refer to membership as "citizenship" here.

of universal human rights and the democratic idea of a popular will that may or may not accede to human rights.

In Section 5, I suggest that the dilemma can be resolved by history and not by philosophical analysis. In this context we shall discuss and draw lessons with regard to (a) whether we need to enrich the concept of democracy beyond the Schumpeterian conception; (b) how religion needs to be understood in the context of a democratic, human rights-respecting regime; and (c) whether it is possible to view the grounding concepts of democracy and human rights as having a certain "religious" aspect, in that they may be found to depend more on faith than reason. Answers to these questions will be brought together in this conclusion: human rights may be viewed as a secularized version of a religion that has been made to live up to its vision of human equality and human dignity in the context of a value-laden (as opposed to a purely procedural) conception of democracy. This vision is not to be taken as a proven philosophical view but as a historical goal which is worth striving for.

2. Democracy as a Method of Decision-making

Democracy is an "essentially contested concept," in that it is a concept "around which there are disputes which are perfectly genuine; which, although not resolvable by argument of any kind, are nevertheless sustained by perfectly respectable arguments and evidence" (Gallie 1956, 169). That democracy fits this definition of "essentially contested concepts" is demonstrated by the fact that there are plausible theories of democracy that are the object of lively debates which show no sign of abating.[4]

It is neither practical nor useful for our purposes to review these theories. Therefore, we shall take as our starting point the relatively simple and abstract conception of democracy that was adumbrated by Joseph Schumpeter in the mid-20th century. According to the Schumpeterian conception,

> democracy may be viewed as a political method, that is to say, a certain type of institutional arrangement for arriving at political—legislative and administrative—decisions and hence incapable of being an end in itself, irrespective of what decisions it will produce under given historical conditions.
>
> (Schumpeter 1976, 242)

There are two main ideas to be considered here: the idea that democracy is a decision-making method and the idea that democracy is incapable of being an end in itself. The two ideas are related in that the second seems to be a consequence of the first, as suggested by the word *hence*. The first idea is fairly clear and familiar: Schumpeter means to refer to democratic processes and

4 See, for example, Dahl 1989; Held 2006.

institutions, which include free elections, parliaments, majority rule, and the like.[5] It is implicitly understood that the citizens are equal and free to advocate different programmes of political/social action.

As to the second idea, we take it to mean that the democratic method is value-neutral, so it may produce different results when applied in different historical, social, and/or cultural conditions. Applied in a liberal type of society, the democratic method will produce results of a liberal kind; applied in a religious type of society, it will produce results of a religious kind; and so on. This is what we find Schumpeter saying a little later in his book, thereby drawing a sharp distinction between the democratic method and the "good"/"bad" decisions it may produce:

> Communities which most of us would readily recognize as democracies have burned heretics at the stake—the republic of Geneva did in Calvin's time—or otherwise persecuted them in a manner repulsive to our moral standards. . . . [T]here have been nations that practiced discrimination of the kind alluded to [discrimination on the basis of wealth, sex, and religion] and nevertheless displayed most of those characteristics which are usually associated with democracy. . . . We may disapprove of [such practices] to be sure. But if we do so we should in good logic disapprove of the theories about the importance of property, religion, sex, race and so on, rather than call such societies undemocratic.
>
> (Schumpeter 1976, 240–41, 244, 245)

It may seem puzzling to view Schumpeter as offering a theory of democracy when he expressly allows that a democracy may discriminate on the basis of gender, wealth, and religion. In fact, there should be no great puzzle here or, if there is one, it is not peculiar to Schumpeter or to democratic thought in particular. For the fact of the matter is that, at various times and locations throughout history, great many political communities and associations have come to exist, but in no instance has it been the case that discrimination and exclusion were absent—so much so that this may be viewed as the norm rather than the exception.

Democracy, in Schumpeter's view, is not an exception to this rule. Exclusion of children (on the basis of age) and lunatics (mental incapacity) was always and continues to be taken for granted. But many other criteria have been used. Thus, democratic Athens excluded slaves, women, and transients. In Britain it was not until 1918 that all men over twenty-one could vote, regardless of wealth or property. In the United States it was not until 1919 that Congress ratified the 19th Amendment, which granted women the right

5 Elsewhere Schumpeter (1976, 269) says that "the democratic method is that institutional arrangement for arriving at political decisions in which individuals acquire the power to decide by means of a competitive struggle for the people's vote."

to vote. Examples can be multiplied to no end, attesting to the fact the question of who is to be included in the political community was always a historical/cultural question, inevitably subject to a certain degree of relativism.

Not finding clear and compelling grounds for inclusion and exclusion, Schumpeter concluded that "the *populus*" (his term for the self-governing political community) must be allowed to define itself however it chooses. It is worth noting that Schumpeter uses a somewhat extreme and thus implausible example to drive his point home. The previously quoted passage continues thus:

> Religious fervor, for instance, is certainly compatible with democracy however we define the latter. There is a type of religious attitude to which a heretic seems worse than a madman. Does it not follow that the heretic should be barred from participation in political decisions as is the lunatic? Must we not leave it to every *populus* to define itself?
>
> (Ibid., 245)

In following this line of thought, Schumpeter was in effect prescribing that the question of inclusion in the political community lies outside the scope of the theory of democracy. For him it was a question over which democracy remains silent. Of course, members of the political community are supposed to be free, equal, and self-governing. But who these people are and how they are to be delimited are separate questions which democratic theory cannot answer.

Schumpeter's position on the question of inclusion proved to be one of the most controversial aspects of his theory of democracy. We shall have a chance to examine this aspect of Schumpeter's view of democracy in Section 4, but for the time being let us explore how religion and human rights fare on this simple, minimalist, and procedural conception of democracy. In this way we hope to gain an understanding of the points at which democracy, religion, and human rights converge and diverge.

Consider democracy (as characterized by Schumpeter) in relation to religion. Some religions (and the communities they define) tolerate the existence of different interpretations of dogma and permissible practice. Others may consider the slightest deviation from established orthodoxy a heresy. Recalling Schumpeter's extreme example, some religions may view the so-called heretic as a mentally deranged person. Or, less benignly, they may view this character as an existential threat to the community. Such religions will not draw a line between the religious and the political. Nevertheless, a political life based on such intolerant religions may be democratic in Schumpeter's light, because it follows "the democratic method" of decision-making.

Democracy is also compatible with religions which are in and of themselves tolerant or which may over time have come to be so. In fact, it could be said that Schumpeterian democracy is equally compatible with atheism or any type of doctrine, including (for example) social-economic doctrines such as capitalism and socialism. The title of Schumpeter's book, *Capitalism, Socialism and*

Democracy, suggests this much retrospectively to someone who reads the book in its entirety. Toward the end of the book, Schumpeter claims that democracy is no less compatible with socialism than capitalism, and that if socialism were to succeed capitalism, this need not mean the end of democracy. According to Schumpeter, there is

> no reason why [the forms and organs of democratic procedure] should have to disappear along with capitalism. General elections, parties, parliaments, cabinets and prime ministers may still prove to be the most convenient instruments for dealing with the agenda that the socialist order may reserve for political decision. The list of these agenda will be relieved of all those items that at present arise from the clash of private interests and from the necessity of regulating them. Instead there will be new ones. There will be such questions to decide as what the volume of investment should be or how existing rules for the distribution of the social product should be amended and so on.
>
> (Ibid., 301)

What matters in the end is not what religion or doctrine is practiced but the fact that the community abides by the rules of democratic procedure in its political life. Exclusions from the political process are "valid" as long as they are "admitted" by the society in question:

> it is not relevant whether we, the observers, admit the validity of those reasons or of the practical rules by which they are made to exclude portions of the population; all that matters is that the society in question admits it.
>
> (Ibid., 244)

However, matters become more complicated when we consider the relation between Schumpeterian democracy and human rights. To disentangle the issues to some degree, it is useful to distinguish between the notion of *rights*—considered in itself—and the notion of *human rights*.[6] For it could be said that democracy, as conceived by Schumpeter, can accommodate systems (schemes) of rights in pretty much the same way as it accommodates different religions. The scheme of rights that was operative in Athenian democracy differed from the scheme of rights that was operative in the polities which Schumpeter mentions—"democratic" Geneva, colonial Massachusetts, or late-19th-century Britain. But the notion of human rights is altogether different in one respect, namely, human rights are commonly viewed as being objective, universally valid, and binding, regardless of culture and history. It is on account of this

6 This is not to say that the two notions are unrelated. Of course, they *are* related, and it should be possible to extend bridges between the two.

facet of human rights that tensions begin to appear in the context of democracy as conceived by Schumpeter. Were we to remain at the level of rights *simpliciter*, there would be no more incompatibility between democracy and the most morally repugnant scheme of rights than between democracy and the most fanatical type of religion.

Schumpeter's conception of democracy allows political communities to "choose" themselves, that is, to define their values and identity however they choose. But given the fact that human rights are universally valid, and given the fact that democracy (as conceived by Schumpeter) allows for political communities to have their own schemes of rights (not human rights), it is conceivable, even likely, for there to be "democratic" political communities that violate human rights. This is how we retrospectively view the Athenian and the other democracies to which Schumpeter refers.

From the perspective of our modern moral sensibilities, we find it hard to attribute democracy to a political community that permits exclusion on the basis of sex, wealth, race, or religion. But to view such a community as *undemocratic* is the same as taking issue with Schumpeter's conception of democracy. In so doing one stipulates that democracy cannot be silent on the question of who can participate in the political process. Not only must democratic theory answer this question, but it must do so in a way that is consistent with the doctrine of human rights. This is as much as to say that democracy must be *constrained* by human rights.

At this point many questions raise themselves. First, is it fair to burden the theory of democracy with the task of deciding on questions of membership in the political community? Second, is "democracy" a value-neutral descriptive concept, or is it a normative concept, one that can be used to fault regimes that fail to comply with human rights? Third, how are we to view human rights? Is it possible to view them as a doctrine of sorts, a normative ethical view, even a religion of some kind? And, if so, what is to prevent Schumpeter from claiming that democracy, properly conceived, cannot accord them any special treatment?

These are some of the questions we shall discuss in the rest of this chapter. In the meantime, it will be instructive to discuss Islamic democracy as a concrete illustration of the difficulties to be found at the intersection of democracy, religion and human rights.

3 Two Models of Islamic Democracy

Muslim thinkers first became acquainted with modern Western democratic political ideas and practices in the second half of the 19th century. Ever since that time, their grasp and appreciation of the complexities of the subject have been steadily growing. Not surprisingly, many views about the relation between democracy and Islam were developed during this long process of maturation. We shall, however, focus on the views of moderate and liberal Islamists, to the exclusion those of the fundamentalists who do not have any substantive notion of self-government.

Unlike the fundamentalists, the moderates and the liberals belong to the modernist/reformist camp of modern Islamic thought. Such thinkers tend to perceive Islam in terms of "openness" and "dynamism" (Stowasser 1993, 3); they also tend to interpret Islam "creatively" (Azmeh 1993, 33), which is to say that they tend to prefer *ijtihad* (independent interpretation) over *taqlid* (tradition-following) (Kurzman 1998, 8). Hourani (1983, 344) went as far as to claim that they were intent upon "reinterpret[ing] Islamic concepts so as to make them equivalent to the guiding principles of European thought."

Nevertheless, moderate and liberal Islamists differ amongst themselves in their interpretation of Islam. Whereas the liberals tend to understand Islam in exclusively spiritual/ethical terms, the moderates believe that while Islam can be understood in spiritual/ethical terms, there is nevertheless a doctrinal (dogmatic) aspect which places limits on any spiritual/ethical understanding of the religion. As we shall see presently, the differences between the moderates and the liberals translate into differences over their conception of the constitution and their understanding of democracy and human rights.

We begin with two thinkers of moderate Islamism whose conception of democracy can be readily understood in terms of Schumpeter's abstract scheme. These two thinkers are Rashid al-Ghannushi—the well-known Tunisian political thinker and leader—and Mohammad Khatami, the first president of the Islamic Republic of Iran. According to al-Ghannushi,

> it is possible for the mechanisms of democracy . . . to operate in different cultural milieus. Secularism, nationalism, . . . and the deification of man . . . are not inevitable consequences of democracy, inasmuch as this latter resolves itself into popular sovereignty, equality between citizens . . . and recognition of the majority's right to rule. There is nothing in these procedures which is necessarily in conflict with Islamic values. On the contrary, the democratic apparatus is the best available method for realizing these values.
>
> (Al-Ghannushi 1993, 88, my translation)

More briefly but somewhat less clearly, Khatami says:

> Democracy is a way to achieve [political] stability. This means that democracy is a mechanism, and that the will of the people decides the form of government. Now, in the West, the popular will has led to secularism and liberalism. In Islamic societies, the popular will is bound to produce a form of government which is in line with the people's Islamic thought.
>
> (Khatami 1998, 103, my translation)

Thus, both thinkers understand democracy to be a "mechanism" for implementing the will of the people. To their minds, the method must be distinguished from the types of decisions that are reached, these being matters for the popular will to determine. Thus, according to al-Ghannushi and Khatami, in the West, the will of the people has chosen to follow the path of secularism, nationalism, materialism, and other this-worldly values. But none of these (Islamically unacceptable paths) is to be viewed as an outcome of the democratic mechanism as such. Rather, they are the outcome of a popular will that upholds a certain conception of value and meaning, operating in accordance with one and the same democratic mechanism. Were the democratic mechanism to operate in an Islamic context, different types of decisions and policies would result.

Both Schumpeter and the moderate Islamists view the democratic method of decision-making as normatively neutral. Thus, al-Ghannushi and Khatami are able to declare that democracy is compatible with Islam. According to this view, one may speak of Islamic democracy as naturally as one may speak of socialist, liberal, Christian, or Jewish democracy. The similarities between Schumpeter and these two moderate Islamic thinkers are real. As we have no evidence that al-Ghannushi and Khatami were acquainted with the writings of Schumpeter, we must assume that they must have reached their conclusions through their own reflection on the variety of past and present democratic systems and practices. This may well have been the way Schumpeter himself arrived at his own view in the first place.

As in the case of Schumpeter, the question of membership in the political community (citizenship) eventually arises for al-Ghannushi and Khatami. Who is to be included in the political community—which al-Ghannushi and other Islamic writers call the *umma*—and on what grounds? Members of the *umma* are supposed to be equal, free, and able to participate in governing themselves (in accordance with Islamic laws). Children and the mentally incapacitated are excluded as on most accounts of democracy and for the same reasons. Exclusion on the basis of wealth and race is prohibited, in accordance with the Islamic religious ideal of human equality. Finally, there are no slaves to be excluded from the political process either.[7]

Still, there are certain types of exclusions that thinkers such al-Ghannushi and Khatami need to grapple with: these include women, non-Muslims, apostates, secularists, atheists, and people with religiously prohibited lifestyles. In the case of non-Muslim members of the Islamic state, we find al-Ghannushi saying:

> Citizenship [of the non-Muslim] will always have a special character which cannot be lifted until the person becomes a Muslim. . . . He cannot occupy high office where this reflects on the identity of the state (such as the office of the president).
>
> (al-Ghannushi 1993, 290, my translation)

7 We saw a revival of slavery at the hands of the militant brand of Islamic fundamentalism known as ISIS, the "Islamic State" which ruled in parts of Syria and Iraq from 2013 to 2018. But this need not deter us here because the Islamic State never laid claim to being democratic, and neither has anyone claimed democracy on its behalf, as Schumpeter does for the Republic of Geneva and for colonial Massachusetts.

With regard to the inclusion of women in the political process, some restrictions apply. Women are not allowed to occupy the highest political office, even though they may sit in Parliament. Even at the parliamentary level, al-Ghannushi finds it necessary to reassure his anxious readers that there is no danger of women ever becoming a majority in Parliament, in such a way as to affect the overall character of the decision-making process:

> The number of women who run for Parliament will always be limited. The majority of members of Parliament, which makes decisions, will always be male, so it cannot be said that allowing women to run for Parliament will cause men to lose their role of leadership (*qiwama*) over women.
>
> (Al-Ghannushi 2000, 119)

This, then, is how Islamic democracy emerges within the conceptual framework advocated by Schumpeter and accepted by al-Ghannushi and Khatami. Strictly speaking, membership of the political community will be male, adult, believing Muslims. The criteria for something being a *democracy* are satisfied in Schumpeter's light, for Schumpeter poses no objection to the political community defining itself the way it chooses. Moreover, the criteria for *Islamicity* are satisfied in al-Ghannushi's and Khatami's light, because the democratic process in and of itself does not violate Islamic teachings. Thus, to all appearances, Islamic democracy seems to be a coherent idea.[8]

However, when we bring the concept of human rights into the discussion, the position of Islamic democracy begins to look problematic. For the idea of human equality, despite its religious roots, does not seem to be taken very seriously in the idea of Islamic democracy thus conceived, on account of exclusions and/or restrictions on the basis of religion and sex. Consequently, advocates of human rights who join the discussion at this stage may do one of two things. They may fault Schumpeter's conception of democracy because it *permits* exclusions on the basis of religion and sex, or they may fault Islam (or, more accurately, certain interpretations thereof) for *accepting* what Schumpeter's conception merely permits. Or they may do both.

As we saw earlier, Schumpeter places the blame squarely on the views that place great value on religion, sex, colour, or wealth, etc. Accepting for now (but just for now) Schumpeter's defence of his own position, we may ask: what can the advocates of religion say in their own defence? There are two paths they can follow: an easy path and a hard one. We shall discuss the easy path in the remainder of this section, leaving discussion of the hard one to the next.

The easy path is taken by the liberal Islamists. It is mainly based on emphasizing the spiritual/ethical aspect of Islam at the expense of the doctrinal/dogmatic elements which may stand in the way of unconditional acceptance of

8 For a fuller discussion the conceptual viability of Islamic Democracy, see Bahlul 2004.

human rights. Briefly stated, their strategy is to interpret Islam so that it fully complies with human rights, thereby solving the problem of inclusion in one short step.

Who are the liberal Islamists, and what do they have to say on the matter of democracy and human rights? Ali Abdel Razeq (1888–1966) may be mentioned first, not only because he is probably the first writer to break with traditional Islamic political thought but because of his conception of Islam as a spiritual call:

> Islam is a religious predication: a summons to God. It is a system that aspires to a reformation of the human condition; to redirect humanity to the path leading to God. It is a means to the attainment of everlasting beatitude, the reward, promised by God, to the most righteous among His subjects. It is a religious union, one that God has willed for all of humanity, encompassing all the lands on earth.
>
> (Abdel Razeq 2012, 92–93)

Fazlur Rahman (1919–1988) adds ethics to spirituality. According to him, the totality of Islamic teachings aims at the establishment of a "community of justice and goodness" (Rahman 1982, 13). This enables him to distinguish between legal enactments and moral principles. He regards the latter as having a more authoritative status, because, in his view, the Qur'an is not to be conceived of as a law book (ibid., 47).

Along the same lines but combining the ethical and the spiritual, Khaled Abou El-Fadl has said that *Shari'a* (Islamic law) should not be viewed as a set of particular, historically conditioned legal enactments; rather, it should be understood in terms of divine intentions and of principles of divine mercy and justice: "it ought to stand in an Islamic polity as a symbolic construct for the divine perfection that is unreachable by human effort" (Abou El-Fadl 2004, 22, 33).

Emphasis on the spiritual/ethical core of Islam does not entail allegiance to any specific political order. Thus, at the end of his book we find Abdel Razeq saying:

> Nothing stops [Muslims] from building their state and their system of government on the basis of past constructions of human reason, of systems whose sturdiness has stood the test of time, which the experience of nations has shown to be effective.
>
> (Abdel Razeq 2012, 118)

What Abdel Razeq left to choice, the later liberal-minded thinkers specified in no equivocal terms: democracy is the political order which Muslims should seek to establish. One of these thinkers is Abou El-Fadl. He gives traditionally interpreted Shari'a its due by saying that its endorsement of the ideas of the rule of law and constitutionalism signifies its acceptance of "core elements of modern democratic practice." But Abou El-Fadl does not stop at this:

> In a democracy, the *people* are the source of the law, and the law in turn ensures the fundamental rights that protect the well-being and interests of the individual members of the sovereignty.
>
> (Abou El-Fadl 2004, 4, italics added)

It has fallen to Adullahi An-Na'im's lot to complete the picture of a Liberal Islamic democracy by offering an interpretation of the Qur'anic revelation so as to bring it into conformity with our modern understanding of universal human rights. An-Na'im, in effect, calls for the abrogation of the extant Shari'a and its replacement by one that is based on the ethical-humanistic message contained in the Qur'anic revelations of the (earlier) Meccan period of Islam.[9] According to An-Na'im, the "Meccan" message of Islam

> [emphasized] the inherent dignity of all human beings, regardless of gender, religious belief, race and so forth. That message was characterized by equality between men and women and complete freedom of choice in matters of religion and faith.
>
> (Na'im 1990, 52)

An-Na'im goes on to urge that the time has come to revert to the earlier message of Islam, which is compatible with our modern notion of human rights:

> Unless the basis of modern Islamic law is shifted away from those texts of the Qur'an and Sunna of the Medina stage . . . there is no way of avoiding drastic and serious violation of human rights.
>
> (Na'im 1990, 179)

What An-Na'im is proposing is no less than an Islamic Reformation, one that would make recognition and adherence to universal human rights an integral part of the faith.

Our discussion so far seems to have left Schumpeter in the clear; moderate Islamic democracy remains on the defensive on account of the human rights criticism, while advocates of human rights and their liberal Islamic partners seem to have escaped all criticism. But matters are not that simple—for neither Schumpeter's conception of democracy nor the position of the advocates of

9 After preaching for twelve years with little success in his home city of Mecca, the Prophet of Islam migrated to neighbouring Medina, where he established the first Islamic polity. The extant Shari'a is supposed to be based mainly on the (later) Medinan revelations, which tend to be legalistic and formalistic.

universal human rights is beyond reproach. These are the matters to which we turn our attention in the next section, beginning with criticism of Schumpeter's conception of democracy.

4. The Dilemma of Democracy and Human Rights

As things stand, the conception which Schumpeter offers allows us to ascribe democracy to a gang of a hundred members which conducts its affairs democratically (voting on which banks to rob, how income is to be distributed among the gang members, etc.). The term can equally apply to a charitable organization. Such general applicability may be thought to count in favour of Schumpeter's theory, but instituting democracy for political communities comprising millions or tens of millions of members is a different matter. The injunction to let "the subjects of a democracy" choose for themselves as they please might work for a gang of robbers, a social club, or a charitable organization, but it can lead to absurdities once it is contemplated for masses of human beings who, not necessarily by choice, live together in a certain territory.

The point was forcefully made by Robert Dahl, who criticized Schumpeter for "conflating" these two statements:

> System X is democratic in relation to its own demos [its own "people"].
> System X is democratic in relation to everyone subject to its rules.
> (Dahl 1989, 122)

This is a plausible distinction, but suppose we *reject* it by insisting that the Apartheid regime of South Africa, where at one time white people made up only 13 percent of the total population, was democratic *sans phrase*. At what point would we need to stop as the percentage decreases? Dahl asks:

> Is there not some number or proportion of a population below which a "people" is not a demos but rather an aristocracy, oligarchy, or despotism? If the rulers numbered 100 in a population of 100 million, would we call the rulers a demos and the system a democracy?
> (Ibid., 122)

It is no use for Schumpeter to say here that we should criticize the theory to which white South Africans subscribed about the importance of race and colour. Schumpeter has a conceptual problem now. He has to be able to distinguish among distinct types of regimes such as oligarchy, aristocracy, democracy, despotism, and the rest. A theory of democracy which cannot make the distinction is hardly worth its salt.

Dahl's own view is that "the demos should include all adult subjects of the binding collective decisions of the association" (ibid., 120). How can one justify this proposal? One would be hard pressed to think of a justification that does not at some point refer to the idea of human rights. The reason is that for others to subject you to laws that you had no hand in making is to treat you unequally, in violation of the human right to equal treatment. This, in effect, is what we actually find Dahl saying. His justification is ultimately based on the idea of intrinsic equality, "the common doctrine of Judaism and Christianity (shared also by Islam) that we are equally God's children" (ibid., 86), regardless of race, gender, religion, etc. It is not implausible to take this as an invocation of human rights.

Michael Walzer (1995, 31) also has argued to a similar conclusion, starting from the moral consideration that "[t]he primary good that we distribute to one another is membership in some human community." The conclusion he reaches is that

> the process of self-determination through which a democratic state shapes its internal life must be open, and equally open, to all those men and women who live within its territories, work in the local economy, and are subject to local law.
>
> (Ibid., 60)

The force of this moral consideration ultimately drives Walzer to conclude that when communities are "deeply divided" to the extent of not being able to agree on a common self-definition (which, of course, entails a criterion of membership), "then its territory must be divided, too, before the rights of admission and exclusion can be exercised" (ibid., 62).

It is evident now that the notion of human rights places constraints on how we can conceive of democracy. In the previous section we saw how the same notion of human rights seems to place constraints on our conception of religion. But now that democracy and religion have been subjected to questioning, it is only natural to raise the question of whether the notion of human rights itself can be questioned. How do human rights fare when subjected to examination? Do they fare any better than either democracy or religion?

Those familiar with the debates which the concept of human rights has engendered in philosophical and other intellectual circles are bound to agree that the concept is as much "essentially contested" as democracy and religion themselves. To begin with, we may note that our present idea of universal humanity has emerged only as the outcome of a long historical development of ideas and struggles about who is to count as a human. Claude Lévi-Strauss claims that

> the concept of an all-inclusive humanity, which makes no distinction between races or cultures, appeared very late in the history of mankind, and did not spread very widely across the face of the globe. For the majority of the human species, and for tens of thousands of years, the idea that humanity includes every human being on the face of the earth

> does not exist at all. The designation stops at the border of each tribe, or linguistic group, sometimes even at the edge of a village.
>
> (Lévi-Strauss 1983, vol. 2, p. 329)[10]

No sooner did the idea of universal humanity begin to "spread widely," at least in the modern West, than philosophers began to view it with suspicion. At the start of the debate we find the utilitarian philosopher Jeremy Bentham (1987, 53) claiming that the concept of human rights is nothing but "nonsense upon stilts." Not much later we find Marx saying, in criticism of the 1789 Declaration of the Rights of Man and of the Citizen, that "the so-called rights of man . . . are nothing but the rights of the member of civil society, i.e. egoistic man, man separated from other men and the community" (Marx 1987, 145).

Ever since that time, human rights have been subjected to criticism from diverse points of view—cultural, Marxist, socialist, feminist, communitarian, and religious. It is the last of these which is of greatest interest in the context of determining how religion can position itself in relation to democracy. As we saw in the previous section, liberal Islamists took the easy path by accepting the modern conception of human rights. Moderate Islamists, on the other hand, with their less than fully inclusive conception of political community, are compelled to take a critical position toward human rights, because it is these that stand to make their position "undemocratic."

Challenging the modern conception of human rights with its "open door policy" of admission is the "hard path" alluded to in the previous section. Jeremy Waldon, speaking on behalf of the critics of universal human rights, seeks to reduce the universalist position to absurdity. Moderate Islamists may want to follow his line of argument. Says Waldron:

> If people in a given society have accustomed themselves to monarchical rule and have sought no hand in government, that counts for nothing: they have a right to democratic freedom which is inalienable, it is said, and they must be brought to recognize the fact. If a church has grown so long and deeply into a community that it permeates all customs and manners and it is unthinkable that anyone should question the common faith, that counts for nothing: they have a right to religious freedom which is imprescriptible, whether they want it or not. Though human rights may be mysterious or unintelligible to the people who are said to have them, they are said to have them just the same, and those claims of right are supposed to capture the moral truth about them in a way that their own customs, practices and shared understandings do not.
>
> (Waldron 1987, 167)

10 The point which Lévi-Strauss makes remains valid despite the relative antiquity of the monotheistic religions, which have indeed entertained a concept of universal humanity. For it cannot be said that religion has always, even for the most part, managed to live up to its vision of universal humanity; sadly, more often than not it has relapsed into the position of equating humanity with membership in the believing community.

Waldron starts off from a point where moderate Islamists are not to be found, for they do not agree that people may not want to live under a democratic regime. But the point about a church (or an Islamic institution) having "grown so long and deeply into a community that it permeates all customs and manners" will resonate with them. Thus to ask them to welcome the unbeliever and the non-Muslim into their political life is to ask them to discount religion in their (necessarily public) political life, notwithstanding the fact that religion has always been an essential part of how they live. Moreover, it is not just that having an "imprescriptible" right to freedom of religion stands to make little or no sense to them, but to tell them that the religiously different have a right to participate in their political affairs is bound to sound coercive to them. If acceptance of human rights were to amount to this, they may well view human rights with great scepticism.

The full implementation of human rights is bound to require a clean separation between (public) political life and religion; in other words, religion must become a private affair. Religion may still give society a certain spiritual/ethical aura of the kind that liberal Islamists may be content with, but this is not sufficient for moderate Islamists, who are unwilling to divide their existence between a private religious sphere and a public political sphere. Nicholas Wolterstorff spoke for many religious citizens when he took Rawls to task for assuming that

> though religious people may not be in the habit of dividing their lives into a religious component and a non-religious component, and though some might not be happy doing so, nonetheless, their doing so would in no case be in violation of their religion.
>
> (Wolterstorff 1997, 116)

According to Wolterstorff, this assumption in unfair:

> [Rawls] is wrong about this. It is when we bring into the picture people for whom it is a matter of religious conviction that they ought to strive for a religiously integrated existence—then especially, though not only then, does the unfairness of the liberal position [read: adherence to the doctrine of human rights] to religion come to light.
>
> (Ibid.)

Waldron and Wolterstorff seem to be suggesting that the definition of what is right, good, or just may be community-specific. This is what we find Walzer saying in clearer terms:

> We cannot say what is due to this person or that one until we know how these people relate to one another through the things they make and distribute. . . . A given society is just if its substantive life is lived in a certain way—that is, in a way faithful to the shared understandings of

> the members. . . . Every substantive account of distributive justice is a local account.
>
> (Walzer 1995, 312–14)

When adherence to human rights becomes a constitutive element of democracy, democracy becomes similar to, if not the same as, "liberal/constitutional democracy," which moderate Islamists are bound to reject. At this point a dilemma of sorts begins to take shape. Standing on one horn of the dilemma, we face the prospect of coercing religious believers into leading a "divided existence" (Wolterstorff's words) and to live in accordance with the doctrine of universal human rights, in a manner reminiscent of Rousseau's repellent idea of "forcing someone to be free" (Rousseau 2002, bk. 1, chap. 7, p. 166). Standing on the other horn, giving full rein to popular sovereignty, we face the prospect of morally unacceptable exclusions whereby nonreligious individuals are treated as second-class citizens or no citizens at all.

Are human rights, therefore, undemocratic? Or should democracy, after all, be sharply distinguished from human rights, in accordance with Schumpeter's conception? These are some of the hard questions we will discuss in the final section of this chapter.

5. A Role for History

In his *Political Liberalism*, John Rawls raised the following question:

> how is it possible for there to exist over time a just and stable society of free and equal citizens, who remain profoundly divided by reasonable religious, philosophical, and moral doctrines?
>
> (Rawls 1993, 4)

The question is doubly difficult. The desiderata of justice and stability are hard enough, but when they are desired for societies where citizens are "profoundly divided" by religious, philosophical, and moral doctrines, the matter becomes harder still. Rawls makes the answer seem easier than it actually is by speaking of *reasonable* doctrines, suggesting that we do not need to worry about "unreasonable" doctrines.[11] Only when we remember Schumpeter's statement about the religious attitude which views the heretic as worse than the madman (Schumpeter 1976, 245) does the thought occur to us that there may be different conceptions of reasonableness—that while some conceptions of reasonableness may themselves be reasonable, others (like that of Schumpeter's religious fanatic) may not be. The problem is that we may not be able to

11 In fact, Rawls speaks rather harshly of such doctrines, saying that "a society may also contain unreasonable and irrational, and even mad, comprehensive doctrines. In their case, the problem is to contain them so that they do not undermine the unity and justice of society" (Rawls 1993, xix).

agree on what makes a religious, philosophical, or moral doctrine unreasonable. We may agree that it is unreasonable to view someone who forsakes his or her religious faith for another as mad, but what are we to say about a religious people who stoutly refuse to lead a "divided existence" between a public political sphere and a private religious sphere? Are they being unreasonable? The answer is not clear.

The idea that societies will continue, at least for the foreseeable future, to be "profoundly divided" by religious, philosophical, and moral doctrines is something that most people nowadays accept. This is as much a fruit of historical developments as of our realization of the importance of democracy and human rights. Some people may find in this realization grounds for criticizing the moderate Islamist view for being somewhat unreasonable. With the notion of reciprocity in the back of their minds, they may address the moderate Islamists by saying: "Imagine yourselves in the place of the Christian, Jew, or atheist to whom you are unwilling to extend full membership in the political community. Doesn't this seem unjust?" Some moderates may surprise us by saying, "No, it is not unjust," or "We cannot imagine ourselves in those places you are asking us to visit in our imagination." This is because their religion is part of who they are—it is constitutive of their identity. From this point onward the discussion becomes quite philosophical, as all discussions of identity are bound to become, with no promise of yielding conclusive results.

For this reason, it may be reasonable to suggest that the dilemma with which we ended the last section is not one that can be resolved within philosophy but one that only history (time) can resolve. We can begin to form a sense of what this suggestion amounts to by initially looking at the situation of human rights at the present historical moment. It is obvious that such notions as equality and freedom, as well as other elements of human rights, are not actual realities and that struggles for equality, freedom, and human rights are still ongoing, in the hope that they *will* become actual in the future.

True, we learned from modern political philosophers to speak of humans as being free and equal, having once lived in a "state of nature" out of which they emerged through a "social contract" that somehow preserved their "natural" freedom and "natural" equality. This notion, according to Margaret Canovan (1990, 16), is still to be found in Rawls's theory, "in which the ghost of the State of Nature walks again in the guise of the 'Original Position.'" In the words of Talal Asad (2003, 57), we seem to have learned to think of this "original" or "natural" condition as some kind of "deep reality," "a realm more real than the social world."

But is the idea that humans are *really* equal, free, and possessed of inalienable rights more than a myth, perhaps comparable to Plato's myth of the cave, or Marx's belief in the iron laws of history which will ultimately lead to Communism? Says Canovan in this regard:

> As countless critics have pointed out, it is not common sense to suppose that all men are created equal or that they are endowed with inalienable

> rights to life, liberty and the pursuit of happiness. Quite the reverse: an unprejudiced observer surveying the human condition would conclude that there is nothing in the least self-evident about human equality.
>
> (Canovan 1990, 9)

This being so, Canovan goes on to suggest that liberalism (and, by implication, human rights) should be viewed as projects to be realized in the future. According to her, "liberalism never has been an account of the world but a project to be realized" (ibid., 16). There is thus a role for history to play. Much work has to be done to realize the project of human rights: our conceptions of ourselves and our actions as individuals and social beings have to change; our sensibilities, too, have to evolve. Richard Rorty (1994, 179) went as far as to pin our hopes for a human-rights-respecting future not on philosophy and logical arguments but on nurturing pro-human-rights sentiments in "generations of nice, tolerant, well-off, secure, other-respecting students . . . in all parts of the world."

What applies to liberalism and human rights may not seem to apply to religion and democracy, but in fact it does. We saw evidence of this in the work of liberal Islamists, who are seeking to formulate a more historically advanced understanding of Islam. Even the moderate Islamists, with their limits on membership in the political community, may need to be surpassed. Liberal Islam may be viewed as a historical project, one which, in the view of writers such as An-Na'im, will make full peace with human rights.

The rapprochement between religion and human rights is not unidirectional, for in the eyes of thinkers such Canovan and Rorty there may be nothing wrong with viewing human rights as some kind of "religion," for there are elements of myth and faith to be found in our belief in human rights. In fact, the doctrine of human rights may be viewed as a secularized kind of religion, where the mysterious religious idea of "equal standing before God" is replaced by the equally mysterious idea of humans having rights by nature or in some "deep reality" that is more fundamental than social, human-invented reality. Conversely, we may view human rights as a traditional religion that has been made to live up to its own vision of human equality and dignity.

In this historical project, democracy, too, will fall into place. For the terms *equality* and *freedom* which we use when we think about human rights—and which Plato, Aristotle, and Schumpeter use to describe democracy—do not have completely different meanings. The dictionary does not list different entries for *freedom* and *equality*, one for Plato and Aristotle, one for Schumpeter and one for the human rights advocate. *Freedom* and *equality* are not lexically ambiguous words, like *bank*, *party*, and *bat*. Instead, they are what we have called "contested concepts." People disagree, often with good reason, over their range and the proper way to employ them.

There is nothing in the nature of democracy which mandates exclusions. Schumpeter seems to have meant his conception of democracy to be purely descriptive—describing, in effect, how democracy has been practiced up to this point in history. But democracy need not be captive to its history any more than religion needs to be. In sum, the tensions which we have highlighted throughout this chapter may be only of a temporary nature. Their resolution will be a historical task, one in which philosophy stands to play an important, even if inconclusive, role.

Works Cited

Abdel Razeq, Ali. 2012. *Islam and the Foundations of Political Power.* Translated by Maryam Loutfi. Edinburgh: Edinburgh University Press.

Abou El-Fadl, Khaled. 2004. *Islam and the Challenge of Democracy.* Princeton, NJ: Princeton University Press.

Al-Ghannushi, Rashid. 1993. *Al-Hurriyat al-ʿAmmah fi al-Dawlah al-Islamiyyah* (Public Liberties in the Islamic State). Beirut: Markaz Dirasat al-Wihdah al-Arabiyyah.

Al-Ghannushi, Rashid. 2000. *Al-Mar'ah baina al-Qur'an wa Waqi' al-Muslimin.* London: Maghreb Center for Research and Translation.

Arberry, A. J. 1964. *The Koran Interpreted.* Oxford: Oxford University Press.

Aristotle. 1962. *The Politics.* Translated by T. A. Sinclair. London: Penguin Books.

Asad, Talal. 2003. *Formations of the Secular: Christianity, Islam, Modernity.* Palo Alto, CA: Stanford University Press.

Azmeh, Aziz Al. 1993. "Islamism and the Arabs." In *Islams and Modernities*, 18–38. London: Verso.

Bahlul, Raja. 2004. "Democracy Without Secularism? Reflections on the Idea of Islamic Democracy." Chap. 5 in *Islam, Judaism, and the Political Role of Religions in the Middle East*, edited by John Bunzl, 99–117. Gainesville, FL: University Press of Florida.

Bentham, Jeremy. (1796) 1987. "Anarchical Fallacies." In *"Nonsense Upon Stilts": Bentham, Burke, and Marx on the Rights of Man*, edited by Jeremy Waldron, 46–76. London: Methuen.

Canovan, Margaret. 1990. "On Being Economical with the Truth: Some Liberal Reflections." *Political Studies* 38: 5–19. https://doi.org/10.1111/j.1467-9248.1990.tb00566.x.

Dahl, Robert A. 1989. *Democracy and Its Critics.* New Haven, CT: Yale University Press.

Gallie, W. B. 1956. "Essentially Contested Concepts." *Proceedings of the Aristotelian Society* 65 (1): 167–98. https://doi.org/10.1093/aristotelian/56.1.167.

Held, David. 2006. *Models of Democracy.* Cambridge: Polity Press.

Hourani, Albert. 1983. *Arabic Thought in the Liberal Age, 1798–1939.* Cambridge: Cambridge University Press. https://doi.org/10.1017/CBO9780511801990.

Khatami, Mohammad. 1998. *Mutalaʿat fi al-Din wal-Islam wal-ʿAsr.* Beirut: Dar al-Jadid.

Kurzman, Charles, ed. 1998. *Liberal Islam: A Sourcebook.* Oxford: Oxford University Press. https://doi.org/10.1093/acref/9780195116212.001.0001.

Lévi-Strauss, Claude. 1983. *Structural Anthropology.* Translated by Monique Layton. Chicago: University of Chicago Press.

Marx, Karl. (1843) 1987. "On the Jewish Question." In *"Nonsense upon Stilts": Bentham, Burke, and Marx on the Rights of Man*, edited by Jeremy Waldron, 137–50. London: Methuen.

Na'im, Adullahi Ahmed. 1990. *Toward an Islamic Reformation: Civil Liberties, Human Rights, and International Law.* Syracuse, NY: Syracuse University Press.

Plato. 1941. *The Republic of Plato.* Translated by Francis Macdonald Cornford. Oxford: Clarendon Press.

Rahman, Fazlur. 1980. *Major Themes of the Qur'an.* Chicago: Bibliotheca Islamica.

Rahman, Fazlur. 1982. *Islam and Modernity: Transformation of an Intellectual Tradition*. Chicago: University of Chicago Press.
Rawls, John. 1993. *Political Liberalism*. New York: Columbia University Press.
Rorty, Richard. 1994. "Human Rights, Rationality, and Sentimentality." In *Truth and Progress, Vol. 3 of Philosophical Papers*, chap. 9, 167–85. Cambridge: Cambridge University Press. https://doi.org/10.1017/CBO9780511625404.010.
Rousseau, Jean-Jacques. (1762) 2002. "The Social Contract." In *The Social Contract and the First and Second Discourses*, edited by Susan Dunn, 149–254. New Haven, CT: Yale University Press.
Schumpeter, Joseph A. 1976. *Capitalism, Socialism and Democracy*. New York: Harper and Row.
Stowasser, B. 1993. "Women's Issues in Modern Islamic Thought." In *Arab Women: Old Boundaries, New Frontiers*, edited by Judith E. Tucker, 3–28. Bloomington and Indianapolis: Indiana University Press.
Waldron, Jeremy. 1987. "Nonsense Upon Stilts? A Reply." In *"Nonsense Upon Stilts": Bentham, Burke, and Marx on the Rights of Man*, edited by Jeremy Waldron, 151–209. London: Methuen.
Walzer, Michael. 1995. *Spheres of Justice: A Defense of Pluralism and Equality*. Oxford: Blackwell.
Wolterstorff, Nicholas. 1997. "The Role of Religion in Decision and Discussion of Political Issues." In *Religion in the Public Square: The Place of Religious Convictions in Political Debate*, edited by Robert Audi and Nicholas Wolterstorff, 67–120. Lanham, MD: Rowman & Littlefield.

6 The Inadequacies of the Algerian Political System—or the Impossibility of a Democratic Transition

Nacer-Eddine Ghozali

1. Introduction

On the eve of independence, Algeria stood out as a rare example of a country enviably positioned for success in the concert of nations, with so much going for it: a national consensus born of the struggle for independence, coupled with promising agricultural, mineral, and oil resources.[1] Yet now, after sixty years of existence as a sovereign state, the country finds itself in a difficult situation.[2] It

1 Algeria is ranked 10th in the world among producers of natural gas, with 2.2 percent of world production. Its export potential is considerable. Its exports reached a peak of 65 billion cubic meters of natural gas in 2005, which had fallen to 49 billion in 2020 (BAD 2022).

2 Algeria often figures in the lower tiers in the country rankings that specialized international organizations compile using various metrics of prosperity. Thus, in the 2021 Human Development Index (HDI), Algeria ranks 91st out of a total of 191 countries (having dropped from 87th place in 2014). In 2003, Algeria made a bid to join the BRICS bloc, but the request was denied. President Tebboune nonetheless stated on national media that "the year 2023 will be crowned by Algeria's entry into BRICS" (Alilat 2023). In the Social Capital Index, measuring "the sum of social stability and the well-being (perceived or real) of the entire population," Algeria was ranked 109th in the world in 2023 out of 167, just above three countries in sub-Saharan Africa: Burkina Faso, Niger, and Senegal. In the 2022 Social Progress Index (SPI), Algeria ranks 95th out of 196 (well ahead of neighbouring Tunisia in 72nd place). In the Prosperity Index, published by the Legatum Institute, Algeria is ranked 109th (compare Morocco in 96th place). In the 2020 Global Knowledge Index (GKI), compiled by the Mohamed Ben Rachid Al Maktoum Foundation, it is ranked 103rd out of 138. It falls below the majority of Arab countries in Cornell University's 2020 Global Innovation Index (GII). In the indexes compiled by the Institut Européen d'Administration des Affaires (INSEAD) and the World Intellectual Property Organization (WIPO), Algeria takes an inglorious 135th place out of 147, though it ranks ahead of its neighbours and other African countries, such as Zimbabwe, Cameroon, Burkina Faso, and Nigeria. In the 2022 Economic Freedom of the World Index, established by the Fraser Institute and considered a benchmark for measuring government investment and the freedom to trade internationally, Algeria ranks 157th out of 165, far behind some very poor countries, such as Niger (135th). This index, conceptualized by Nobel laureate Milton Friedman, is considered the first scientific standard for measuring economic freedom, in turn considered the basic background condition for well-being, health, education, and peace. In the 2022 Global Skills Index (GSI), which measures workforce training and the readiness of workers to adapt to emerging trends in the global marketplace, Algeria ranks just 100th out of 120, having dropped by 11 positions over the previous year. And, finally, there is the Global Talent Competitiveness Index, which measures the ability of countries worldwide to attract and retain

DOI: 10.4324/9781003431206-10

is failing in almost every respect.[3] Economic backsliding and social deterioration are undermining the national consensus. The model of the rentier state based mainly on oil revenues is coming undone. The gap between the elites and the population is widening. And for evidence of the breakdown in social consensus, we need only look at corruption, the bloated bureaucracy, the growth of the underground economy, the lack of mobility, the declining quality of life, and the flow of emigration (with a negative net migration rate), among other factors (see esp. Garon 1994).

The country's multidimensional crisis has a long history. It dates back to the early years of the struggle for independence, when the military chieftains increasingly imposed their own hegemony and their idea of legitimacy. They even used coercion to secure that hegemony.[4] In July 1962, on the eve of independence, when the nation-state had not yet been established, Colonel Boumédiène, commander of the National Liberation Army (Armée de Libération Nationale, or ALN), the military wing of the National Liberation Front (Front de Libération Nationale, or FLN), disbanded the Provisional Government of the Algerian Republic (Gouvernement Provisoire de la République Algérienne, or GPRA). From then on, the army set itself up as the embodiment of power, its vigilant guardian and custodian. It made power into its characteristic makeup—hence the impossibility of a transition toward democracy, where power is given an institutional form, which in turn was deemed unacceptable.

For over six decades, from the country's independence to the present day, power has not issued from society or from its freely expressed will except through artificial constructs. From the outset, power has been based on the extraction of rent from resources (including legacy rent-generating resources) and operates on the basis of patronage, cronyism, and co-optation. Operating

---

talent and which was established by three organizations, namely, INSEAD (France), the Portulans Institute (United States), and the Human Capital Leadership Institute (Singapore): here Algeria was ranked 104th in 2022, behind neighbouring Tunisia (91st) and Morocco (96th).

3 Algeria's per capita GDP was USD 4,343 in 2022, and according to the World Bank it is expected to drop to USD 3,768 in 2024.

4 Evidence of such coercive tendencies while the Algerian War of Independence was still underway comes from one of its leading figures, Larbi Ben M'Hidi, who after his capture spoke these ominously foreboding words to his arresting officer, Colonel Bigeard: "When we are free, terrible things will happen. All the suffering of our people will be forgotten in a fight for advantage. There will be a power struggle. We're in the middle of a war and some people already have their sights on that. Yes, I'd like to die fighting before the end." These remarks were reported by Ferhat Abbas (1980, 174), the first president of the Provisional Government of the Algerian Republic (Gouvernement Provisoire de la République Algérienne, or GPRA), who also reported comments made to him in 1960 by Colonel Lotfi, head of Wilaya V, after a meeting of the National Council of the Algerian Revolution (Conseil National de la Révolution Algérienne, or CNRA). Lotfi went so far as to denounce the "fascist tendencies" of certain revolutionary military leaders who, in his words, "dream of being sultans with absolute power." Even more pointedly, he said, "behind their quarrels, I see a serious danger for independent Algeria. . . . I would rather die in the maquis than live with these wolves" (quoted in Berrouane 2015, 206–7, my translation, here as well as throughout this chapter).

in a vacuum, power is self-sufficient. Allergic to doubt and challenge, it has every reason to distrust free and transparent elections. Like the constitution, elections serve only to mask their own lack of representation, as well as that of the state's institutions. The people are thus reduced to resigning themselves to plebiscitary voting. The lack of legitimacy is addressed, where necessary, by repression, using the police and military force to provide security and the system of justice to stifle opposition.

2. The Nationalist Route for Conferring Legitimacy on the System

Since the war of national liberation, Algeria's fundamental legal texts have all been imbued with nationalism, in turn coloured with populism and the Arab-Islamic tradition. For example, the preamble to the current constitution of 2020 contains a good amount of grandiloquent language devoted to celebrating the country's tradition of resistance throughout its history, not without indulging in a certain angelicalness:

> The Algerian people are a free people; and they are resolved to remain so. Stretching back over thousands of years, their history is marked by a progression of exertion and struggle that has turned Algeria into an everlasting seedbed of freedom and a land of glory and dignity.

As much as it was imperative for the struggle for independence to appeal to the epic of war and to nationalist ideology, this appeal has since served as a tool by which to legitimize power and the interests it protects (Labat 2003, 7). Apart from making permanent the epic narrative of the war of national liberation and the awe it is meant to inspire, the system pursues a twofold aim: to lend credence to the myth of unanimity, all the while denying that there exist any social and political contradictions. In essence, the system seeks to erase "socio-cultural pluralism" and sideline "any opposition by ruling out any demand for a rotation of power" (Benchikh 2003, 8; cf. Addi 2020). This timid nationalism, so characteristic of governance since independence, is not unrelated to the rent-seeking legacy. In any case, nationalist ideology remains a sure-fire way to protect the system and its penchant for exclusive representation.

3. The Army's Central Role in the Political System

During the struggle for independence, the army exerted its authority over the various institutions of the FLN and steered the nation's destiny. In this sense, the army can be said to have preceded the state (Daguzan 2020) and has since held a tight grip on power, so much so that the relation between the two is inextricable (Zartmann 1967; cf. Daguzan 2020): the army is so "consubstantial" with power that "the boundary between politics and military force is beyond blurred" (Aït Kaki 2004). The army certainly remains removed from the country's daily life, but it jealously guards the system so as to preserve it. Through its Department of Intelligence and Security (Département du Renseignement et de la Sécurité, or DRS), the army exercises tight control over the entire political, economic, and social system (Benchikh 2003, 63–64; Addi 1999; Catusse 2006; Sifaoui 2012). The DRS selects "all state officials, from the highest level—from the President of the Republic—to the head of 'daïra' (under-prefecture), and even below. No one can be appointed without the consent of the security services": these are the words of former Prime Minister Sid Ahmed Ghozali (quoted in *El Watan*, 11 January 2012; cf. *El Watan*, April 14, 2014), who likens these services to "a political army" (quoted in Daoud 2010).[5] In short, as the phrase goes, this power was exercised in Algeria by the "college of praetorians" in keeping with the institutional structure that during the revolutionary war, under a set of unwritten rules,[6] had been established by the so-called triumvirate.[7] Obviously, whenever there emerges a crisis or threat deemed to pose a serious danger to the existing order, the army openly intervenes, even if that means running the affairs of the country. This was the case during the crisis that in February 2019 was precipitated by the Hirak demonstrations held in protest of an announced fifth term for Abdelaziz Bouteflika. De facto power fell into the hands of the all-powerful general Ahmed Gaïd Salah, acting as chief of staff of the Algerian People's National Army (Armée Nationale Populaire Algérienne, or ANP) and deputy minister of national defence: so strong was his grip on power that he could dictate the agenda for ending the crisis and its terms—a task otherwise reserved for the regime as a whole and which in that official capacity he personally saw to completion.

An omnipresent figure on the political scene, Gaïd Salah energetically called for a referral to the Constitutional Council in order to have President

5 Consider the words of Belaïd Abdeslam, who served as chairman of the High Council of State (Haut Comité d'État, or BCE, a collective transitional presidency set up in 1992), in which capacity he candidly remarked: "It was the army that put me here, and only the army can make me leave. . . . Who could have believed that [Mohamed] Boudiaf [his predecessor as chairman of the BCE] could have come here of his own free will?" (quoted in Graïne 2001).

6 See Benchikh 2003, 54. Just recently, in 2023, a military appeals court heard the case of the former director general of internal security, General Wassini Bouazza, who had been indicted for unjust enrichment, malfeasance in office, and obstruction of justice. Along with four of his subordinates, he was found guilty of having interfered in the presidential election of 12 December 2019, during which he attempted to tilt the outcome in favour of his candidate of choice, Azzedine Mihoubi—former Secretary-general of the Democratic National Rally (Rassemblement National Démocratique, or RND)—to the detriment of other candidates (*Algérie 360°*, 4 June 2023). After the fall of Abdelaziz Bouteflika in 2019, he was sentenced to eight years in prison. See Alilat 2020a.

7 The triumvirate consisted of Colonels Krim Belkacem (commander of Wilaya III), Abdelhafid Boussouf (commander of Wilaya V), and Lakhdar Bentobbal (former head of Wilaya II). It was this triumvirate—otherwise known as "the three B's"—that during the War of Algerian Independence imposed their diktat on the leaders of the revolution.

Bouteflika declared unfit for office on grounds of incapacity in accordance with Article 102 of the Constitution (this happened on 26 March 2019). The country's strongman then ordered the arrest of regime oligarchs and members of the Bouteflika clan under a "clean hands operation" (May 2019); he made an appeal urging the country not to "waste any more time"; he rejected the appeasement measures taken by the interim president, Abdelkader Bensalah, describing these measures as "diktats" and "poisoned ideas" (July 30); he denounced the advocates of a democratic transition and the idea of calling for early elections to amend the constitution (August 26); determined to hold a presidential election before the end of 2019, he ruled out the idea of amending the electoral law (September 2) before deciding on a date for the presidential election, despite a massive rejection of the ballot by the population. The candidate he endorsed, Abdelmadjid Tebboune, was elected in the first round (12 December).

In a way, this sovereign and original role of the army has recently been codified by the Constitution of 20 December 2020. In the form of a veritable legal revolution, the document stipulates that "the National People's Army shall protect vital and strategic interests in accordance with constitutional provisions" (Art. 30). This notion of vital interests is sufficiently vague to lend itself to all sorts of interpretations. In any case, there is nothing to prevent the army from taking whatever action it deems necessary in view of such interests. This is what on several occasions has been implied by the successor to General Gaïd Salah, General Saïd Chengriha, in statements he has made publicly in the political arena.

4. Algerian Ultra-presidentialism

Under the current constitution in Algeria, the head of state (president) benefits from a presidentialist system taken to extremes. In addition to the explicitly enumerated constitutional powers, the head of state can count on the parliamentary support provided by the mechanical majority constituted by the parties aligned with the president (the FLN and the RND) and their satellite groups. Neither the legislature nor the judiciary can lay claim to any role of significant power: they are constrained in their legislative and judicial functions, acting under pressure, which means that the separation of powers expressly provided for in the constitution is doomed to remain fictional. Nor is there any autonomy for intermediate bodies, such as political parties, unions, and various other groups and organizations. This setup essentially lines up with the logic of an authoritarian political system, one that tolerates neither counterbalancing forces nor any effective opposition and whose core nature traces back to the beginnings of the Algerian Republic. In that connection, the power that for twenty years, from 1999 to 2019, was embodied in the presidential monarch Abdelaziz Bouteflika is a power of rulelessness. As former Prime Minister (head of government) Ali Benflis has remarked, his power comes down to an "absence of rules. He knows neither what a Prime Minister nor a Chamber of Deputies is: he doesn't want to know—he alone counts" (quoted in Levet and Tolila 2023, 68), so much so that through his exercise of power this constant theme of Algerian presidentialism translates into a caricature of itself. More than with any leader, his "obsession with power for its own sake" (Alilat 2020b) led him to follow him ambition and modify the constitution, bending it to his boundless political appetites and in this sense "personalizing" the state and its institutions. His former head of government (prime minister), Ali Benflis, does not hesitate to describe Bouteflika's rule as a "reign of arbitrariness . . . scaled up to the point where it invests the whole country" (ibid., 69). Despite the physical ordeals that clearly incapacitated him, he did not hold back from seeking a fifth term in office—an ambition to which the cathartic reaction of the popular Hirak Movement of February 2019 put an end.

5. Constitutionalism as Facade

All Algerian constitutions are the product of crises coming to a head or looming in the horizon.[8] These crises have forced the government to equip the country with new institutions or to grant reforms without fundamentally altering its own makeup—and not without exerting control over the process and its outcome. Invariably, the manner of constitution-writing is authoritarian (see Benchikh 2009, 254–55) and not too transparent (see Boussoumah 2009, 9). Formally, it checks all the democratic boxes, establishing the separation of powers, providing for judicial review and an independent judiciary, and guaranteeing the rights and freedoms enshrined in universal instruments. But in reality, contrary to this rhetoric, the constitution's only vital function is to legitimize the ruling regime and enable it to project an image of civility domestically as well as internationally, so as to "please the West."[9] In practice, the constitution is constructed so as to provide the powers that be with their cherished instruments of power, securing the system's ability to maintain and reproduce itself and to control and limit access to positions of governmental power. This is why the references the constitution makes to power are purely instrumental, its main purpose being to maintain the illusion that governmental action and policy have a legal basis in the constitution itself. The formal constitution is therefore irrelevant to understanding the real functioning of the regime. Contrary to what the constitution proclaims in its preamble, it is not the "fundamental law" of the country. It is not designed to achieve a democratic transition. For the most part, it is disembodied—an empty shell.

8 Algeria has had several constitutions and constitutional amendments since independence: the 1963 constitution, suspended in June 1965 following the coup d'état of that same month; the 1976 constitution, amended in 1979, 1980, and 1988; the 1989 constitution, adopted after the events of 5 October 1988; the 1996 constitution, amended in 2002, 2008, and 2016; and the 2020 constitution.

9 This last comment and assessment is from Mehdi Adimi, spokesman for the Talae El-Hourriet party (Freedoms in the Vanguard), as quoted in *Liberté*, 26 December 2018.

6. A Fake Multiparty System

Historically, at its founding, the Algerian political system rested on the rule of a single party, the National Liberation Front (FLN), which left a deep imprint on the country. Monocracy was abandoned only in the wake of the 1988 October Riots, which prompted President Chadli Bendjedid to grant reforms. The 1989 constitution and the law of 5 July 1989 on political associations were accordingly enacted as a matter of urgency. As a result, although the single-party system was abolished after twenty-seven years of existence, the process was rushed, having come in response to the popular unrest. For this reason, party pluralism is tightly controlled. It is not intended to allow a free political contest or the possibility of a political alternative (Amrani 2007). Consequently, the only parties that stand a fair chance at participating in the democratic process and winning elections are the ones that have the regime's backing.

For this reason, the powers that be do not bother to form a party from scratch in a bid to win over the electorate. This was the case with the National Democratic Rally (the RND), made to order by relatives of President Liamine Zéroual: it was founded on 21 February 1997, and then on 5 June 1997, not even five months after its "founding," it won parliamentary elections.[10] Like its twin brother, the FLN, it played the part assigned to it as loyal supporter of the regime, pledging allegiance to the head of state. This "submission" of the two parties to the system takes the place of a political platform based on content. The automatic parliamentary majority they are called upon to form is reinforced by a constellation of Lilliputian formations. These are mere by-products of the FLN, orbiting around it more-or-less like satellites. Devoid of popular support, these satellite parties are incapable of influencing public affairs. They are more concerned with their own existence, hoping to gain some political or administrative advantage in return for their allegiance to power, for they are aware that elections are political machinations: when the votes come in, so do the revenues that get divided up among the parties (Hachemaoui 2003, 40ff.). This is why in the disorderly abolition of the single-party system, some parties were greenlighted to participate in elections even if they did not have the regime's backing: they were thus confined to the margins of political life, and this was the case for the Socialist Forces Front (Front des Forces Socialistes, or FFS) and the Rally for Culture and Democracy (Rassemblement pour la Culture et la Démocratie, or RCD).[11] They can only engage in occasional criticism against the regime. We must therefore recognize that the pluralism put on display is nothing more

10 What prompted the RND's creation was the need to provide President Zéroual with a party after the state-controlled party, the FLN, defected in opposition to the policies pursued against the Islamist insurrection.

11 For twenty years, the secretaries-general of these two parties were appointed directly by President Bouteflika.

than that—a facade behind which to conceal the true nature of the multi-party system, "a pure creation functional to the regime's need to showcase itself" (AW 2009).

This tightly controlled party-alignment system is in keeping with the constraints of a closed authoritarian regime whose first concern is its own preservation. "As long as I am here, there will be no new political party, no new television or radio channel," declared President Bouteflika during the 2004 presidential campaign, referring to the 1989 reforms ending single-party rule and the state's monopoly over the media as a "serious error" (quoted in *Le Soir d'Algérie*, 8 July 2010). In keeping with this logic—and in order to exert greater control over the party system—he introduced a law (enacted on 12 January 2012) that considerably tightened the conditions for creating political parties. The authorization process was placed in the sole discretion of the Ministry of the Interior, which is now free to fast-track applications submitted by groups deemed to be aligned with the ministry itself,[12] while slow-tracking those deemed to be unaligned,[13] this in clear violation of the law,[14] even going to the extreme of prohibiting parties from undertaking any political activity.[15] The ministry pushed this line to its limit when it announced that it would henceforth decide to authorize or stop authorizing the formation of new parties at will.[16] The ministry sometimes points to the political nature of the problem (*Le Soir d'Algérie*, 8 July 2010) and sometimes to "inconsistencies in the paperwork or a process underway to draft a new law" (*El Watan*, 2 November 2011). Moreover, repressive measures have been taken against pluralism, already severely limited and strictly regulated. Under the false pretext of noncompliance with Law No. 12–04, opposition parties find themselves in the crosshairs of the authorities. They suffer harassment, as happened to the Rassemblement pour la Culture et la Démocratie (RCD) and the Union pour

12 In the leadup to the parliamentary elections of 10 May 2012, sixteen minor parties were greenlighted in the most haphazard way.

13 One of the delay tactics the ministry resorts to consists in denying an application without notifying the applicant or providing a reasoned decision for the denial, as the law requires, thereby denying the applicant an opportunity to appeal the decision.

14 In some cases, these parties were unable to submit their applications. In other cases, the ministry refused to grant them authorization to hold their constituent congresses after they had been authorized to make those submissions, as happened to Ahmed Taleb Ibrahimi's Wafaa party, Karim Tabbou's Union Démocratique et Sociale (UDS), and Sadek Temmache's Front National pour l'Authenticité et le Renouveau (FNAR), among others.

15 The most glaring example is that of the Front Démocratique (FD), founded by Sid Ahmed Ghozali, who in an interview published on 28 September 2015 in *Tout sur l'Algérie* (TSA), noted that the party's formation had been authorized sixteen years earlier under Article 22 of a 1997 law, and yet a ban was still being enforced to prevent the party from engaging in any political activity.

16 "No authorization for new parties is being considered at this time." This is a remark that Dahou Ould Kablia, Minister of the Interior and of Local Authorities, made on national radio in February 2011 (as quoted in *La Dépêche de Kabylie*, 26 February 2011).

le Changement et le Progrès (UCP).[17] These practices are clearly integral to the agenda the authorities are pushing to neutralize any independent political expression by the parties and to control the political landscape.

The upshot is that the country is now deprived of a genuine pluralist party system capable of driving political life, which was already constrained before the fall of President Bouteflika—for it mainly revolved around the two sister parties allied with the regime: the National Liberation Front (FLN) and the Democratic National Rally (RND)—and is now sluggish. This is due to the disrepute the FLN and the RND fell into with the end of the Bouteflika era in 2019. Inflexibly committed to Bouteflika and to his rent-seeking policy and logic of loyalty, these two parties were also consigned to oblivion by the popular Hirak Movement that began on 16 February 2019. What is more, in the ensuing presidential elections of 12 December 2020, they made the mistake of running Azzedine Mihoubi, who in that election would go on to lose to Abdelmadjid Tebboune, hence the stiff corruption sentences handed down to their former leaders and allies.[18]

7. An Electoral and Fraudulent Authoritarianism

Elections in Algeria have rarely been carried out in keeping with universal international principles and standards. Electoral practices pay little heed to standards of honesty and transparency. These practices depend mainly on the regime's political aims. As a result, the electoral function has been hijacked, and elections are conducted entirely under the watchful eye of the government. Voting in Algeria does not mean democratically electing one's representatives or expressing an opinion about the regime's past and future policies but simply giving the regime the support it needs to ensure its own legitimacy. Uncertainty of outcome does not factor into Algerian electoral practice.

In fact, the government is doing everything it can to keep control of the electoral process so as to ensure that nothing of consequence should happen that might foster political alternation. To this end, it uses various means, without any check on its activity: these include mobilizing the regime's traditional proxy parties (the FLN, the RND, and their satellite parties); mobilizing social and professional groups and organizations with nationwide

17 Examples include the "temporary" suspension of the Socialist Workers' Party (Parti Socialiste des Travailleurs, or PST)—which happened on 20 January 2022 at the hands of the Council of State (Conseil d'État, Algeria's highest administrative court), forcing it to shut down all operations and close its premises—and a clampdown on the Democratic and Social Movement (Mouvement Démocratique et Social, or MDS), whose operations were frozen on 23 February 2023 under an order the same Council of State issued acting at the behest of the Ministry of the Interior (see Amnesty International 2022).

18 These included prison sentences handed down, in particular, to Djamel Ould Abbès and Mohammed Djemaï (former Secretary-general of the FLN) and to Ahmed Ouyahia (former Secretary-general of the RND as well as former Prime Minister).

reach, such as the *anciens moudjahidines* (veterans) and *chouhadas* (children of people killed in war), the Scouts, the General Union of Algerian Workers (Union Générale des Travailleurs Algériens, or UGTA), and the employers' organization formerly known as Forum des Chefs d'Entreprise (FCE), now Confédération Algérienne du Patronat Citoyen (CAPC); and acting through the state's administrative and ideological apparatus (state media, mosques, zawiyas). The tactics used by the government also include voter intimidation,[19] tampering with voter rolls,[20] setting up fake polling stations, engaging in political bribery,[21] ballot-box stuffing,[22] large-scale fraud,[23] and

19 During the 2014 presidential election, for example, the *wali* (governor) of Algiers went on an inspection of shantytowns warning that "there will be no rehousing for those who do not vote." Similarly, according to several eyewitness accounts at signature drives for the incumbent president, Bouteflika, some civil servants were threatened with dismissal unless they signed the petition (Chellali 2014).

20 In 2012, EU election observers were denied access to the entire voter registration roll on "data protection" grounds.

21 Following the May 2017 parliamentary elections, Moussa Touati revealed that his party—the Algerian National Front (Front National Algérien)—had to pay money to claim a seat in the lower house, the People's National Assembly (Assemblée Populaire Nationale, or APN): "We were forced to pay money to government agents to gain access to the election returns we needed in order to challenge the official results for the Blida seat" (quoted in *Algérie Patriotique*, 14 September 2017).

22 Following the May 2017 parliamentary elections, videos began to circulate on social media providing evidence of numerous alleged cases of election fraud: on some occasions, a light would be switched off by someone trying to pass unobserved while stuffing the ballot box; on other occasions, the number of ballots collected from the ballot box exceeded the total vote tally announced for that polling station.

23 On one occasion, a few days before the 1999 presidential election, a former *wali* (governor) from Blida named Bachir Frik publicly admitted to having participated in electoral fraud in his district, saying that he was acting on an order from his campaign director, Ali Benflis, so as to help Bouteflika win (*Courrier International*, 11 April 2014).

According to Saïd Sadi, Secretary-general of the Rassemblement pour la Culture et la Démocratie (RCD), the voter participation rate in the election held on 9 April 2009 did not exceed 18 percent. He reports that in Blida, for example, at the Douzia polling station, only twenty-one women had voted out of 430 who were registered to vote, and this was just two hours before the polls closed. "But then the *wali* arrives and evacuates everyone, and the participation rate increases to 82%." According to Krim Tabou, Secretary-general of the Front des Forces Socialistes (FFS), if we plot the vote count as it progressed over the course of election day, we have to irrefutably conclude that at midday "an order from the top" had been given to proceed with ballot stuffing and rigging. According to Louisa Hanoune, Secretary-general of the Parti des Travailleurs (PT), the "fraud was massive and widespread," and in the capital even her campaign director had the unpleasant surprise of finding that people had voted in her place (Tlemçani 2012, 163).

The regime-backed parties themselves accused each other of brazen election fraud: the FLN in the parliamentary elections of 2012 and the RND in the parliamentary and local elections of 1997 (Ghozali 2020, 22–23).

vote-buying,[24] among others. All of these practices undermine the integrity and credibility of elections (Ghozali 2022, 175–76). The principle of democratic representation is thus effectively gutted. It loses all meaning.

This is noted in part by the Electoral Integrity Project, whose 2019–2021 global report rates the integrity of Algerian elections as poor: Algeria is relegated to 114th place out of 139, with a PEI index (Perception of Electoral Integrity) of 43 (Garnett, James, and MacGregor 2022).[25] Similar assessments come from the EU Election Observation Missions (EOMs), even if they are so cautious in their reporting. After the parliamentary elections held in May 2012, an EOM report came out highlighting numerous problems whose net effect was, in essence, to "undermine the transparency of the electoral process," with structural weaknesses in voter rolls, human rights violations, arrests, convictions, and the like (EU EOM 2012, résumé, point 11). Also damning is the EOM report issued after the May 2017 elections (EU EOM 2017). Finally, the EOM report on the presidential election of April 2014 notes that "even if it was expected that Bouteflika would seek a fourth term in office and be on the ballot, owing in particular to the balance of power and to campaign conditions, the results were surprising in virtue of the landslide in the first round" (with 81.49 percent of the votes).[26] The 2014 EOM report details the upstream measures taken by President Bouteflika to ensure re-election.[27] As the former Prime Minister Sid-Ahmed Ghozali once remarked, "elections were simply an electoral parody" (quoted in *El Watan*, 20 January 2008).

In the view of former Prime Minister Mokdad Sifi, "the electoral system systematically fails with proven fraud in elections" (letter to Abdelkader Bensalah, Chargé des Consultations Relatives aux Réformes Politiques, *El Watan*, 20 January 2008).

24 Several examples attest to such fraud. One of these was the 2018 election for staggered renewal of membership in the senate (the Council of the Nation). Nadia Benakli (2018) reports that it would have cost around 10 billion dinars to buy the votes needed to win a senate seat. An elected official from the Parti des Travailleurs (PT) said in 2018, "I know a candidate who offered 1 billion dinars to become a senator. An elected official promised him 10 votes" (quoted in *El Watan*, 24 December 2018). Likewise, Farid Alilat (2018) reports that in December 2018, during the staggered senate elections, "certain candidates offered up to 30 million dinars (about 220,000 euros) to buy votes." See also Lyes 2018. The parliamentary elections of May 2017 highlighted the role of Algerian magnates already involved in efforts to influence politics even in the lower house (the Assemblée Populaire Nationale). In particular, a scandal highlighting the links between the business world and the political world concerned Wafi Ould Abbès, the son of the FLN's secretary-general, who was accused of influence peddling for having sold electoral lists to businessmen (Baroudi 2017).

25 This assessment lines up with Algeria's poor rating in the 2020 democracy index drawn up by the Economist Intelligence Unit (EIU 2020), in which the country was ranked 115th out of 167.

26 The report concludes that "in view of the lack of traceability in verifying the results, it is difficult to say whether the results announced by the Constitutional Council are credible" (*El Watan*, 18 March 2014).

27 In its report, the EU EOM noted that "the announcement of this candidacy took place against the backdrop of a takeover of key government positions in the agencies and institutions of the Republic, among them the Constitutional Council."

Such methods undermine the credibility of elections, the legitimacy of the institutions, and "people's trust in those who govern them."[28] This is why voter turnout is low. In fact, abstention is a clear trend whose significance the official figures themselves are increasingly unable to play down, with a 61.75 percent abstention rate for the parliamentary elections of 4 May 2017 and 77 percent for the constitutional referendum of 1 November 2020. The current president, Abdelmadjid Tebboune, was elected on 12 December 2019 with a very low turnout (39.83 percent)[29]—the lowest on record for a multiparty presidential election. The downward trend continued with the parliamentary elections of 12 June 2021, and when the question was put to Tebboune, Bouteflika's successor, his take was that "the turnout is of little importance. The most important thing is that the ballot boxes produce representatives of the people who have sufficient legitimacy to assume legislative power."[30]

Be that as it may, abstention is undeniably a form of political protest and a sign of distrust of public affairs and of those in power. It is because citizens are aware of the futility of their vote—and of their inability to genuinely exercise their right to participate in the conduct of their own affairs—that they show their disaffection by taking refuge in abstention and indifference. In the end, they are unable to exercise their right to self-determination and to participate in the process that is its direct expression, namely, democracy.

8. The Political Influence of the Moneyed Powers and the Gangrene of Corruption and Predation

In the 1990s, a new development emerged in Algerian political life. A new crop of entrepreneurs was taking advantage of the considerable revenues coming in from the state's oil exports and the cash flow generated by a flourishing informal economy. Thanks to some huge outlays the government budgeted to finance economic stimulus programmes, the new entrepreneurial class, ever more aggressive, gradually took over the political arena. They understood the advantages of putting money into elections, spending liberally to buy municipal offices,[31] and even parliamentary seats,[32] sometimes with the complicity

28 From a statement by former Prime Minister Mokdad Sifi (quoted in *El Watan*, 3 May 2011).

29 This election day of 12 December 2019 itself fell on the 43rd consecutive Friday of Hirak protests. Thousands of people took to the streets of Algiers and other cities across the country, shouting "No vote! We want freedom!" (*Jeune Afrique*, 13 December 2019).

30 The remark was made at a press conference held on election day (quoted in *Maghreb Émergent*, 12 June 2021).

31 The spokesperson for the Algerian chapter of Transparency International reports that mayoral offices have been bought by big business as a lucrative return on investment (Abéga 2003).

32 This happened, for example, with the parliamentary elections held in May 2017 (see Chahed 2017), as well as with the staggered senate elections held in November 2018, during which "some candidates offered up to 30 million dinars (about 220,000 euros) to buy votes" (Alilat 2018; see also Lyes 2018). In 2020, a trial was held for two business magnates—Baha Eddine Tliba, who had been a member of parliament and then became Vice President of the lower

of government officials.[33] A number of candidates from business circles thus began to gain access to seats in the National Assembly (APN) and the Senate (the Conseil de la Nation),[34] seizing the opportunity to increase their wealth, while at the same time securing parliamentary immunity for themselves.

In this regard, when Bouteflika was first running for president in 1999, he spoke out against "these bandits who have become the rulers and the rulers the bandits" (quoted in *Le Matin d'Algérie*, 6 April 1999). Soon after taking in office, he came back to the issue in a speech delivered on 30 August 1999 in which he acknowledged that "Algeria is beset by corruption." However, more than a decade later, in June of 2012, his Prime Minister and Secretary-general of the Rassemblement National Démocratique (RND), Ahmed Ouyahia, had to sound the alarm once more by acknowledging that "money rules in Algeria" and that it was beginning to "govern and become Mafia-like" (Benakli 2012; cf. Guemache 2012). Indeed, there has never been a period so conducive to corruption and embezzlement of public funds as that which spans Bouteflika's twenty years of authoritarian rule (Hadjadj 2003, § 7ff.). With the complicity of government officials and the support and acquiescence of those in power, businessmen close to the president's inner circle obtained lucrative government contracts, loans, and considerable tax breaks.[35] Mafia-like networks were set up in the shadows of the decision-making centres, funnelling part of the dirty money back to them.[36] In a way, they become the economic guardians of

house (the National Assembly) and who was indicted on charges of "money laundering as part of a criminal outfit" and "influence peddling to obtain undue advantages," and Djamel Ould Abbès, the former head of the Front de Libération Nationale (FLN), along with his two sons—and during the trial it was revealed that the FLN's electoral lists were exorbitantly expensive: the list leader (at the top of the ticket) for the 2017 parliamentary elections was a seat that was sold for 7 billion dinars (about 165,000 euros) (Meddi 2020).

33 According to Djillali Hadjadj, president of the Algerian Association for the Fight Against Corruption (Association Algérienne de Lutte Contre la Corruption, or AALC), "intermediaries who [in the mid-1990s] were already involved in illegal dealings were working with senior interior and local officials. These bosses had a direct hand in selecting and appointing unelected mayors" (Hadjadj 2003, § 36ff.).

34 A typical case is that of the previously mentioned billionaire Baha Eddine Tliba, member of parliament for El Oued and then Annaba, nicknamed "the Emir of Qatar of Annaba," who became "the system's protégé." He entered the prime minister's inner circle. He spoke as he pleased, claiming to speak on behalf of those in power. "His wealth and connections gave him influence over the 462 MPs who make up the National Assembly (APN)." He became a member of the FLN's central committee and was appointed Vice President of the APN (Hamdi 2019).

35 "They were awarded government contracts and received land, bank loans, and numerous tax breaks," while those "who refused to put their hand in their pocket to support Bouteflika's candidacy were blacklisted" (Alilat 2020c). In a statement in October 2017, Prime Minister Abdelmadjid Tebboune acknowledged that the state had granted more than 50 billion dinars in aid, subsidies, and bank loans to private companies over the past fifteen years (Alilat 2017).

36 According to Djillali Hadjadj, speaking in 2018, the amount of bribes paid for various government contracts awarded by the Algerian government, in which individuals close to the government are involved, reached 60 billion dollars (Mahmoudi 2018).

government payouts (Guenanfa 2019). In any case, corruption ends up affecting the government's entire apparatus, across all its branches, even working its way into the highest echelons of power itself.[37]

The cases brought against former ministers, prime ministers, senior army officers, *walis*, judges, party leaders, and businessmen close to former President Bouteflika after his exit from power in 2019 have brought to light the extent of the revolving door between money and politics.[38] Corruption has since found all the more reason to flourish because the institutions that oversee the management of the country's resources (Parliament, the Inspectorate General of Finance, and the Court of Accounts)[39] have been deliberately put on hold. At the same time, decision-making processes have become increasingly opaque.

The moneyed powers—looking to protect their privileges while enabling the government to maintain its grip on power—did not hold back from pumping considerable amounts of money into the presidential campaigns held in 2004, 2009, 2014, and 2019.[40] As if to confirm a tacit agreement, the president's inner circle, not wishing to alienate these precious backers, did not hesitate to decide to sack Prime Minister Abdelmadjid Tebboune in August of 2017. He had taken the liberty of "firing a warning shot" at the robber barons of the informal economy by proposing to separate money and power: "The state is the state, and money is money," he emphatically remarked (quoted in *Maghreb Émergent*, 21 June 2017). In so doing, he was attacking the oligarchs, who were too entrenched in the president's inner circle to be sanctioned by the authorities. He had crossed a kind of red line.[41] In the eyes of the president of the republic, those close to him should not, under any circumstance, be subject to the laws of the republic itself. This meant, for example, seeking judicial impunity and "clearing" the name of a close friend who had been prosecuted for corruption and rehabilitating him.[42]

37 In his memoir recounting his experience as former French ambassador to Algeria, from 2006 to 2008, Bernard Bajolet (2018) reveals, "I was shocked by the heights that corruption had reached, even within the family of the head of state" (*Algeria Watch*, 24 September 2018).

38 Embroiled in the corruption were three former prime ministers and at least fifteen former ministers.

39 According to Abdelkader Benmarouf, president of the Algerian Court of Accounts, the court "never published its annual reports during the era of former President Abdelaziz Bouteflika" (quoted in *Inter Lignes*, 15 May 2019). In fact, Bouteflika did not let go of the fact that he had been ordered by this court to pay several hundred thousand Swiss francs to the Treasury for having kept a "secret account" resulting from surplus cash generated from diplomatic and consular missions in the period from 1965 to 1978, while serving as minister of foreign affairs.

40 The corruption trials brought against the ruling elite and business magnates after Bouteflika's failure to win a fifth term in office revealed that their ill-gotten gains amounted to more than 7 billion dinars (52.8 million euros) (*El Watan*, 29 November 2019).

41 At the forefront of the push to have Tebboune dismissed was Ali Haddad, President of the powerful Forum des Chefs d'Entreprise (FCE) (*Le Point Afrique*, 15 August 2017).

42 Perhaps no one exemplifies this playbook better than Chakib Khelil, a loyal backer of the regime who went on to serve as minister of energy and mines for ten years (from 1999 to 2010) and was then prosecuted on graft charges in 2013 (in the Sonatrach 1 and 2 affairs).

Ultimately, as AALC president Djillali Hadjadj has commented, everything happens as if the policy in force under Bouteflika's regime was captured in the motto "Enrich yourself and let us enrich ourselves" (quoted in *Le Point*, 22 May 2019). This has prompted a Hirak activist to say that "the only thing Bouteflika has succeeded in democratizing is corruption and nepotism" (quoted in Mann 2019), which have become "an Algerian sport from top to bottom" (Levet and Tolila 2023, 123). It is therefore quite logical that in Transparency International's global Corruption Perceptions Index (CPI), Algeria appeared in 117th place out of 180 countries in 2021, down by thirteen places relative to 2020 (when it was ranked 104th) and far from its North African neighbours (Tunisia, ranked 70th in 2021, and Morocco, 87th). To be sure, the latest data from the 2023 CPI shows some improvement (putting Algeria in 104th place), but that doesn't change the overall picture, in which Algeria clearly figures among the most corrupt countries in the world. What is more, this pathology has worsened since Tebboune's accession to power, despite the publicity and numerous trials held against oligarchs and other figures associated with the old regime. On the other hand, Algeria has been a signatory to the 2003 UN Convention Against Corruption since 2004, as well as to the 2006 African Union Convention on Preventing and Combating Corruption and the 2010 Arab Anti-Corruption Convention. But, then again, Algeria's own anti-corruption agency, the Organe National de Prévention et de Lutte Contre la Corruption (ONPLC), established 2012, has been placed under supervision and has not been able to effectively function, this for purely political reasons linked to corruption cases involving senior government officials and the government-affiliated parties (the FLN and the RND).[43]

9. Protected Rights and Freedoms

As early as 1989, the constitution enshrined a wide range of human rights, to which it devoted an entire chapter (Chapter IV). These were recognized as "the common heritage of all Algerian men and women, who shall assume the task of transmitting it from generation to generation so that they may preserve its integrity and inviolability" (Art. 31 of the constitution of 23 February 1989, reinst. 1996, rev. 2016) and "infringements of rights and freedoms . . . shall be punishable by law" (Chapter IV, Arts. 29–44). The 2020 constitution (in force since 30 December 2020) emphatically enshrines

---

The minister of justice, Mohammed Charfi, was consequently replaced with someone close to the head of state (Tayeb Louh), who had the case buried. Khelil was subsequently rehabilitated, and he triumphantly returned to the country in 2016 (Levet and Tolila 2023, 123–24; *Jeune Afrique*, 19 January 2023).

43 The agency was subsequently placed under presidential supervision and then under the Ministry of Justice. It has worked on a number of cases, in particular the embezzlement of national solidarity funds and the misappropriation of money from the National Agricultural Development Programme (PNDA), respectively involving the former minister for national solidarity, Djamel Ould Abbès, and the former secretary-general of the FLN, Amar Saadani (Siouane 2019).

the same rights and freedoms (Title II, Chapter I): freedom of opinion and worship (Art. 51), freedom of expression and assembly (Art. 52), freedom of association (Art. 53), freedom of the press (Art. 54), and the right to establish political parties (Art. 57), among several others. Algeria is also a signatory to the 1966 International Covenant on Civil and Political Rights (ICCPR), having acceded in 1989. None of this formal recognition of rights and freedoms, however, translates into practice: *de jure* these rights and freedoms may have the force of law, but *de facto* they have been bracketed.

10. A Judiciary Lacking Independence

In 1976, Algeria enacted a second constitution geared toward socialism, and in it the judicial branch of government was accordingly identified by its "function" (*fonction*). The 1989 and 1996 constitutions pivoted to liberalism, and the administration of justice was elevated to the status of a "power" (*pouvoir*). In reality, contrary to these constitutional proclamations, Algerian justice has never truly been conceived as a power—much less, therefore, as an "independent power," in which the "independent judge obeys only the law," which in turn "protects society and the freedoms and rights of citizens" (Art. 163 of the 1996 constitution, consolidated version of 30 December 2020). In reality, Algerian judges lack the independence they need to decide cases solely on the basis of the law (Bekhchi 2013, 188). They are constantly at the mercy of "various interferences that prevent them from fulfilling their judicial duty" (Mahiou 2011, 393). They are often forced to submit to political decisions. This dependence of the Algerian judge is such that the judiciary has been described as an "instrumentalized justice system" (Badi 2020).

The courts are increasingly seen as places where those in power sit in judgment of their adversaries and less and less as places where justice is administered. In that same vein, consider that when former President Bouteflika came to power, he did not hesitate to confide, "I don't believe in any independent justice. Justice, that's me."[44] Understood in this way, justice can only be primarily political. "It is a cog in the system" (Levet and Tolila 2023, 59). This is borne out by some major decisions handed down by the Constitutional Council as well as by administrative and civil judges.

11. The Constitutional Court

While this body is described in the 1989 constitution as "an independent institution in charge of monitoring the observance of the Constitution" (Art. 153), in practice, at least over the course of the twenty years spanning Bouteflika's presidency (when the court existed as the Constitutional Council), its

44 "Je ne crois pas à l'indépendance de la justice. La justice, c'est moi." This is a remark that Abdelaziz Bouteflika is reported to have made to his chief of staff, Ali Benflis, in April of 2001 at the presentation of the report drawn up by the investigative committee chaired by Mohand Issad and charged with looking into the events in Kabylia (Alilat and Poletti 2019).

decisions do not argue in favour of any judicial independence. More often than not, this court was content to give its legal backing to all presidential initiatives, including those that were unquestionably contrary to the Constitution. Suffice it to cite four examples.

The first concerns the Constitutional Council's opinion of 8 November 2008, in which this body unconditionally endorsed Bouteflika's demands for amendments to the Constitution that would open the door to a lifetime presidency for him, while appropriating all executive power for himself.[45]

The second example concerns the Constitutional Council's opinion of 28 January 2016, endorsing the constitutional amendment requiring "Algerian nationality of origin for access to high government and political office."[46] This opinion frontally contradicts several provisions of the Constitution enshrining a key principle of the rule of law, namely, equality among all citizens, and it also breaks with precedent that has been clear and consistent since 1989.

The third example concerns the Constitutional Council's refusal to initiate the presidential disability proceedings under Article 102 of the Constitution, under which the presidency can be declared vacant if the president is found to be incapacitated. President Bouteflika stayed in office until April of 2019, when he resigned amid the Hirak protests, sparked by his announcement that he would seek a fifth term in office.

Finally, more recently, the Constitutional Council took up the case of the constitutionality of Ordinance 21-08 of 8 June 2021, Article 2 of which provides a new definition of terrorism whose effect is to amplify the already broad and vague definition of a terrorist act set forth in Article 87 of the Algerian Criminal Code. The court held that this ordinance is constitutional in both form and substance.[47] And as the UN Human Rights Council notes with concern, this provision will allow "for the prosecution of actions that might constitute exercise of the freedom of expression or peaceful assembly" (UNHRC 2018, 17).

12. Administrative Courts

In taking so-called sensitive cases, administrative courts do not appear to be any bolder. Knowing that in these cases they are being carefully watched, they are inclined to adjudicate in such a way as to please the ruling elites, a prime example being their effort to stall Ali Benflis in his bid to run for president against

45 Avis n° 01/08 A.RC/CC/du 7 Novembre 2008 relatif au projet de loi portant révision constitutionnelle, *JORA* no. 63 of 16 November 2008, www.joradp.dz/FTP/jo-francais/2008/F2008063.pdf. In this regard, see Benadji 2009, paras. 51–99.

46 Avis n° 01/16 A.RC/CC/du 28 janvier 2016 relatif au projet de loi portant révision de la Constitution, *JORA* no. 6 of 3 February 2016, www.joradp.dz/FTP/jo-francais/2016/F2016006.pdf.

47 Décision du Conseil Constitutionnel n° 23/D.CC/21 du 7 Juin 2021 relative au contrôle de la constitutionnalité de l'ordonnance modifiant et complétant l'ordonnance n° 66-156 du 8 juin 1966 portant code pénal, *JORA* no. 45 of 9 June 2021, www.joradp.dz/FTP/jo-francais/2021/F2021045.pdf.

Bouteflika in 2004: Benflis had recently been appointed Secretary-General of the FLN and had just ended his term as prime minister, and even though he was qualified to enter the race, he met with resistance from an administrative court that to this end went so far as to pull a surprise on the contender by doing its work at night.[48] A veritable operation to "normalize" the president's party (the FLN) was undertaken to put the president back into play, including by exerting pressure on the judiciary. "Only he [Bouteflika] can be elected." This is "a typical example of politicians forcefully interfering in the activity of the judiciary," writes former magistrate Leïla Aslaoui (2007, par. 5). Even after Bouteflika's resignation, the administrative courts continued to perform the same function of judicially instrumentalizing government policies targeting opposition groups: this included political parties,[49] as well as civil society organizations that had taken an active part in the Hirak Movement.[50]

As for the civil courts' subservience to political power, this is amply illustrated by the immunity these courts have recognized for regime loyalists implicated in corruption scandals, even in cases of proven large-scale corruption.[51] Like their counterparts in administrative justice, ordinary courts play a role in the political scene whether they like it or not: they are forced to

48 In the notorious case of the FLN's eighth party congress, held in March of 2003, the administrative court in Algiers intervened with a surprise decision delivered on 30 December 2003, invalidating all congress proceedings undertaken since March. The president of the administrative chamber was summoned in the middle of the night with her two magistrates, without the presence of either a public prosecutor or the defendant, to deliver a nightly decision: the eighth congress was found to be null and void, and all party assets and activities were thereby frozen.

49 On 20 January 2022, the Council of State (Conseil d'État) ordered the "temporary suspension" of the Socialist Workers' Party (PST), forcing it to cease all its activities and close its premises. The same happened on 23 February 2023 with the Democratic and Social Movement (MDS), whose leader, Fethi Ghares, was also sentenced to two years in prison and was fined 200,000 dinars (see Amnesty International 2022).

50 On 23 February 2023, the Council of State upheld on appeal the ban which the lower administrative court in Algiers had imposed on the main Algerian youth association—the Rassemblement Actions Jeunesse—on charges of "violating the law on associations and activities in contradiction with the objectives listed in the statutes." This put an end to the association, which had been at the forefront of the Hirak protests and whose activities the government had been clamping down on since October 2019. Eleven of the association's members were prosecuted, nine of whom were imprisoned for publishing "documents likely to harm the national interest" (see Hamdi 2023). On 16 April 2021, the SOS Bal El Oued association was disbanded on "foreign funding" charges, and its president, who was actively involved in the Hirak Movement, was sent to prison (Hamdi 2021). And on 29 June 2022 came the breakup of the Algerian League for the Protection of Human Rights (Ligue Algérienne des Défense des Droits de l'Homme, or LADDH) (see Bobin 2023).

51 A prime example here is that of former energy minister Chakib Khelil and his family. They have been prosecuted for corruption in a number of cases, most notably in connection with Algeria's national oil company, Sonatrach (the Sonatrach 1 and 2 scandals that broke out in 2010 and 2013: cf. note 42). Most recently, in 2022, Khelil was tried and sentenced in absentia to twenty years in prison on charges related to his time as energy minister from 2000 to 2020.

provide legal cover for the government's repressive policies. This has been so in many cases in which "the judge plays politics,"[52] as the former communications minister Abdelaziz Rahabi has denounced.[53] Neither did the fall of the Bouteflika regime put an end to these practices. The measures taken against the free press, in particular, are so severe that there are no longer any truly independent media outlets.[54] Unfair and disproportionate sentences have also been handed down to journalists, party activists, bloggers, and civil-society players. Almost four years after the peaceful Hirak uprising of February 2019, the regime has stepped up its repression of the last remaining protest groups. The regime's criminalization of any civic engagement affects all organizations that are independent of the regime (LDH 2023). This practice is indicative of the closure of the political landscape.

13. Enshrining Rights and Freedoms

Since 1989, the year of political openness, the Constitution has recognized a wide range of human rights, to which it devotes the whole of Chapter IV, with a strong emphasis on "fundamental freedoms, human rights and rights of the citizen" (Art. 31 of the constitution of 23 February 1989, reinst. 1996, rev. 2016), stating as well that "infringements of rights and freedoms . . . shall be punishable by law" (Art. 34). In grandiloquent style, which we will not enter into, the 2020 constitution (in force since 30 December 2020) emphatically enshrines the same rights and freedoms (Title II, Chapter I), reaffirming the universally recognized civil and political rights: freedom of opinion and worship (Art. 51), freedom of expression and assembly (Art. 52), freedom of association (Art. 53), freedom of the press (Art. 54), and the right to establish political parties (Art. 57), among several others.

Algeria is also a signatory to the 1966 International Covenant on Civil and Political Rights (ICCPR), having acceded in 1989. But it is one thing for the country to formally recognize these basic rights and freedoms and to commit to protecting the internationally binding rights set forth in the ICCPR and another thing to stand by these commitments and genuinely protect the formally recognized constitutional rights. And in this regard the country's track record is very poor, with more than an ample supply of violations,

52 Emblematic is the example of Mohamed Benchicou, executive editor of the independent daily *Le Matin*, who was sentenced to two years in prison even if the real reason behind his imprisonment was the publication of his book *Bouteflika: Une Imposture* (Benchicou 2004).

53 In an interview with Hakim Laâlam published on 13 December 2020 in *Le Soir d'Algérie* (see Abdelaziz 2020).

54 In April 2022, the daily newspaper *Liberté* was shut down by its owner after its editorial line came under strong criticism from President Tebboune himself. And in May 2023, Ihsane El Kadi, founder and editor-in-chief of *Radio M* and the *Maghreb Émergent* news website, was sentenced to three years in prison, at the same time as all his assets were seized and the parent company of these two outlets was dissolved.

ranging from forced disappearances to arbitrary detention and torture (see UNHRC 2019). For all these reasons, Algeria comes under regular criticism from United Nations bodies, notably the UN Human Rights Council (see UNHRC 2008, 2010, 2011, 2017, 2019), the Office of the United Nations High Commissioner for Human Rights (OHCHR 2020), and the UN Committee against Torture (in 2011, 2013, 2015, and 2018);[55] from the European Union, particularly the European Parliament (EP 2018, 2020, 2023);[56] and from nongovernmental organizations, both international—specifically Amnesty International (2008, 2018, 2021, 2022, 2023)—and national.[57] This prompted the Human Rights Committee, at its 122nd session, to "suspend follow-up dialogue" with Algeria, citing the country's "unsatisfactory implementation" of the committee's decisions (UN Human Rights Committee 2018; see also UN Human Rights Committee 2007a, in the case of *Kimouche v. Algeria* and UN Human Rights Committee 2007b, paras. 7, 8, and 13).

In response to the peaceful popular Hirak uprising of 2019, calling for radical change in the political system, the regime responded by taking a repressive stance. We can see this in the amendments introduced to the Algerian Criminal Code under Presidential Ordinance 21-08 of 9 June 2021. These amendments include a definition of terrorism so broad and ambiguous that it could conceivably be read to encompass almost any kind of political activity. Indeed, terrorism is defined as "any targeting of state security, national unity, or the stability and normal functioning of the institutions by any action or incitement intended to advance, by any means whatsoever, the goal of accessing power or bringing about any change in the system of governance by nonconstitutional means" (§ 14).[58] According to international observers, these provisions have led to an upsurge in acts of intimidation and repression against civil society

55 See in particular the decision the Committee Against Torture issued in 2011 under Art. 22(7) of the Convention against Torture and Other Cruel, Inhuman or Degrading Treatment or Punishment (CAT 2011).

56 In a resolution of 25 November 2020, the European Parliament "strongly condemns the escalation of arbitrary and unlawful arrests, detentions and judicial harassment of journalists, human rights defenders, trade unionists, lawyers, civil society and peaceful activists in Algeria" (EP 2020).

57 On the occasion marking the 70th anniversary of the Universal Declaration of Human Rights, the Algerian section of Amnesty International, the Algerian League for Human Rights (Ligue Algérienne des Droits de l'Homme, or LADH), and the Algerian League for the Defence of Human Rights (Ligue Algérienne pour la Défense des Droits de l'Homme, or LADDH) expressed their concern about "violations of the rights to freedom of expression, association, and peaceful demonstration, as well as of the right to unionize, despite the fact that these rights and freedoms are all constitutionally protected" (*Maghreb Émergent*, 9 December 2018).

58 The French text of the provision: "tout acte visant la sûreté de l'État, l'unité nationale et la stabilité et le fonctionnement normal des institutions par toute action ayant pour objet d'œuvrer ou inciter, par quelque moyen que ce soit, à accéder au pouvoir ou à changer le système de gouvernance par des moyens non constitutionnels."

(FIDH 2023; Alilat 2021), the human rights movement,[59] and independent media,[60] and indeed against all forms of dissent across the board.[61]

14. Epilogue

Four years after the Hirak uprising of 2019, Bouteflika's twenty-year regime collapsed. The movement rallied behind two slogans: "Yetnahaw Gaa!" ("Let them all go!") and "Dawla madania machi askaria" ("A civilian state, not a military one"). They reflect the people's hunger for radical change in the system. This demand for freedom was not favoured by the army's chief of staff, General Gaïd Salah, the intransigent guardian of the system of which he was the embodiment. With a narrow focus on political and military power—and having seen in the unrest an opportunity to force the resignation of President Bouteflika, of whom he was among the most loyal supporters—he was determined to carry out his own resilient plan for ending the crisis. After a long struggle with the popular Hirak Movement, the regime's strongman succeeded in organizing the presidential election for 12 December 2019.

Clearly, the elections took place in a tense climate of unrest, and the new head of state, Abdelmadjid Tebboune, constantly paid tribute to the "Blessed Hirak," voicing support for the project of building a "New Algeria." Very quickly after the election, however, he reversed course, aggressively strengthening the authoritarian order, all the while carrying out a policy of judicial

59 Addressing the situation in Algeria, Mary Lawlor, UN Special Rapporteur on the Situation of Human Rights Defenders, emphatically stated in February of 2023 that "acts of intimidation, silencing and repression against the human rights movement must end," a statement she made in response the dissolution of two prominent human rights associations in Algeria: the Ligue Algérienne pour la Défense des Droits de l'Homme (LADDH) and the Rassemblement Actions Jeunesse (RAJ) (OHCHR 2023). The statement was endorsed by Clément Nyaletsossi Voule, Special Rapporteur on Freedom of Peaceful Assembly and of Association, and Irene Khan, Special Rapporteur on Freedom of Opinion and Expression.

60 On 11 May 2023 the European Parliament adopted by an overwhelming majority (536 votes in favour, 4 against) an emergency resolution openly condemning the repression of freedom of the press and calling for an end to the arrest and detention of political activists, journalists, human rights activists, and trade unionists (EP 2023). Applauded by Reporters Without Borders (Reporters sans Frontières) (RWB 2023a), this resolution sparked an outcry in Algeria.

On the occasion of World Press Freedom Day (3 May 2023), President Tebboune himself felt compelled to say, "We have no journalists in prison" (quoted in Boumaza 2023), delivering this remark in response to the publication of the 2023 World Press Freedom Index compiled by Reporters Without Borders, whose work Tebboune regarded as libellous because it ranked Algeria in 136th place, citing a "growing authoritarianism in Algeria . . . where the situation continues to be classified as 'bad'" (RWB 2023b).

61 New repressive laws were enacted on 28 April 2020. These introduced, in particular, two offences into the Algerian Criminal Code: one for spreading "fake news" (Art. 196 bis), the other for engaging in "solidarity" (Art. 95 bis). And, as noted, Ordinance No. 21-08 of 8 June 2021 extended the definition of terrorism to include any act aimed at "accessing power or bringing about any change in the system of governance by nonconstitutional means" (Criminal Code, Art. 87 bis). On this point, see Cherbi 2023 and Human Rights Watch 2023.

repression (Bobin and Zerrouky 2023). Opposition political parties were crushed and those involved in the Hirak hunted down. Journalists, trade unionists, lawyers, students, and community activists were subjected to a repression never before seen (Belkaïd 2022; Dris 2022). So severe is the repression that many people are thinking only about surviving or emigrating. This authoritarian crackdown is creating a climate of disenchantment and national depression. In short, the country is once again facing the same structural challenges it was facing decades ago.

Works Cited

Abbas, Ferhat. 1980. *L'Indépendance Confisquée, 1962–1978*. Paris: Jeune Afrique.

Abdelaziz, Merzouk. 2020. "Pour Abdelaziz Rahabi, 'le juge fait de la politique en Algérie.'" *Algérie 360°*, December 13, 2020. www.algerie360.com/20201213-algerie-droits-de-lhomme-detenus-dopinion-abdelaziz-rahabi/.

Abéga, Séverin Cécile. 2003. "La violence endémique en Afrique." *Bulletin de l'APAD* 25. https://doi.org/10.4000/apad.199.

Addi, Lahouari. 1999. "L'armée, la nation et l'État en Algérie." *Confluences Méditerranée* 29: 39–46. HAL Open Science repository, June 25, 2009. https://shs.hal.science/halshs-00398898.

Addi, Lahouari. 2020. "Le système de pouvoir en Algérie, ses origines et son évolution." *Confluence Méditerranée* 4 (115): 103–13. https://doi.org/10.3917/come.115.0105.

Aït Kaki, Maxime. 2004. "Armée, pouvoir et processus de décision en Algérie." *Politique Étrangère* 69 (2): 427–39.

Alilat, Farid. 2017. "Algérie: Ahmed Ouyahia, l'éternel recours de Bouteflika." *Jeune Afrique*, September 4, 2017. www.jeuneafrique.com/mag/468593/politique/algerie-ahmed-ouyahia-leternel-recours-de-bouteflika/.

Alilat, Farid. 2018. "Algérie: Les élections sénatoriales du 29 décembre, dernier tour de chauffe avant la présidentielle." *Jeune Afrique*, December 16, 2018. www.jeuneafrique.com/mag/685424/politique/algerie-les-elections-senatoriales-du-29-decembre-dernier-tour-de-chauffe-avant-la-presidentielle/.

Alilat, Farid. 2020a. "Algérie: La chute du général Wassini Bouazza, tout-puissant patron de la sécurité intérieure." *Jeune Afrique*, July 1, 2020. www.jeuneafrique.com/1009041/politique/algerie-la-chute-du-general-wassini-bouazza-tout-puissant-patron-de-la-securite-interieure/.

Alilat, Farid. 2020b. *Bouteflika, l'Histoire Secrète*. Monaco: Éditions du Rocher.

Alilat, Farid. 2020c. "Algérie: Enquête au cœur du système Bouteflika." *Jeune Afrique*, October 5, 2020. www.jeuneafrique.com/mag/1049038/politique/algerie-enquete-au-coeur-du-systeme-bouteflika/.

Alilat, Farid. 2021. "Algérie: La répression sous Tebboune est-elle plus sévère que sous Bouteflika?" *Jeune Afrique*, June 29, 2021. www.jeuneafrique.com/1190038/politique/algerie-la-repression-sous-tebboune-est-elle-plus-severe-que-sous-bouteflika/.

Alilat, Farid. 2023. "L'Algérie refusée par les Brics: Pour Abdelmadjid Tebboune, un revers symbolique." *Jeune Afrique*, August 24, 2023. www.jeuneafrique.com/1476064/politique/lalgerie-refusee-par-les-brics-pour-abdelmadjid-tebboune-un-revers-symbolique/.

Alilat, Farid, and Arianna Poletti. 2019. "Algérie: Incarcération de Tayeb Louh, dernier ministre de la Justice d'Abdelaziz Bouteflika." *Jeune Afrique*, August 22, 2019. www.jeuneafrique.com/818944/societe/algerie-tayeb-louh-dernier-ministre-de-la-justice-dabdelaziz-bouteflika-incarcere/.

Amnesty International. 2008. "Algeria: Briefing to the Committee Against Torture." April 17, 2008, Index No. MDE 28/001/2008. www.amnesty.org/en/documents/mde28/001/2008/en/.

Amnesty International. 2018. "Amnesty International Report 2017/18: The State of the World's Human Rights, Algeria." February 22, 2018, Index No. POL 10/6700/2018, pp. 71–73. www.amnesty.org/en/documents/pol10/6700/2018/en/.

Amnesty International. 2021. "Amnesty International Report 2020/21: The State of the World's Human Rights, Algeria." April 7, 2021, Index No. POL 10/3202/2021, pp. 62–65. www.amnesty.org/en/documents/pol10/3202/2021/en/.

Amnesty International. 2022. "Algeria: Authorities Target Political Parties in Their Latest Clampdown." February 9, 2022. www.amnesty.org/en/latest/news/2022/02/algeria-authorities-target-political-parties-in-their-latest-clampdown/.

Amnesty International. 2023. "Amnesty International Report 2022/23: The State of the World's Human Rights, Algeria." March 27, 2023, Index No. POL 10/5670/2023, pp. 68–71. www.amnesty.org/en/documents/pol10/5670/2023/en/.

Amrani, Hafnaoui, Secretary General of the Council of the Nation of Algeria. 2007. "L'Algérie: Du monopartisme au multipartisme." In *Le passage d'un système de parti unique au multipartisme*. Union interparlementaire, Association des Secrétaires Généraux de Parlement, Nusa Dua session, April–May 2007.

Aslaoui, Leïla. 2007. "Pouvoir ou simple fonction? Justice et société." In "Dossier de recherche: Justice, politique et société en Afrique du Nord. II, Justice et politisation." Special issue, *L'Année du Maghreb* 3: 135–40. https://doi.org/10.4000/anneemaghreb.361.

AW. 2009. "Partis politiques en Algérie: La confidence de Sid-Ahmed Ghozali." *Algeria Watch*, December 13, 2009. https://algeria-watch.org/?p=39077.

BAD (Groupe de la Banque Africaine de Développement). 2022. *Perspectives économiques en Algérie: Évolutions macroéconomiques et financières récentes*. BAD.

Badi, Abdelghani. 2020. "Entretien: Une répression ciblée, la justice instrumentalisée." Chap. 11 in *Hirak en Algérie: L'Invention d'un Soulèvement*, edited by Omar Benderra, François Gèze, Rafik Lebdjaoui, and Salima Mellah, 145–51. Paris: La Fabrique Éditions. https://doi.org/10.3917/lafab.azouz.2020.01.0145.

Bajolet, Bernard. 2018. *Le Soleil ne se Lève Plus à l'Est: Mémoires d'Orient d'un Ambassadeur peu Diplomate*. Paris: Plon.

Baroudi, Sofiane. 2017. "L'influence politique occulte des patrons algériens." *Orient XXI*, April 26, 2017. https://orientxxi.info/magazine/l-influence-politique-occulte-des-patrons-algeriens/1829.

Bekhchi, Abdelwahab. 2013. "Variations autour d'un demi-siècle de production juridique algérienne: Le long chemin vers la construction d'un système juridique pour le développement et la bonne gouvernance." In Vol. 1 of *L'Algérie, Cinquante Ans Après: La Part du Droit*, edited by Walid Laggoune, 2 vols. Algiers: Éditions AJED.

Belkaïd, Akram. 2022. "Algérie: Une restauration musclée." *Politique Étrangère* 87 (2): 83–93.

Benadji, Chérif. 2009. "Révision de la Constitution: Vers une présidence à vie?" In "S'opposer au Maghreb." Special issue, *L'Année du Maghreb* 6: 225–61. https://doi.org/10.4000/anneemaghreb.587.

Benakli, Nadia. 2012. "Ouyahia au conseil national du RND: 'Oui, je dérange.'" *L'Expression*, June 3, 2012. www.lexpressiondz.com/nationale/oui-je-derange-154687.

Benakli, Nadia. 2018. "Enquête: Magouilles, passe-droits et argent sale. La jungle des sénatoriales." *L'Expression*, November 8, 2018. www.lexpression.dz/nationale/la-jungle-des-senatoriales-303449.

Benchicou, Mohamed. 2004. *Bouteflika: Une Imposture*. Paris: Jean Picollec.

Benchikh, Madjid. 2003. *Algérie: Un Système Politique Militarisé*. Paris: L'Harmattan.

Benchikh, Madjid. 2009. "Constitutions démocratiques et réalités autoritaires au Maghreb: La démocratie de façade." In *Le Débat Juridique au Maghreb: De l'Étatisme à l'État de Droit*, edited by Yadh Benachour, Jean-Robert Henry, and Rostane Mehdi, 242–59. Paris: Éditions Publisud-Iremam.

Berrouane, Abderrahmane. 2015. *Aux Origines du MALG: Témoignage d'un Compagnon de Boussouf.* Algiers: Barzakh.

Bobin, Frédéric. 2023. "En Algérie, la dissolution de la Ligue des Droits de l'Homme illustre l'escalade répressive du régime." *Le Monde*, February 1, 2023. www.lemonde.fr/afrique/article/2023/02/01/en-algerie-la-dissolution-de-la-ligue-des-droits-de-l-homme-illustre-l-escalade-repressive-du-regime_6160088_3212.html.

Bobin, Frédéric, and Madjid Zerrouky. 2023. "Du Hirak à la répression, l'Algérie bascule dans une nouvelle ère." *Le Monde Afrique*, February 10, 2023. www.lemonde.fr/afrique/article/2023/02/10/du-hirak-a-la-repression-l-algerie-bascule-dans-une-nouvelle-ere_6161333_3212.html.

Boumaza, Ania. 2023. "Tebboune: 'Nous n'avons pas de journalistes en prison.'" *Algérie 360°*, May 6, 2023. www.algerie360.com/tebboune-nous-navons-pas-de-journalistes-en-prison/.

Boussoumah, Mohammed. 2009. *L'opération Constituante de 1996.* Algiers: OPU.

CAT (UN Committee Against Torture). 2011. "Decision: Communication No. 341/2008. Decision of the Committee Against Torture Under Article 22 of the Convention Against Torture and Other Cruel, Inhuman or Degrading Treatment or Punishment." 46th sess., May 9–June 3, 2011. UN Doc. CAT/C/46/D/341/2008.

Catusse, Myriam, ed. 2006. "Les partis politiques dans les pays arabes. Tome 2, Le Maghreb." *Remmm: Revue des Mondes Musulmans et de la Méditerranée* 11–12. https://doi.org/10.4000/remmm.2852.

Chahed, Nadia. 2017. "Algérie: La mafia de l'argent sale à l'assaut des législatives." *Anadolu Ajansı*, March 20, 2017. https://bit.ly/anadolu-ajansı-chahed-2017-algerie-mafia-argent-assaut-legislatives.

Chellali, Salsabil. 2014. "Algérie: Une leçon de fraude électorale." *El Watan*, April 19, 2014. www.courrierinternational.com/article/2014/04/19/une-lecon-de-fraude-electorale.

Cherbi, Massensen. 2023. "Le Hirak algérien à quatre ans du 22 février 2019: Entre répression judiciaire et renforcement de l'ordre autoritaire." *Arab Reform Initiative*, February 22, 2023. www.arab-reform.net/fr/publication/le-hirak-algerien-a-quatre-ans-du-22-fevrier-2019-entre-repression-judiciaire-et-renforcement-de-lordre-autoritaire/.

Daguzan, Jean-François. 2020. "L'armée algérienne au défi de la transformation." *Maghreb – Machrek* 2 (244): 77–97. https://doi.org/10.3917/machr.244.0077.

Daoud, Kamel. 2010. "Sid Ahmed Ghozali: Les 'harkis du système,' l'armée politique et la question iranienne." *Le Quotidien d'Oran*, October 18, 2010.

Dris, Chérif. 2022. "Les limites d'un régime résilient." Chap. 5 in *Cheminements Révolutionnaires: Un An de Mobilisations en Algérie (2019–2020)*, edited by Amin Allal, Layla Baamara, Leyla Dakhli, and Giulia Fabbiano, 117–48. Paris: CNRS Éditions. https://books.openedition.org/editionscnrs/56564.

EIU. 2020. *Democracy Index 2020: In Sickness and in Health?* The Economic Intelligence Unit.

EP (European Parliament). 2020. "Resolution on the Deteriorating Situation of Human Rights in Algeria, in Particular the Case of Journalist Khaled Drareni." Procedure reference: 2020/2880(RSP). Text adopted in Brussels on November 26, 2020. https://oeil.secure.europarl.europa.eu/oeil/popups/ficheprocedure.do?lang=en&reference=2020/2880(RSP).

EP (European Parliament). 2023. "Resolution on Media Freedom and Freedom of Expression in Algeria: The Case of Journalist Ihsane El-Kadi." Procedure reference: 2023/2661(RSP). Text adopted in Strasbourg on May 11, 2023. https://oeil.

secure.europarl.europa.eu/oeil/popups/ficheprocedure.do?lang=en&reference=2023/2661(RSP).

EP (European Parliament Think Thank). 2018. "Algeria and the EU: Challenges Before the Elections." *Briefing*, December 5, 2018. www.europarl.europa.eu/thinktank/en/document/EPRS_BRI(2018)630328.

EU EOM (Election Observation Mission). 2012. *Élections Législatives: Algérie 2012. Rapport Final.* EU EOM. https://ec.europa.eu/info/strategy/relations-non-eu-countries/types-relations-and-partnerships/election-observation/mission-recommendations-repository/missions/167.

EU EOM (Election Observation Mission). 2017. *Élections législatives: Algérie 2017. Rapport Final.* EU EOM.

FIDH (Fédération Internationale pour les Droits Humains). 2023. "Algérie: Après quatre ans de contestation, la société civile à l'agonie." February 23, 2023. www.fidh.org/fr/themes/defenseurs-des-droits-humains/algerie-apres-quatre-ans-de-contestation-la-societe-civile-a-l-agonie.

Garnett, Holly Ann, Toby S. James, and Madison MacGregor. 2022. *Year in Elections Global Report: 2019–2021.* The Electoral Integrity Project. www.electoralintegrity-project.com/globalreport2019-2021.

Garon, Lise. 1994. "Crise économique et consensus en État rentier: Le cas de l'Algérie socialiste." *Études Internationales* 25 (1): 1–22. https://doi.org/10.7202/703278ar.

Ghozali, Nacer-Eddine. 2020. "Algérie." In *Constitutions et Lois Fondamentales des Pays Arabes*, edited by Eric Canal-Forgues, Maïa-Oumeïma Hamrouni, and Feriel Ait-Ouyahia, Vol. 1, 19–124. Paris: A. Pedone.

Ghozali, Nacer-Eddine. 2022. "Algérie: Des résiliences autocratiques et des pathologies politiques à la captation de l'État: 20 ans de règne de Abdelaziz Bouteflika." In *Mélanges en l'Honneur du Doyen Mohamed Larbi Fadhel Moussa.* Munich: Hanns-Seidel-Stiftung.

Graïne, Larbi. 2001. "L'Armée, Bouteflika et les petites phrases de Belaïd Abdesselam." *La Tribune*, March 17, 2001.

Guemache, Hamid. 2012. "Le Premier ministre accuse la mafia de chercher à contrôler l'économie du pays." *La Tribune*, June 4, 2012. www.latribune.fr/actualites/economie/international/20120604trib000701917/le-premier-ministre-algerien-accuse-la-mafia-de-chercher-a-controler-l-economie-du-pays.html.

Guenanfa, Hadjer. 2019. "Algérie – Djilali Hadjadj: 'La prédation a été systématique à tous les niveaux.'" *Le Point*, May 22, 2019. www.lepoint.fr/afrique/algerie-djilali-hadjadj-la-predation-a-ete-systematique-a-tous-les-niveaux-22-05-2019-2314270_3826.php.

Hachemaoui, Mohammed. 2003. "La représentation politique en Algérie entre médiation clientéliste et prédation (1997–2002)." *Revue Française de Science Politique* 53 (1): 35–72. www.persee.fr/doc/rfsp_0035-2950_2003_num_53_1_395688.

Hadjadj, Djilali. 2003. "Violence et corruption: Cas de l'Algérie." *Bulletin de l'APAD* 25. https://doi.org/10.4000/apad.203.

Hamdi, Rania. 2019. "Algérie: Arrestation de Baha Eddine Tliba, l'enfant gâté du système 'lâché' par Gaïd Salah." *Jeune Afrique*, October 17, 2019. www.jeuneafrique.com/843990/politique/algerie-arrestation-de-baha-eddine-tliba-lenfant-gate-du-systeme-lache-par-gaid-salah/.

Hamdi, Rania. 2021. "Algérie: SOS Bab-el-Oued a-t-elle bénéficié d'un 'financement étranger'?" *Jeune Afrique*, April 29, 2021. www.jeuneafrique.com/1163192/politique/algerie-sos-bab-el-oued-a-t-elle-vraiment-beneficie-dun-financement-etranger/.

Hamdi, Rania. 2023. "En Algérie, Dissolution du RAJ, une ONG emblématique du Hirak." *Jeune Afrique*, February 27, 2023. www.jeuneafrique.com/1421053/politique/en-algerie-dissolution-du-raj-une-ong-emblematique-du-hirak/.

Human Rights Watch. 2023. *2023 World Report. Algeria: Events of 2022.* Edited by Tirana Hassan. www.hrw.org/world-report/2023/country-chapters/algeria.

Labat, Séverine. 2003. "Islamiste et mouvement social en Algérie." *Vingtième Siècle: Revue d'Histoire* 3 (79): 3–18. https://doi.org/10.3917/ving.079.0003.
LDH (Ligue des Droits de l'Homme). 2023. "Urgence Algérie: Contre la répression, solidarité internationale." Communiqué commun LDH, FDIH et l'Organisation Mondiale Contre la Torture (OMCT), dans le cadre de l'Observatoire pour la Protection des Défenseurs des Droits Humains, January 23, 2023. www.ldh-france.org/urgence-algerie-contre-la-repression-solidarite-internationale/.
Levet, Jean-Louis, and Paul Tolila. 2023. *Le Mal Algérien*. Paris: Bouquins.
Lyes, B. 2018. "Vote aux sénatoriales: Un smartphone, ou un téléviseur, pour une voix." *Algérie éco*, December 30, 2018. www.algerie-eco.com/2018/12/30/vote-aux-senatoriales-un-smartphone-ou-un-televiseur-pour-une-voix/.
Mahiou, Ahmed. 2011. "A propos de l'indépendance de la justice algérienne." In *L'exigence et le Droit, Mélanges en l'Honneur du Professeur Mohand Issad*, edited by Ali Bencheneb and Chérif Bennadji. Algiers: Éditions AJED.
Mahmoudi, R. 2018. "Affaire Chikhi: Silence pesant de l'Organe de lutte contre la corruption." *Algérie Patriotique*, July 26, 2018. www.algeriepatriotique.com/2018/07/26/affaire-chikhi-silence-pesant-de-lobservatoire-de-lutte-contre-corruption/.
Mann, Nathan. 2019. "Algérie: La seule chose que Bouteflika a réussi à démocratiser c'est la corruption et le népotisme." *Libération*, March 1, 2019. www.liberation.fr/planete/2019/03/01/algerie-la-seule-chose-que-bouteflika-a-reussi-a-democratiser-c-est-la-corruption-et-le-nepotisme_1712411/.
Meddi, Adlène. 2020. "Faut-il dissoudre le Parlement (et le FLN)?" *Le Point*, September 8–9, 2020. www.lepoint.fr/afrique/algerie-faut-il-dissoudre-le-parlement-et-le-fln-08-09-2020-2390935_3826.php.
OHCHR (Office of the United Nations High Commissioner for Human Rights). 2020. "UN Experts Condemn Jail Sentence Against Algerian Journalist and Call for His Release." Press release, Geneva, September 16, 2020. www.ohchr.org/en/press-releases/2020/09/un-experts-condemn-jail-sentence-against-algerian-journalistand-call-his.
OHCHR (Office of the United Nations High Commissioner for Human Rights). 2023. "Algeria: UN Expert Says Crackdown on Civil Society and Human Rights Defenders Must End." Press release, Geneva, February 22, 2023. www.ohchr.org/en/press-releases/2023/02/algeria-un-expert-says-crackdown-civil-society-and-human-rights-defenders.
RWB (Reporters Without Borders). 2023a. "European Parliament Calls on Algeria to Release Journalist Ihsane El Kadi and Respect Press Freedom." May 11, 2023. https://rsf.org/en/european-parliament-calls-algeria-release-journalist-ihsane-el-kadi-and-respect-press-freedom.
RWB (Reporters Without Borders). 2023b. "2023 World Press Freedom Index: Journalism Threatened by Fake Content Industry." https://rsf.org/en/2023-world-press-freedom-index-journalism-threatened-fake-content-industry.
Sifaoui, Mohamed. 2012. *Histoire Secrète de l'Algérie Indépendante: L'État-DRS*. Nouveau Monde Éditions.
Siouane, Zoheir. 2019. "Après la nomination de Tarek Krour président de l'ONPLC. Anticorruption: Défaut de bilan en attendant les actions." *Algérie 360°*, May 16, 2019. www.algerie360.com/apres-la-nomination-de-tarek-krour-president-de-lonplc-anticorruption-defaut-de-bilan-en-attendant-les-actions/.
Tlemçani, Rachid. 2012. "Un autoritarisme électoral." *Tumultes* 1–2 (38–39): 149–71. https://doi.org/10.3917/tumu.038.0149.
UNHRC (United Nations Human Rights Council). 2008. "Report of the Special Rapporteur on Violence against Women, Its Causes and Consequences, Yakin Ertürk. Addendum: Mission to Algeria." 7th sess., February 13, 2008. UN Doc. A/HRC/7/6/Add.2.

UNHRC (United Nations Human Rights Council). 2010. "Report of the Special Rapporteur on Violence against Women, Its Causes and Consequences, Rashida Manjoo. Addendum: Mission to Algeria." 17th sess., May 19, 2011. UN Doc. A/HRC/17/26/Add.3.

UNHRC (United Nations Human Rights Council). 2011. "Report of the Special Rapporteur on Adequate Housing as a Component of the Right to Adequate Standard of Living, and the Right to Non-discrimination in This Context, Raquel Rolnik. Addendum: Mission to Algeria." 19th sess., December 26, 2011. UN Doc. A/HRC/19/53/Add.2.

UNHRC (United Nations Human Rights Council). 2017. "Report of the Special Rapporteur on the Right of Everyone to the Enjoyment of the Highest Attainable Standard of Physical and Mental Health on his Visit to Algeria, Dainius Pūras." 35th sess., April 20, 2017. UN Doc. A/HRC/35/21/Add.1.

UNHRC (United Nations Human Rights Council). 2018. "Concluding Observations on the Fourth Periodic Report of Algeria." 123rd sess., August 7, 2018. UN Doc. CCPR/C/DZA/CO/4.

UNHRC (United Nations Human Rights Council). 2019. "Report of the Working Group on Enforced or Involuntary Disappearances." 42nd sess., July 30, 2019. UN Doc. A/HRC/42/40.

UN Human Rights Committee. 2007a. "Views: Communication No. 1328/2004. Communication Submitted on October 7, 2004 by Messaouda Kimouche, née Cheraitia, and Mokhtar Kimouche (Represented by Counsel, Nassera Dutour)." View adopted on July 10, 2007. State Party: Algeria. Subject Matter: Disappearance, Detention Incommunicado. 90th sess., July 9–27, 2007. UN Doc. CCPR/C/90/D/1328/2004.

UN Human Rights Committee. 2007b. "Consideration of Reports Submitted by States Parties Under Article 40 of the International Covenant on Civil and Political Rights. Concluding Observations of the Human Rights Committee: Algeria." 91st sess., December 2, 2007. UN Doc. CCPR/C/DZA/CO/3.

UN Human Rights Committee. 2018. "Follow-Up to Views Under the Optional Protocol to the International Covenant on Civil and Political Rights. Advance Unedited Version, Restricted Distribution." 122nd sess., May 29, 2018. UN Doc. CCPR/C/122/R.2.

Zartmann, William. 1967. "L'armée dans la politique algérienne." *Annuaire de l'Afrique du Nord* 6: 265–78.

Part III

Islam and the Mediterranean Today

7 Redefining Ourselves So as to Make the Mediterranean a *Mare Nostrum*

Hande Orhon Özdağ and Erhan Doğan

1. Introduction

In the 1946 preface that Fernand Braudel wrote to the first edition of his magnum opus, *La Méditerranée et le Monde Méditerranéen à l'Époque de Philippe II* (Braudel 1972), he emphasized the need to look at the Mediterranean as a historical entity. The nomenclature attributed to this geographical region provides us with an inherent clue to its historical character. Across numerous languages, the Mediterranean is designated by its geographic position.[1] In the majority of languages, the name for the Mediterranean reflects its encompassing and continent-connecting nature, with words whose literal meaning is "the middle sea" or "the sea between lands," for example. The Romans called the Mediterranean the *mare nostrum*—"our sea."

Over the course of time, it has become apparent that the Roman concept of *mare nostrum* transcended a mere spatial placement "between" or "in the middle of" lands. Furthermore, the concept has served as a nexus for an array of religions, ethnicities, and languages—fostering connections among these diverse entities, while also drawing divisions. Presently, individuals hailing from the Balkans, southern Europe, northern Africa, the Middle East, and Anatolia, representing various strands of Judaism, Christianity, Islam, and other faiths, coexist within the orbit of this sea. Consequently, the Mediterranean has evolved into a sea that accommodates numerous "us" and "them" identities.

Historians and anthropologists of the modern age have made a valuable effort to understand and explain this living stage of history. Sometimes they have tried to explain, as Braudel formidably did, how the geography of the Mediterranean region affects the development of various civilizations (Abulafia 2005). Sometimes they have argued that what gives coherence to

1 For instance, the name for the Mediterranean in Turkish is *Akdeniz*, which combines the morphemes *deniz* (sea) and *ak* (white). In Turkish, therefore, the name immediately calls to mind not so much an area as a colour—or the idea of "the white sea"—literally "the sea which is white." In the ancient Turkish tradition, however, directions were designated by colour, and so *Akdeniz* meant "the western sea" or "the sea in the west."

DOI: 10.4324/9781003431206-12

the "Mediterranean system" are not its similarities but its "complementary differences" (Bromberger 2006, 99). Sometimes they have drawn a distinction between the history *of* the Mediterranean and history *in* the Mediterranean (Horden and Purcell 2000, 9), looking at this history as one of "diversity in unity" (Abulafia 2005).

In this chapter, we harness this idea from the standpoint of international relations, exploring the feasibility of reconstructing the Mediterranean as a *mare nostrum*: we accordingly argue for a potential transformation of the region into a collective entity representing its diverse population. Our focus falls on the adaptable aspects of the region-building and identity-construction processes. We contend that before we can reshape the Mediterranean into a *mare nostrum*, we first have to carefully examine the region and resolve its internal and external challenges. Furthermore, we posit that a full understanding of the factors contributing to past failures in the region-building process could prove instrumental in shaping the success of future endeavours. We thus begin, in Section 2, by clarifying the role of the Mediterranean region as a "subject"—or entity—within the realm of international relations. We then turn to the current situation, in Section 3, where we assess the state of the Mediterranean as it currently exists, highlighting its most problematic features. In Section 4 we go into the main reasons why the region-building process has so far failed. And finally, in Section 5, we draw a narrow roadmap that we think can effectively guide the effort to make the Mediterranean a *mare nostrum*.

2. The Mediterranean as a Subject of International Relations

Before we can even discuss the prospects for redefining a collective identity for the Mediterranean, we have to be able to form a clear picture of the Mediterranean region itself. While the region can be identified by its geography and certainly cannot be understood without some sense of its boundaries (Cantori and Spiegel 1969, 362; Nye 1968, vii; Russet 1967, 11), the very act of geographically delineating the Mediterranean is not without complexities. The most important question in delineating the Mediterranean has to do with the foundation on which we should base our understanding: is it the waters, coastlines, and islands that essentially shape the Mediterranean, or should the emphasis instead fall on the civilizations and states that have been invariably influenced by these geographically defined contours (Abulafia 2005)?

Within the realm of international relations, geographical proximity or commonalities, while necessary, do not in themselves suffice for delineating a region. This understanding naturally directs our attention toward the intricate social and political dimensions intrinsic to a region's definition. Ethnic, linguistic, social, and historical commonalities and interactions (Cantori and Spiegel 1969, 362), along with cultural similarities and economic interdependence (Russet 1967, 11), figure as crucial characteristics in delineating a geographical formation as a region—the very essence of international relations. Furthermore, beyond their geographical underpinnings, regions undergo political construction through the implementation of social and economic regionalization strategies (Katzenstein 2003, 215). Consequently, the delineation of the Mediterranean region transcends the realm of geography, emerging as a multifaceted sociopolitical challenge.

As a subject within the realm of international relations, the Mediterranean encompasses southern EU countries in addition to Turkey, the northern African countries (Algeria, Libya, Mauritania, Morocco, Tunisia), and the Levant countries (Egypt, Israel, Palestine, Jordan, Lebanon, Syria) (Pace 2005, 2). Yet, these countries are also integral components of other distinct "regions," such as Europe, the Balkans, and the Middle East and North Africa (MENA). Consequently, the Mediterranean assumes the role of an intersection wherein various regions converge, essentially forming a region made up of subregions. Additionally, the involvement of extraregional countries, particularly the United States, Russia, and more recently China, introduces a layer of complexity as they endeavour to exert influence within the Mediterranean. These efforts sometimes extend to operations conducted beyond EU-affiliated parts of the region, potentially jeopardizing the interests of Mediterranean countries. The presence of these extraregional actors further adds intricacy to the overall dynamics within the region.

Ana Bojinović Fenko summarizes the three most frequently used definitions of the Mediterranean in international relations: "(a) as a neighbouring area and thus a foreign policy object of Europe, (b) as an inter-regional space, where diversity derives from different sub-regional units and (c) as an area of autonomous regionalisation process" (Bojinović Fenko 2015, 81). Indeed, the confluence of these three primary usages, considered in conjunction with the aforementioned definitional and scope-related complexities, brings to light the quandary pertaining to the appropriate level of analysis when examining the Mediterranean. At what level should our scrutiny be directed: the state level, the regional level, or the international-system level? Given that the intricacies of Mediterranean politics have perpetually arisen from the interplay of domestic, regional, and international dynamics (Jünemann 2004, 1), none of these levels can be disregarded. Consequently, it is imperative to take a considerably comprehensive approach in order to fully comprehend the Mediterranean phenomenon.

3. The Mediterranean in Existence

Evaluating the Mediterranean as a single unit proves to be a complex endeavour (Bromberger 2006, 91). Beyond shared aspects such as lifestyle patterns, climate conditions, and dietary practices, the region's coherence remains elusive when we delve into the dimensions of ethnicity, language, religion, and culture. In essence, if we should characterize the Mediterranean strictly on the basis of definitions predicated on homogeneity and resemblance, the bona fide picture of the "region" we would consequently get would become a challenging proposition to defend. This challenge stems from the historical reality that the Mediterranean has consistently been a crucible of sorts, with its confluence of diverse social, economic, religious, and political forces, making it a nexus for both conflict and collaboration, discord and cohabitation (Xenakis 1999, 63).

The Mediterranean region has undergone a multifaceted and ever-evolving process of formation. Four primary regionalization processes can be identified in the region, spanning from the 19th century to the 1990s and succinctly outlined by Kerem Öktem (2010, 23) as follows: (a) the dissolution of dominant empires, namely, the Ottoman and Habsburg empires, which had exerted their influence over the region for prolonged periods; (b) the era of European regionalization that emerged in the aftermath of World War II; (c) the postcolonial epoch; and (d) the postcommunist period. Hence, pivotal junctures in the global arena, encompassing episodes like the two world wars and the end of the Cold War, along with broader regional reconfigurations, concurrently acted as transformative forces in shaping the Mediterranean at different phases. The era characterized by the emergence of nation-states in the 19th and early 20th centuries, the post-WWII interplay of imperialism and anti-imperialist resistance, the dynamics of the Cold War, and the surge of ethnic nationalisms in the wake of communism's demise, collectively make up driving forces perpetually moulding the contours of the Mediterranean region.

These periods also laid the foundation for the prevailing characteristics of relations among the Mediterranean littoral states. Alongside these regionalization phases, novel dimensions were introduced by the deepening forces of globalization and the escalating instability within the MENA region post 9/11 and during the Arab uprisings of the 2010s. Presently, any analysis of relations within the Mediterranean basin makes it necessary to closely examine four problems as follows: (a) bilateral disputes between littoral states; (b) subregional fragmentation; (c) uncontrolled migration from south to north; and (d) challenges in distributing resources. Let us take these up in turn.

3.1. Bilateral Disputes Between Littoral States

Numerous countries situated around the Mediterranean Sea are grappling with historical and contemporary conflicts. Notable examples of such bilateral challenges include the enduring disagreement between Greece and Turkey over matters like the Aegean islands, Cyprus, and minority rights, as well as the claims over northern and southern Cyprus; the conflict between Israel and Palestine; the deeply entrenched difficulties involving Israel and Lebanon; and the controversies between Algeria and Morocco regarding the issue of Western Sahara (Chivvis and Fishman 2017, 5). However, these bilateral issues also unmistakably highlight the divergence and even conflicting nature of regional security priorities among states in the region, thereby underscoring that the Mediterranean region is far from embodying a cohesive "security complex" (Aliboni 2001, 2).

3.2. Subregional Fragmentation

Contrary to the perception of the Mediterranean as a homogeneous and harmonious entity (Öktem 2010, 7), its composition is notably characterized by pronounced fragmentation. This fragmentation becomes starkly apparent across political, economic, and cultural dimensions. In fact, it proves instructive to employ global geopolitical dichotomies in grasping the complexities of Mediterranean fragmentation: both the ideologically driven West-East division and the economically oriented North-South divides have exerted significant influence on the ongoing reconfiguration of the region. Following World War II, a distinctive dichotomy emerged within the Mediterranean region. While the northwestern periphery experienced a gradual process of liberal democratization, the Balkans embarked on a path toward communism under Yugoslavia. Simultaneously, the North African rims witnessed an intensified nation-building process rooted in socialist-statist principles (ibid., 28). Notably, the southern reaches of the Mediterranean were characterized by liberation struggles waged against their colonizers, among which were not only distant powers but also immediate neighbours across the northern Mediterranean expanse. In tandem with cultural disparities, ideological rifts further cement the political disunion within the region. Spanning an extensive spectrum of political trajectories, ranging from fascism to socialism and from colonialism to nationalism (Halliday 2008, 19), the enduring legacy comprises relatively democratic and secular administrations prevailing in the northern expanse, juxtaposed with predominantly nondemocratic regimes characterized by robust religious inclinations in the southern realms.

In the Mediterranean region, one of the most significant and striking examples of fragmentation lies in the economic disparity between its northern and southern parts. As documented in Daniele and Malanima (2016, 19), this economic divide is exemplified by a substantial per capita GDP gap between the highest-ranking country, France and the lowest-ranking country, France's former colony Algeria. Specifically, per capita GDP in France in 2016 was about six times that of Algeria. When we approach the year 2022, we can see from World Bank data that there remains a remarkably wide PPP-based GDP per capita gap (current international dollar)[2] between the highest-ranking country, France and the lowest-ranking country, Morocco (also a former colony of France). France's per capita GDP is nearly six times greater than that of Morocco, underscoring the persistent economic disparities in the Mediterranean region (World Bank 2024). While income disparities within Mediterranean nations may be less pronounced in relation to developmental parameters, it is noteworthy that non-European Mediterranean countries show greater inequality than their Euro-Mediterranean counterparts (Amendola and Dell'Anno 2014, 39–40).

Furthermore, the southern Mediterranean's enduring peripheral status (Wallerstein 2004, 29) has persisted over time. Characterized by a rentier structure, the economy of the southern rims hinges crucially on the export

2 The concept here is that of GDP per capita based on purchasing power parity (PPP). As the World Bank (2017) explains in its Metadata Glossary, "PPP GDP is gross domestic product converted to international dollars using purchasing power parity rates. An international dollar has the same purchasing power over GDP as the US dollar has in the United States."

of energy resources and raw materials (Corm 2011, 128). Intraregional trade dynamics are also disappointing. Bearing in mind that the Mediterranean region is among the least economically integrated regions in the world, it shouldn't be surprising that economic integration is unevenly developed. For instance, according to the data the Union for the Mediterranean published in its first report on Euro-Mediterranean regional integration (UfM 2021), when it comes to trade, the European Union accounts for more than 95 percent of merchandise exports within the area (OECD 2021, 25). The Mediterranean region sees 70 percent of its cargo traffic occurring between European ports, while 15 percent involves trade between Europe and North Africa. A mere 5 percent of the traffic pertains to trade between countries in the MENA region (OECD 2021, 103; UfM 2021). In light of this, it becomes evident that despite various economic initiatives, meaningful economic interaction within the region remains constrained. Moreover, the current state of economic interaction perpetuates the disadvantaged status of certain Mediterranean countries.

Within the region, a mosaic of coexistence encompasses Catholic Latin populations, Orthodox Balkan communities, Arab Muslims, and Jews, forming a complex cultural fabric (Bromberger 2006, 92). And yet we cannot easily assert that that this coexistence unfolds in perpetual seamlessness. On the contrary, the Mediterranean's demographic composition has fostered an enduring tradition of cultural otherness, consistently underpinning the region's social composition (Halliday 2008, 18–19). This cultural otherness is magnified by the prevailing political circumstances, with certain political entities unfortunately resorting to manipulating it as a tool by which to further diverse political objectives. Starting with the conflicts amid the disintegration of Yugoslavia and continuing through the 2003 invasion of Iraq and the Arab uprisings of the 2010s, the Mediterranean has not remained immune to the exploitation of cultural differences. This tendency has become particularly pronounced, tracking the ascent of Islamic terrorism in the southern Mediterranean and the emergence of far-right political leanings in the northern Mediterranean countries (BBC 2019), ultimately giving rise to the phenomenon of cultural otherness, which now operates as a defining cultural divide among the inhabitants of the Mediterranean region.

3.3. Migration

Migration in the Mediterranean presents itself as a multidimensional challenge, encompassing at least two distinct dimensions. Between 2015 and 2016, the Mediterranean witnessed a staggering influx of people crossing into Europe, with the number reaching 1.4 million (MMRP 2017, 1). During this time, which concomitantly gave rise to a circumstance known as the European migration crisis, the EU undertook proactive measures in response to irregular migration phenomena. Noteworthy among these measures are the Malta Declaration, addressing the Central Mediterranean Route (EC 2017);

the EU Action Plan for the Central Mediterranean Route (EC 2022); the EU-Morocco Partnership and the Valletta Process for the Western Mediterranean Route (EC 2024); and the EU-Turkey Statement (EC 2016), all of which were implemented by the European Union. As noted by Bojinović Fenko (2015, 80), whether through the eastern, western, or central routes, the longstanding migratory movement from south to north remains resistant to comprehensive control. As reported by the International Organization for Migration, the count of arrivals of irregular migrants through the Mediterranean migration routes witnessed a resurgence after a low point in 2020. Notably, the year 2021 saw an influx of nearly 145,000 migrants who undertook voyages across the Mediterranean and arrived in Greece, Italy, and Spain (Buchholz 2023). In 2020, 2021, and 2022, the Mediterranean crossing claimed the lives of 1,881, 3,231, and 3,017 individuals, respectively, as they endeavoured to cross its waters (UNHCR ODP 2024).

According to the latest data from the International Organization for Migration (IOM) and the UN Refugee Agency (UNHCR), an estimated 144,200 attempts are reported to have been made to reach Europe from across the central Mediterranean Sea in 2022 by migrants and refugees making the perilous journey from Tunisia (79,800), Libya (58,900), and Algeria (5,500). This was a 33 percent increase compared to known departures in 2021 and marks the highest number of departures since 2017 (IOM and UNHCR 2023).

As is widely recognized, the primary drivers behind migration in this region encompass economic challenges, instability, and conflicts within the MENA. However, this phenomenon took on new characteristics with the Arab uprisings that swept across the Mediterranean's southern peripheries in the 2010s, along with their widespread impact across nearly all Arab states and the persistent state of instability. The concurrent interplay of economic crisis and escalating instability in the southern reaches of the region (Awad 2013, 13) compelled a considerable number of individuals to seek new prospects and livelihoods in the north. To illustrate, before the uprisings in Libya and the escalating turmoil that followed, the country was a destination for migrants from Africa (MMRP 2017, 3). However, as humanitarian conditions within the country increasingly deteriorated, migrants pressed on to find more secure havens further north (ibid.). While the majority of migrants originating from Syria are indeed themselves Syrian, it is noteworthy that migrants who seek refuge in Syria from other countries, such as Iraq and Palestine, also endeavour to navigate routes to Europe. Consequently, the instability and inadequate security in the region have brought about a situation where the southern Mediterranean states can no longer act as a buffer zone between European Mediterranean states—particularly in the EU—and the MENA region.

Migration flows within the Mediterranean represent a pivotal facet of people-to-people interactions (Helly 2017, 308) among the Mediterranean population. Still, even if migration does in fact contribute to fostering such interaction, it does not appear to be making a positive impact in redefining a collective identity for the Mediterranean. Quite the contrary, migration acts as a notable catalyst for the resurgence of far-right political parties, which draw support from anti-immigration sentiments (Rodriguez-Aguilera 2014, 1) not only in Europe's Mediterranean countries but also across a considerable swath of the EU (Davis and Deole 2017, 15). Consequently, the unmitigated spread of migration within or across the Mediterranean region inadvertently amplifies processes of othering, thereby accentuating distinctions and divisions within the region.

A prominent example showcasing the simultaneous rise of far-right ideology and an anti-immigrant stance is discernible in the 2022 appointment of far-right leader Giorgia Meloni as prime minister of Italy. The electoral campaign prominently featured anti-immigration messaging, with particular emphasis on efforts to curtail irregular migration, as evidenced by her endeavours—and those of her party—to halt the movement of migrant boats (Balmer 2022). In the wake of the 2015 refugee crisis, with migration flowing primarily out of Syria, the Sweden Democrats' far-right anti-immigration party became ascendant, going mainstream with their electoral triumph in 2022, and this too offers a significant example of the intricate interplay between migration dynamics and the emergence of far-right political movements in the European context (Moran 2022). The challenges originating within the Mediterranean region can therefore be said to extend beyond its borders, implying that their repercussions transcend geographical boundaries.

3.4. Resource-distribution Challenges

The allocation of resources stands as a foremost regional concern, bearing significant import both in terms of environmental pressures and entwined geopolitical struggles, often enmeshed with the issue of sovereignty. Climate change exerts a notably amplified impact on the Mediterranean region compared to the global mean. While the global average air temperature has risen by approximately 1.1°C relative to preindustrial eras, the Mediterranean region experiences an even more pronounced increase, exceeding 1.5°C (UNEP/MAP and Plan Bleu 2020, 6). Population densities along coastal areas have persistently surged at rates that defy sustainability norms throughout the preceding decade. Between 1965 and 2015, the encroachments of urbanization intensified across 75 percent of Mediterranean countries, with built-up regions experiencing a twofold or even more substantial expansion (ibid.). This burgeoning trend has inevitably exacted a toll on biodiversity, notably compromising the integrity of coastal ecosystems. The Mediterranean region is particularly affected due to factors like water scarcity, population growth, poor management, and climate change. Many water resources are shared across countries, complicating the issue internationally.

As Ayşegül Kibaroğlu has stated (2017, 276), prominent cross-border river basins within the Mediterranean context, specifically including the Jordan, Nile, and Euphrates-Tigris Rivers, find themselves situated within subregions marked by pronounced geopolitical strains. These complex political dynamics have served to exacerbate historical disagreements over water resources, which conceivably could have found resolution under more propitious political conditions. In essence, conflicts pertaining to water allocation were either compounded, or at the very least impacted, by interstate disputes over matters such as security and territorial boundaries, as well as other multifaceted issues (Kibaroğlu 2017, 276).

Another significant resource-allocation concern is that of the eastern Mediterranean issue, which was precipitated by the discovery of gas reserves in the 2010s and reached an apex in 2020–2021. Although the struggle seems limited to Turkey, Greece, and southern Cyprus, it also involves Egypt, Libya, Israel, France, and the EU, as well as the United States. The driving factors behind the current dispute are rooted in disagreements over territorial waters, exclusive economic zones, and unresolved issues related to Cyprus (Dalay 2021). However, also driving the conflict in key ways are Egypt's discovery of the Zohr gas field and its efforts to become an energy hub, Israel's ambition to export gas via the EastMed pipeline, and Turkey's desire to secure energy independence and regional influence. Presently, a discernible shift is underway in the geopolitical landscape of the eastern Mediterranean, which is transitioning from a state of conflict to one of coexistence. This transformation can largely be attributed to a convergence of factors, including Turkey's economic imperatives, global considerations related to energy and economics, and the dynamic evolution of regional relationships (ibid.). It is noteworthy that, in spite of these favourable trends, the eastern Mediterranean issue retains the capacity to escalate into a far-reaching conflict unless a comprehensive resolution is achieved.

4. Factors Contributing to the Failure of Region-building Processes

Numerous notable endeavours have been undertaken to foster the transformation of the Mediterranean into a more interconnected and interdependent region, a development that undeniably contributes to regional harmony and the cultivation of a shared Mediterranean identity. Within this trajectory, pivotal junctures of the European integration process have exerted a significant influence on the progress of these initiatives, primarily by way of two distinct avenues: (a) the process of enlargement and (b) the nuances of the perceived threat to strategic interests within the European Union. In the period from 1972 to 1974, the then European Economic Community (EEC), propelled by its Global Mediterranean Policy and Euro-Arab Dialogue, embraced a policy that treated the Mediterranean as a cohesive entity, effectively contributing to the conceptual "invention" of the Mediterranean in this sense (Bicci 2007, 63).

It is notable that in the post-imperial era, when the initial strides were being made toward a reimagined Mediterranean, none of the Mediterranean littoral states apart from Italy and France took part in this endeavour. Even so, in the 1980s the landscape underwent a noteworthy evolution that gradually culminated in a new paradigm under which the European Union expanded its membership to encompass not merely two but a total of eight Mediterranean littoral states. In this way, the geographical encirclement of the Mediterranean by the EU facilitated an intertwined trajectory through which the course of European integration became increasingly imbued with a Mediterranean character over the span of subsequent decades.

The transformation of the Mediterranean has been significantly influenced by shifts in the international arena and the evolving threat perceptions within the EU. Marked by the end of the Cold War, the tragic events of 9/11, and the Arab uprisings of the 2010s, these critical junctures presented substantial challenges demanding adequate responses. The EU actively engaged in these processes through mechanisms like the Euro-Mediterranean Partnership (EMP), the European Neighbourhood Policy (ENP), and the Union for the Mediterranean (UfM) (Horst 2013, 79). However, while the non-European parts of the Mediterranean largely embraced these initiatives, they encountered distinct and potentially more formidable obstacles. Despite concerted efforts toward region-building, the outcomes have so far have fallen short of achieving the "objective of turning the Mediterranean basin into an area of dialogue, exchange and cooperation guaranteeing peace, stability and prosperity" (Barcelona Declaration 1995) or realizing the aspiration of forging a harmonized and cohesive Mediterranean.

A pivotal factor significantly responsible for this lack of success can be found in the EU's approach toward the Mediterranean. The EU's stance is notably influenced by its threat perceptions, economic vested interests, and security-oriented perspective—all elements that culminate in a largely instrumental and hegemonic approach to the Mediterranean. In the Cold War era, as is known, western European countries were concerned with the threat posed by the power of their eastern neighbours, but this paradigm has since shifted, with the European countries coming to identify their *southern* counterparts as the perceived source of threat and vulnerability (Jünemann 2004, 5). This perception is notably galvanized by apprehensions surrounding migration, terrorism, Islamic fundamentalism, and the potential spread of weapons of mass destruction (Adler and Crawford 2006, 20). Collectively, these issues are viewed as challenges that need to be overcome with a view to protecting European interests (Horst 2013, 83).

The Mediterranean has been subjected by the EU to a process of othering that extends to its Mediterranean member states as well (Pace 2005, 101–3). This is borne out by the discourse analysis conducted by Michelle Pace, who reveals how the Mediterranean is set in striking contrast to Europe, the former referred to as "uncivilized" as opposed to "civilized" Europe, with parallel oppositions between "undeveloped" versus "developed," "dependent" versus "independent," "colonized" versus "colonizer," "periphery" versus "centre," and "unstable" versus "stable" (ibid., 103). This othering is defined by Annette Jünemann (2004, 8) as the construction of an alien or divergent "other," and if we consider the practice as a fundamental facet of identity formation, it follows that the EU's othering of the Mediterranean constitutes a noteworthy component of the EU's own identity construction, thereby fostering cohesion among the union's members (ibid.), while concurrently "othering" the non-European Mediterranean.

In a parallel vein, the EU's economic stance toward the region serves as another illustration of how its policies fall short of furnishing enduring resolutions to the region's predicaments. A case in point lies within the context of the Euro-Arab dialogue, where European partners offered counsel to their Arab counterparts, advocating a shift toward labour-intensive industries as opposed to capital-intensive ventures (ibid., 3). This advice, while reflecting European apprehensions regarding potential economic rivalry with their Arab counterparts (ibid.), sought at the same time to further entrench the peripheral economic standing of the southern Mediterranean countries.

In the subsequent years, along with the implementation of structural adjustment programmes advocated by the International Monetary Fund and the World Bank, the EU extended economic assistance to the southern Mediterranean states through a multitude of economic initiatives (Corm 2011, 128). Nevertheless, it becomes evident that the endeavours of international financial institutions and the EU were primarily focused on ensuring free trade and fostering free-market policies, rather than on addressing the substantive economic challenges faced by these peripheral states (ibid., 129). The European economic stance when it comes to the economic disparity between the northern and southern regions of the Mediterranean therefore failed to establish a framework based on mutual interests: the interests that did find support were instead, for the most part, the economic ones of the northern countries.

A second prominent factor that holds back the process of region-building lies in the prevailing political turmoil and economic woes affecting the Mediterranean region. An illustrative case in point is the stalling of the Middle East peace process, since this resulted in effectively inhibiting the political component of the Euro-Mediterranean Partnership (EMP), designed to foster a regional framework of political and security cooperation (Gillespie 2004, 21; Horst 2013, 83). Likewise, the protracted Israeli-Palestinian conflict presented a significant barrier to the functioning of the Union for the Mediterranean (UfM) (Seeberg 2013, 63). However, it is noteworthy that the adverse conditions and unfavourable climate within the region are owed in part not only to the challenges originating from the southern Mediterranean but also to the political and economic disruptions experienced in the northern Mediterranean. The EU, as a potent proponent of soft-power initiatives in the region, has encountered setbacks due to these internal instabilities, encompassing events such as the global economic crisis, the Ukrainian crisis, and Brexit (Chivvis and Fishman 2017, 11–12). This volatility has effectively eroded the appeal and capability of the EU (ibid., 12) as an actor dedicated to region-building efforts.

Despite the aspirations, the Arab uprisings of the 2010s had to establish democratic governance in the southern Mediterranean, and despite the optimism it initially kindled for an enhanced regionalization process, the movement failed to yield a pathway to more seamless cooperation and regional community building (Youngs 2015). Instead, it engendered persistent geopolitical complexities among several Mediterranean states, both European and non-European in composition. Standing out as particularly dramatic in this context is the Libyan case. NATO's Operation Unified Protector, orchestrated by France and involving Mediterranean countries such as Turkey and Italy, resulted in the overthrow of the Qaddafi regime. However, this action also precipitated enduring instability within Libya (Eljarh 2020, 78). Likewise, the interactions among certain Mediterranean countries during and after the Arab uprisings of the 2010s gave rise to novel predicaments within the region. For instance, relations between Egypt and Turkey deteriorated, leading to a suspension of diplomatic ties (Al Arabiya 2013). Moreover, Turkey's approach to the Libyan situation came into contradiction with the policies pursued by France, Italy, Egypt, and Israel, further exemplifying the intricate entanglements that emerged in the Mediterranean geopolitical landscape.

In this context, it is rather paradoxical that, instead of contributing to regional cohesion, the Arab uprisings of the 2010s and their aftermath have led to a distinct and divisive impact within the region. Particularly when viewed in conjunction with the eastern Mediterranean issue, the Mediterranean region has encountered noteworthy destabilization subsequent to Turkey's establishment of maritime boundaries through an agreement with Libya's Government of National Accord. This development has catalysed antagonistic competition and assertions of influence among other countries, including Egypt, France, and the United Arab Emirates (Dalay 2021). These power configurations, instead of facilitating regional integration, have obviously introduced novel layers of complexity to the pre-existing geopolitical disputes.

Another disruptive force lies in the rise and radicalization of Islamism, which has exacerbated the pre-existing security challenges within the region, consequently undermining the region-building endeavour. The ascendancy of Islamic fundamentalism has undeniably engendered destabilization across the southern and eastern Mediterranean. Neither is this impact confined to those areas: the growing influence of Islamic fundamentalism has also intermittently unsettled the northern Mediterranean, with crises precipitated by acts of terrorism. Illustrative of this phenomenon are events such as the Charlie Hebdo attack in 2015 and the series of terrorist assaults in Spain in 2017, which vividly underscore the complexities inherent in the region-building process within the

Mediterranean. As is known, some perpetrators of the Charlie Hebdo attack trace their lineage to Algeria (CNN 2018), while a similar linkage exists for eleven of the individuals involved in the terrorist incidents in Spain, a common factor among these perpetrators being their Moroccan descent (Peregil 2017). As much as these tragic events may underscore the imperative of political collaboration among Mediterranean states, they also serve as poignant illustrations of the formidable challenges confronting political cooperation initiatives, particularly at a societal level.

Still another pivotal factor that stands out in explaining region-building shortcomings is the lack of constructive people-to-people interaction. As is known, one of the tripartite components of the Euro-Mediterranean Partnership (EMP) was directed toward cultural and human affairs, aspiring to forge a cultural alliance within the region. However, this facet of the EMP was inherently driven by the European Union's apprehensions about the phenomenon of unwanted immigration (Gillespie 2004, 21–22). Consequently, the EU harnessed the notion of a cultural partnership to address security concerns. Subsequently, the Union for the Mediterranean (UfM), under the Joint Declaration of the Paris Summit for the Mediterranean (CE 2008, 17), recognized the imperative of initiatives anchored in civil society and consequently revised its vision, placing an enhanced emphasis on the civil-society stratum. Regrettably, however, despite these endeavours, a decade has elapsed without yielding a notable reversal in this trajectory.

In this context, the surge of the Arab uprisings of the 2010s ushered forth two distinct yet connected possibilities: (a) an opportunity to mitigate the securitization of predominantly Muslim-populated countries—an opportunity facilitated by the emergence of a novel image capturing the aspirations for freedom among Arab people—and (b) the potential to reinforce the adverse image of violence that some Europeans associate with this geographical expanse (Horst et al. 2013, 3). However, given that the Arab uprisings have precipitated a surge in undesirable migration and engendered region-wide instability and violent conflicts, notably exemplified by the scenarios in Libya and Syria, it becomes increasingly difficult to contend that the former scenario holds greater likelihood.

Consequently, there is among northern Mediterranean inhabitants the prevailing perception that they appear as colonizers, invaders, and infidels in the eyes of their extremist southern counterparts. Conversely, the latter group predominantly regards southern Mediterranean inhabitants as migrants, cheap laborers, and potential terrorists. This unfavourable perception permeates other areas of conflict and contention within the region as well: consider the Israelis and Palestinians, northern and southern Cypriots, and Greeks and Turks. The cumulative effect is that none of the implemented initiatives or unfolding events have engendered a shared "Mediterranean cultural region" or cultivated widespread, mutually experienced people-to-people interactions across the region (Helly 2017, 307–8).

5. Closing Remarks: What Path Forward?

As has been pointed out in recent studies (see, e.g., O'Neil 2022, 3), in recent years the world has been regionalizing in a process where countries that actively fostered engagement with their neighbouring counterparts have gained a distinct competitive advantage. This regionalization paradigm at the same time offers countries a viable way to enhance the economic prosperity of their citizens and local communities. It is evident that neither isolationist economic policies predicated on self-sufficiency nor unchecked global integration is the best or most effective way to pursue economic growth. The prudent approach consists in cultivating and reinforcing interregional connections, in such a way as to equip countries with the means by which to excel within an interconnected and fiercely competitive global arena.

In this study we have shed light on the multifaceted complexities inherent in the Mediterranean region, showing how this necessitates a nuanced understanding in shaping a redefined *mare nostrum*. As we have illustrated, the multiplex challenges confronting the region are intricate and intertwined, calling for a comprehensive and integrated approach. It is inescapably apparent that if the effort to transform the Mediterranean into a shared *mare nostrum* is to succeed, it needs resolute political support and robust policy-making.

And equally apparent, as key to this political will, is the need to rectify the economic disparities among the Mediterranean littoral countries. With apt strategies, the objective remains a plausible one, even if this means taking the long view, enacting a paradigm shift under which the peripheral economies of the underdeveloped littoral countries move away from the rentier model and pivot toward a model based on high-value-added production. This in turn requires a context of stability not only economic but also political. Which brings us to the next point, about political stability.

It seems incontestable that no region-building can succeed in the Mediterranean absent a background of political stability, an essential bedrock on which rests the prospect not only for economic growth but also for political integration or, at the very least, for peace. Indeed, without political stability there can be no basis on which to build the consensus needed to solve regional and bilateral impasses. It warrants emphasis, however, that political stability cannot come at the cost of democratic backsliding and must therefore rein in any attendant hegemonic proclivities. If political stability is to be achieved, in other words, it is necessary to promote democratic and secular ideals within the region, while at the same time holding in check the tendencies of the more developed Mediterranean entities to exert a dominant influence in the region. This means that the European Union, in embracing regional transformation, needs to be able to stand back and give way to initiatives championed by the Mediterranean countries themselves, in such a way that the whole of the Mediterranean can harmoniously coalesce around these initiatives. But what this also means is that democratic ideals need to be nurtured from the grassroots, in an organic, bottom-up approach that, while potentially gradual, is inherently enduring.

This brings us to the last point, which is that no less essential to this transformative roadmap is the integral role of interpersonal exchange. If we recognize the fluid nature of cultural and political identities and of the interactions through which they are forged, we will be in a better position to forestall the "othering" dichotomy these identities can trigger, which in turn underscores the significance of person-to-person engagement. It is by working at this ground level of personal engagement that we can dismantle preconceptions and prejudices and turn negative perceptions into positive ones. In this way we can nurture the collective spirit of the Mediterranean and its people, and if we can translate that spirit into collective agency, we will have moved closer to realizing the aspiration of a Mediterranean *mare nostrum* embodying that spirit.

In conclusion, the strategic trajectory toward a redefined Mediterranean *mare nostrum* is resolute in its call for political resolve, economic equilibrium, political stability, and person-to-person interactions. It is within the crucible of these endeavours that the Mediterranean mosaic, reflective of shared values and aspirations, stands poised for reconstitution through the concerted efforts of its constituents.

Works Cited

Abulafia, David. 2005. "Akdeniz Nedir?" In *Tarih Boyunca Akdeniz Uygarlıkları*, edited by David Abulafia and translated by Nurettin Elhüseyni, 51–69. İstanbul: Oğlak.

Adler, Emanuel, and Beverly Crawford. 2006. "Normative Power: The European Practice of Region-Building and the Case of the Euro-Mediterranean Partnership." In *The Convergence of Civilizations? Constructing a Mediterranean Region*, edited by Emanuel Adler, Federica Bicchi, Beverly Crawford, and Raffaella A. Del Sarto, 3–47. Toronto: University of Toronto Press.

Al Arabiya News (staff writer). 2013. "Egypt, Turkey Downgrade Mutual Ties: Turkey Continues to Support the Muslim Brotherhood and Has Refused to Recognize Egypt's New Rulers as Legitimate." Published November 23, 2013, updated May 20, 2020. https://english.alarabiya.net/News/middle-east/2013/11/23/Egypt-downgrades-relations-with-Turkey-.

Aliboni, Roberto. 2001. *The Role of International Organizations in the Mediterranean*. Institutions & Policies Working Papers. Hellenic Foundation for European & Foreign Policy.

Amendola, Adalgiso, and Roberto Dell'Anno. 2014. "Income Inequality and Economic Growth: An Empirical Investigation in Mediterranean Countries." *Rivista Italiana di Economia Demografia e Statistica* 68 (2): 35–58. https://econpapers.repec.org/article/iteiteeco/140203.htm.

Awad, Ibrahim. 2013. "The Arab Spring and Population Movements in the Mediterranean Region." In *Regional Dynamics in the Mediterranean and Prospects for Transatlantic Cooperation*, 13–24. Mediterranean Paper Series 2013. Washington, DC: The German Marshall Fund of the United States (GMF).

Balmer, Chrispian. 2022. "Migrants Face Tougher Times in Meloni's Italy." *Reuters*, August 29, 2023. www.reuters.com/world/europe/migrants-face-tougher-times-melonis-italy-2022-10-07/.

Barcelona Declaration. 1995. "Barcelona Euro-Mediterranean Conference (November 27–28, 1995): Declaration and Work Programme." European Commission. DOC/95/7. https://ec.europa.eu/commission/presscorner/detail/en/DOC_95_7.

BBC. 2019. "Europe and Nationalism: A Country-by-Country Guide." *BBC News*, November 13, 2019. www.bbc.com/news/world-europe-36130006.

Bicci, Federica. 2007. *European Foreign Policy Making Toward the Mediterranean*. New York: Palgrave Macmillan.

Bojinović Fenko, Ana. 2015. "The Mediterranean Region as a Phenomenon and an Object of Analysis in the Field of International Relations." *International Journal of Euro-Mediterranean Studies (IJEMS)* 8 (2): 75–90. https://emuni.si/wp-content/uploads/2019/11/2015-8-2_75%E2%80%9390.pdf.

Braudel, Fernand. 1972. *The Mediterranean and the Mediterranean World in the Age of Philip II*. Vol. 1, preface to the 1st ed., 17–22 (May 1946). Translated by Siân Reynolds. New York: Harper & Row. Orig. pub. as *La Méditerranée et le Monde Méditerranéen à l'Époque de Philippe II* (Paris: Armand Colin, 1949).

Bromberger, Christian. 2006. "Towards an Anthropology of the Mediterranean." *History and Anthropology* 17 (2): 91–107. https://doi.org/10.1080/02757200600624339.

Buchholz, Katharina. 2023. "Number of Migrants Crossing the Mediterranean Picks Up." *Statista*, April 14, 2023. www.statista.com/chart/18753/migrants-arriving-across-the-mediterranean-in-europe/.

Cantori, Louis J., and Steven L. Spiegel. 1969. "International Regions: A Comparative Approach to Five Subordinate Systems." *International Studies Quarterly* 13 (4) (special issue on international subsystems): 361–80. https://doi.org/10.2307/3013600.

CE (Council of the European Union). 2008. "Joint Declaration of the Paris Summit for the Mediterranean" (Paris, 13 July 2008). Brussels, July 15, 2008, 11887/08 (Presse 213). www.consilium.europa.eu/uedocs/cms_data/docs/pressdata/en/er/101847.pdf.

Chivvis, Christopher S., and Benjamin Fishman. 2017. *Regional Foreign Policy Dynamics and Their Implications for the Mediterranean Region*. Santa Monica, CA: RAND Corporation. www.rand.org/pubs/perspectives/PE223.html.

CNN (Editorial Research). 2018. "2015 Charlie Hebdo Attacks Fast Facts." December 25, 2023. https://edition.cnn.com/2015/01/21/europe/2015-paris-terror-attacks-fast-facts/index.html.

Corm, Georges. 2011. "Economic Evolution in the Mediterranean Countries in a Changing World." *IEMed Mediterranean Yearbook 2011*. www.iemed.org/publication/economic-evolution-in-the-mediterranean-countries-in-a-changing-world/.

Dalay, Galip. 2021. "Turkey, Europe, and the Eastern Mediterranean: Charting a Way Out of the Current Deadlock." Policy briefing, January 2021. Brookings Doha Center. www.brookings.edu/articles/turkey-europe-and-the-eastern-mediterranean-charting-a-way-out-of-the-current-deadlock/.

Daniele, Vittorio, and Paolo Malanima. 2016. "Trends in Mediterranean Inequalities 1950–2015." Munich Personal RePEc Archive. MPRA Paper No. 78324. https://mpra.ub.uni-muenchen.de/78324/.

Davis, Lewis, and Sumit S. Deole. 2017. "Immigration and the Rise of Far-Right Parties in Europe." *IFO DICE Report* 15, no. 4 (December): 11–15. IFO Institute for Economic Research. www.ifo.de/DocDL/dice-report-2017-4-davis-deole-december.pdf.

EC (European Council). 2016. "EU-Turkey Statement." Press release, March 18, 2016. www.consilium.europa.eu/en/press/press-releases/2016/03/18/eu-turkey-statement/.

EC (European Council). 2017. "Malta Declaration by the Members of the European Council on the External Aspects of Migration: Addressing the Central Mediterranean Route." Press release, February 3, 2017. www.consilium.europa.eu/en/press/press-releases/2017/02/03/malta-declaration/.

EC (European Council). 2022. "EU Action Plan for the Central Mediterranean Route." https://home-affairs.ec.europa.eu/eu-action-plan-central-mediterranean_en.

EC (European Council). 2024. "Migration Flows on the Western Routes." Last reviewed January 11, 2024. www.consilium.europa.eu/en/policies/eu-migration-policy/western-routes/#transit.

Eljarh, Mohamed. 2020. "Is Europe Exporting Instability to the Southern Mediterranean? Libya as a Case Study." *09 EUROMED Survey: Changing Euro-Mediterranean Lenses* (December): 78–82. www.iemed.org/?p=6813.

Gillespie, Richard. 2004. "Reshaping the Agenda? The Internal Politics of the Barcelona Process in the Aftermath of September 11." Chap. 2 in *Euro-Mediterranean Relations After September 11: International, Regional and Domestic Dynamics*, edited by Annette Jünemann, 20–35. London and Portland, OR: Frank Cass.

Halliday, Fred. 2008. "The Mediterranean in an Age of Globalisation." IBEI Working Paper 2008/17. Institut Barcelona d'Estudis Internacionals. www.jstor.org/stable/resrep14181.

Helly, Damien. 2017. "Cultural Diplomacy and Cooperation in the Mediterranean: A Constant Investment." *IEMed Mediterranean Yearbook 2017*. www.iemed.org/publication/cultural-diplomacy-and-cooperation-in-the-mediterranean-a-constant-investment/.

Horden, Peregrine, and Nicholas Purcell. 2000. *The Corrupting Sea: A Study of Mediterranean History*. Oxford: Blackwell Publishers.

Horst, Jakob. 2013. "Free Trade, Development and Authoritarianism in a Rentier Economy: Intentions and Reality of the EU's Logic of Action in Algeria." Chap. 5 in *Euro-Mediterranean Relations After the Arab Spring: Persistence in Times of Change*, edited by Jakob Horst, Annette Jünemann, and Delf Rothe. Surrey: Ashgate.

Horst, Jakob, Annette Jünemann, Florian Kühn, Elena M. Maggi, and Delf Rothe. 2013. "Logics of Action in the Euro-Mediterranean Political Space: An Introduction to the Analytical Framework." Chap. 1 in *Euro-Mediterranean Relations After the Arab Spring: Persistence in Times of Change*, edited by Jakob Horst, Annette Jünemann, and Delf Rothe. Surrey: Ashgate.

IOM and UNHCR (International Organization for Migration and Office of the United Nations High Commissioner for Refugees). 2023. *DTM (Displacement Tracking Matrix) Migrant and Refugee Movements Through the Central Mediterranean Sea: Joint Annual Overview for 2022*. Geneva: IOM Europe, November 28, 2023. https://dtm.iom.int/reports/migrant-and-refugee-movements-through-central-mediterranean-sea-joint-annual-overview-2022.

Jünemann, Annette. 2004. "Security Building in the Mediterranean After September 11." Chap. 1 in *Euro-Mediterranean Relations After September 11: International, Regional and Domestic Dynamics*, edited by Annette Jünemann, 1–19. London and Portland, OR: Frank Cass.

Katzenstein, Peter J. 2003. "Japan, Technology and Asian Regionalism in Comparative Perspective." Chap. 6 in *The Resurgence of East Asia: 500, 150 and 50 Year Perspectives*, edited by Giovanni Arrighi, Takeshi Hamashita, and Mark Selden, 214–58. London and New York: Routledge Curzon.

Kibaroğlu, Ayşegül. 2017. "Water Challenges in the Mediterranean." *IEMed Mediterranean Yearbook 2017*. www.iemed.org/publication/water-challenges-in-the-mediterranean/.

MMRP. 2017. "Dynamics of Migration across the Mediterranean." Mediterranean Migration Research Programme (MMRP), Policy briefing, July. Funded by the Economic and Social Research Council (ESRC). https://evimedresearch.wordpress.com/wp-content/uploads/2017/07/mmrp-dynamics-of-migration-july-2017.pdf.

Moran, Jake. 2022. "Climate, Conflict, and Migration: Europe's Next Frontier of Populism." *European Center for Populism Studies (ECPS)*, December 7, 2022. www.populism-studies.org/climate-conflict-and-migration-europes-next-frontier-of-populism/.

Nye, Joseph. 1968. *International Regionalism*. Boston: Little, Brown and Company.

OECD. 2021. *Regional Integration in the Union for the Mediterranean: Progress Report.* Paris: OECD Publishing. https://doi.org/10.1787/325884b3-en.

Öktem, Kerem. 2010. "The Ambivalent Sea: Regionalizing the Mediterranean Differently." Chap. 1 in *Mediterranean Frontiers: Borders, Conflict and Memory in a Transnational World*, edited by Dimitar Bechev and Kalypso Nicolaidis, 13–34. London and New York: Tauris Academic Studies.

O'Neil, Shannon K. 2022. *The Globalization Myth: Why Regions Matter.* New Haven, CT: Yale University Press.

Pace, Michelle. 2005. *The Politics of Regional Identity: Meddling with the Mediterranean.* London and New York: Routledge.

Peregil, Francisco. 2017. "Terror Attacks in Barcelona Put Spotlight on Morocco." *El País*, US edition, August 23, 2017. https://elpais.com/elpais/2017/08/23/inenglish/1503477891_212505.html.

Rodriguez-Aguilera, Cesáreo. 2014. "The Rise of the Far Right in Europe." *IEMed Mediterranean Yearbook 2014.* www.iemed.org/publication/the-rise-of-the-far-right-in-europe/.

Russett, Bruce M. 1967. *International Regions and the International System: A Study in Political Ecology.* Chicago, IL: Rand McNally.

Seeberg, Peter. 2013. "Learning to Cope: The Development of European Immigration Policies Concerning the Mediterranean Caught between National and Supra-national Narratives." Chap. 4 in *Euro-Mediterranean Relations after the Arab Spring: Persistence in Times of Change*, edited by Jakob Horst, Annette Jünemann, and Delf Rothe. Surrey: Ashgate.

UfM (Union for the Mediterranean). 2021. "The UfM Presents Its 1st Report on Euro-Mediterranean Regional Integration." https://ufmsecretariat.org/news-report-regional-integration/.

UNEP/MAP and Plan Bleu (United Nations Environment Programme / Mediterranean Action Plan and Plan Bleu). 2020. *State of the Environment and Development in the Mediterranean: Full Report.* Edited by Elen Lemaitre-Curri and Lina Tode. https://planbleu.org/en/soed-2020-state-of-environment-and-development-in-mediterranean/.

UNHCR ODP (Operational Data Portal of the Office of the United Nations High Commissioner for Refugees). 2024. "Europe Sea Arrivals." https://data.unhcr.org/en/situations/europe-sea-arrivals?id=105.

Wallerstein, Immanuel. 2004. *World-Systems Analysis: An Introduction.* London: Duke University Press.

World Bank. 2017. "GDP Per Capita, PPP (Constant 2017 International $)." World Bank Metadata Glossary. https://databank.worldbank.org/metadataglossary/world-development-indicators/series/NY.GDP.PCAP.PP.KD.

World Bank. 2024. "GDP Per Capita, PPP (Current International $), 1990–2022." International Comparison Program (World Bank), World Development Indicators Database (World Bank), Eurostat-OECD PPP Programme. https://data.worldbank.org/indicator/NY.GDP.PCAP.PP.CD.

Xenakis, Dimitris K. 1999. "Euro-Mediterranean Formations and the Emerging European System: The Case of Cyprus." *The Cyprus Review* 11 (1): 59–82. https://cyprusreview.org/index.php/cr/article/view/461.

Youngs, Richard. 2015. "20 Years of Euro-Mediterranean Partnership." Carnegie Europe, Brussels, Belgium, May 18, 2015. https://carnegieeurope.eu/2015/05/18/20-years-of-euro-mediterranean-partnership-pub-60337.

8 Islamic Economics Versus Euro-Mediterranean Partnership Policies

On Economic Upgrading in the Mediterranean Space

Alessandro Romagnoli

1. Introduction

The Mediterranean is a sea wedged among three continents, its contours outlined by three adjoining shores: those of southern Europe, western Asia, and North Africa. These geographical features have made the Mediterranean a space of inevitable contact for the people living on its shores, where they have accordingly been driven to interact socially, politically, and economically since antiquity. But interaction doesn't necessarily mean cohesion: the historical paths followed by the societies of the three Mediterranean shores are ones that over the course of time have resulted in convergence and division, encounter and collision. The success of capitalism in Europe brought about a deep divide between the northern and the southeastern Mediterranean shores, sowing rifts at once political and social. In particular, capitalism tilted the balance between the two areas in favour of the north, paving the way for colonialism in the 18th century and for mandates and protectorates in the first half of the 19th century. A few decades after the Middle Eastern and North African countries gained their independence, and hence political and economic autonomy, the Muslim states found themselves facing a new form of ideological subordination that intensified to the point of questioning the ability of southeastern Mediterranean societies to rise up to the challenge of the social and economic upgrading connected to the introduction of capitalism. For Muslim societies—which for fourteen centuries had been following a line of development guided by socioeconomic principles based on the Qur'an—that kind of questioning and criticism was received as a downgrading of their identity and character in a way they had already experienced under colonialism, all the more so since their economies were just then experiencing high rates of growth.

This ideological divide came to a head in the 1980s, when the "market fundamentalist" approach was pitted against the "social contract" approach (Romagnoli 2022): the contention was that the economic policies implemented in Muslim countries amounted to a set of measures rooted in a religious and political ideology having nothing to do with economic theory and that this ideology was responsible for the "failed development" of Muslim

DOI: 10.4324/9781003431206-13

economies. From the 2000s on, the ideological conflict over economic policy came to be defined by the "neoliberal agenda"—the basis on which the European Union's Euro-Mediterranean policies have been built—which was set in opposition to the "Islamic economics" to which the Muslim countries were committed. This opposition resulted in a dynamic of mutual recrimination, with the northern countries being accused of pushing neoliberal economics as a way to unilaterally impose their own hegemonistic interests, and the southeastern countries being accused of taking an opportunistically defensive stance. Meanwhile, the increasing economic interdependence brought about by globalization, coupled with the structurally critical conditions of both developed and developing Mediterranean economies, required both groups of countries to find common aims and tools by which to manage the economic conjuncture (Romagnoli 2019): they had to address not only the problems they had in common (such as energy and migration) but also the problems of growth and development distinctive to each country. But this need for a shared perspective meant that policy-makers on both sides had to agree on an analysis of economic problems in the Mediterranean and converge on a common set of economic policies, even if these conditions could not be attained in the context just described.

In the four decades during which this ideological conflict over economic policy grew stronger and stronger, the Mediterranean has seen a series of destabilizing developments brought about by institutional changes in international relations, war, political unrest, and even religious boycotting: witness the accession of some Mediterranean states to the European Union, the wars that broke out in the former Yugoslavia and the Middle East, the protest movements that swept across the Mediterranean Arab countries, the suspicion of the Muslim religion elicited by the emergence of Sunni jihadist groups, and the war against the Islamic State, as well as the intense migratory and refugee flows. These events have involved one or more Mediterranean countries and have spread as circles in the water from one shore to the others, giving rise to further intertwining divides. The economic disparity among people living in these neighbouring countries—a disparity ascribable to the international economic relations between developed and developing countries—is probably the divide to which all the other divides can be traced back. At the centre of this framework is the ideological debate between Islamic economics and Euro-Mediterranean Partnership policies.

If we are to understand the challenge that so-called Islamic economics poses when it comes to managing Mediterranean economic relations, it is essential that we analyse that economic model itself by looking at the environmental conditions under which the debate on that model emerged. It is therefore essential to analyse the social principles at the basis of economic development in Islam and the path that modern Muslim economies have followed in shifting from Islamic principles to an implementation of the social contract, mainly because this analysis will also explain why the social contract can be an effective development model. The next step in this analysis will consist of presenting the structural economic conditions in the Mediterranean space, highlighting the economic needs of developed and developing countries and their possible interconnections. The final step will consist of presenting the overall framework of the EU policies crafted under the Euro-Mediterranean Partnership: this will make it possible to understand both the differences between the Islamic economic policies and the Euro-Med policies aimed at developing the southeastern Mediterranean and the powerlessness of Euro-Med policies to solve either that problem or the common economic problems of the Mediterranean area.

2. What Is "Islamic Economics"

Islamic economics is a way of thinking about economic behaviour and activities, and it is not a well-known discipline except among scholars of Islamic studies who investigate and debate it. Outside this intellectual environment, it does not enjoy much currency, because the prevailing idea about this kind of economic thought is still the one that Timur Kuran outlined in the 1980s, commenting that this

> literature, whose exponents call themselves "Islamic economists," purports to provide the blueprint of an economic system consonant with the original sources of Islam. The central feature of the proposed system is that individuals are guided in their economic decisions by a set of behavior norms, ostensibly derived from the Qur'an and the Sunna. Two other features stand out: *zakāt*, a tax considered the basis of Islamic fiscal policy, and the prohibition of interest, viewed as the centerpiece of Islamic monetary policy.
>
> (Kuran 1986, 135)

In fact, since the birth of the movement in the 1940s, specialists in the subject have mainly debated the epistemology of Islamic economics, that is, the theory, source, and application of the knowledge connected to its vision of economic activity and behaviour (Suar, Meirison, and Nazar 2020). Accordingly, the definition of Islamic economics itself shifts between "a social science that studies society's economic problems inspired by Islamic values" (ibid., 8) and "an effort/struggle to carry out the orders of Allah SWT related to economic affairs in our personal lives (Micro), in our community (Meso), and at the Level of People (Macro)" (ibid., 17). In both definitions, Islamic economics lays out a way of thinking about the courses of action for Muslim people engaged in economic activities and in crafting policies for managing these activities. Economics so characterized is at root religious in nature, being based on the economic prescriptions contained in some surahs in the Qur'an that set forth social and individual behavioural principles to be followed in leading one's life and in building economic institutions (see El-Ashker and Wilson 2006).

It is probably due to this characterization that Islamic economics has by and large been straitjacketed into a discipline essentially concerned with explaining the nexus between religion and capitalism or the role that religious principles played when capitalism took hold,[1] especially when the triggers of capitalist development have been put on trial (Kuran 1997, 2004). The study of this problem can be said to have had its start with Max Weber ([1904/05] 1992), who hypothesized a positive connection between Protestant ethics and the economic success of Protestants in certain contexts, and Werner Sombart ([1911] 2017), who identified a certain "aptitude" for this role in the Jews; unlike the other monotheistic religions, Islam was regarded as a barrier to the introduction of capitalism just when the Muslim countries were emerging as successful economies. The matter was put on the right track by a thriving literature starting from Maxime Rodinson's seminal book on Islam and capitalism, in which it was argued, as to Muslims, that "nothing in their religious tradition was opposed to the adoption of modern and progressive economic methods, or else . . . that tradition tended to favour economic and social justice" (Rodinson 1966, 2). Interest in such a specific relation resurfaced in the mid-1980s (Kuran 1986), stirring up among scholars a debate mainly focused on specific aspects of the topic:

> The first subliterature consists of studies that explore whether Islam affects economic development rates and patterns in the present. . . . The second subliterature is composed of historical investigations on whether Islam affected the economic trajectories of predominantly Muslim societies. . . . The third subliterature focuses on Islam's contemporary political effects, with attention to the economic sources of political patterns. . . . The final subliterature studies the historical sources of authoritarian governance. . . . Two other strands concern attempts to restructure entire economies according to Islamic teachings and Islamic networks.
>
> (Kuran 2018, 1295–6)

These contributions, mainly focused on the development process that unfolded over the last three decades, all investigate the effects on economic

1 As Rodney Wilson (2015, 51) explains, "there are three major lines of inquiry regarding the relationship of economics to religion. The first interprets religious behaviour from an economic perspective, focusing on both individual and group behaviour by, for example, investigating the utility or satisfaction that individuals or households gain from the time they spend on religious pursuits and devotion, as well as the positive externalities that believers can derive from being part of a group of worshipers or members of sects. The second is concerned with the economic consequences of religion, which is not only whether religious beliefs can result in greater economic justice, but whether it can actually contribute to economic efficiency; the hypothesis being that believers are more motivated than nonbelievers. The third approach . . . is concerned with the implications of religious belief for economic policy-making and whether the choices are governed by the moral values of faithful."

performance attributable to religious variables, traditional Islamic institutions (charity and finance), and economic attitudes passed down by Islamic culture (traditions, education). Apart from the works whose aim is to restructure a Muslim economy according to Islamic principles and those concerned with inspecting the relation between Islamic principles and political forms of government in Muslim societies, the studies take place outside the religious field, being developed within economics. Despite that, even if they use some instruments of modern economics (such as cross-country analysis), their perspective is still based on a supposed exclusive causal relation between religious principles and economic performance, since they ascribe that performance in Muslim economies to their adoption of Islamic principles and institutions. In addition, the period considered for analysis presents some self-defeating elements, for the development model that Muslim countries have implemented over the last three decades isn't exclusively based on Islamic principles: the policies adopted by the Muslim countries were the ones that had been pushed onto them by international economic organizations (the International Monetary Fund and the World Bank), and these policies were strongly affected by the political, economic, and cultural developments of the 1970s and 1980s.

This was a time marked by increasing inflation, stagnation, and sovereign debt occasioned by the oil shocks of the period and the crisis of the Fordist manufacturing model. All the while, Keynesian economic theory and policy was being abandoned, and domestic and foreign policy shifts enacted by major economic powers like the United States and the United Kingdom resulted in a climate of international political instability (Romagnoli 2022, 713–19). These developments all conspired to favour the introduction of a new paradigm in economic theory and policy that wiped out any alternative models for interpreting economic facts and managing the economy (Laybourn-Langton and Jacobs 2018). The explanation for the development process and the policies by which to drive that process completely changed: in fact, in the economic analysis, the development process vanished, having been effectively reduced to economic growth. Up to that point the Middle Eastern and North African countries had been implementing policies in some way inspired by Muslim principles and were among the best-performing developing economies (Romagnoli and Mengoni 2014, 97–121), but with these policy changes came a heavy setback: the economic results obtained were disclaimed by the international economic organizations that stood over their "sovereign debt" (Romagnoli 2022) and, under the Washington Consensus, the economic development model adopted after independence was discarded to introduce the new model sponsored by the international economic organizations. For that matter, the new economic paradigm the World Bank and the International Monetary Fund imposed on the MENA countries in order to deal with the crisis did not outperform these countries' traditional development model.

Apart from the literature considered by Kuran, there is another branch of economic studies that has investigated three questions as follows:

(1) The compatibility of Islamic principles with capitalist foundations (Rice 1999) and the ability of Muslim societies to sustain capitalism while adhering to Islamic principles (Tripp 2006).
(2) The implications that religious beliefs carry for economic policy-making (Wilson 2015).
(3) The differences between the principles of Islamic economics and mainstream economics (Askari, Iqbal, and Mirakhor 2015).

The aforementioned disparagement of the Muslim cultural approach to economic problems has prompted a new economic analysis of institutions (principles, habits, traditions, technical methods, economic policies, and laws) on the part of North (1990) and especially Aoki (2007), as well as other scholars (Askari, Iqbal, and Mirakhor 2015; Mirakhor and Askari 2010; Wilson 2015). And, thanks to this work, Islamic economics can now be decoupled from religious doctrine and deservedly be considered in its own right as a set of assumptions underpinning the models of economic development that Middle Eastern and North African countries and other developing economies successfully adopted in their golden age.

Some scholars have examined the Islamic perspective on business ethics, comparing it with the features of capitalism, and they have observed a basic compatibility between them, even if there are differences (Rice 1999). According to Mohammad Taheri (2003), the basic principles structuring the economic activities in capitalism (individual economic freedom, free disposal, and protection of property) in the Qur'an are expressed as follows:

(1) The right of property is conceded in a multifaceted form of ownership: private, public, and state ownership.
(2) Economic freedom is supported by encouraging investment in business enterprises and spending on final goods.
(3) It is acceptable to distinguish between management and workers but not to engage in discriminatory workplace practices, which are not tolerated.
(4) Income inequality is permitted if it is deserved, that is, if it reflects the individual's effort and diligence; as a consequence, this behaviour is considered to be socially appropriate.

All these rights and characteristics of the economic actor need to be compliant with social justice, that is, subordinated to the obligations that the membership of a community requires. Social justice rests on two basic principles: mutual responsibility and social balance. Mutual responsibility calls on all members of society to satisfy the general needs of the community; social balance, for its part, is a principle of economic equality implemented individually through mandatory charitable giving (the *zakāt*) and through the state's responsibility to provide for the basic needs of the community and its members. In this respect it is acceptable to have wealth, but it is desirable for it to circulate by ensuring income redistribution within a community. Everyone is free to consume any good except those forbidden by religion, but no one is allowed to waste or hoard goods, the rationale being to preserve the environment while protecting future generations from shortages. Social justice also requires a balance between private ownership (personal interest) and public welfare (the social interest), so the right to private property is not unlimited: ownership can be limited for the public welfare. Finally, it is forbidden for lenders to charge interest on their loans.

What the Islamic economic ethics just outlined is a picture of is an environment where economic activities are based not on individualism but on membership in a community. The community therefore stands as the reference point for all the activities of its members, while the principles governing these activities are those of mutual responsibility and economic equality. The rights and attributes of the economic actor must be in keeping with those of citizens engaged in any other social activity. And in fact society itself is organized around four principles as follows (Hifazatullah et al. 2011; Sirageldin 2002):

(1) Unity (*tawḥīd*). This is the vertical dimension of the ethical system, governing the freedom of action of each individual acting as an integral part of the whole.
(2) Equilibrium (*al-ʿadl wa'l-iḥsan*). This is the horizontal dimension of ethics, requiring a balance to be obtained between the needs of the present generation and those of future generations.
(3) Free will (*ikhtiyār*). Individuals are free to follow their own paths in social and economic activities, and they can exercise this freedom in ways that suit the needs of the changing times.
(4) Responsibility (*farḍ*). Individuals commit to seeking social aims in carrying out economic activities.

The principles just listed resemble those necessary to build a capitalist economy, but they are framed in light of a different conception of society. At first glance, this subordination of economic activities to the interests of the community appears to run contrary to a proper running of the economy. But an argument can be made that the behaviour of economic actors cleaving to these principles is economically efficient and beneficial as these terms are understood in the traditional language of mainstream economics. As a matter of fact, there are developed capitalist economies whose development has been achieved precisely by following the same basic principles that have been implemented in some Muslim countries (see Clark 2006).

3. From Islamic Economics to the Social Contract: Building a Development Model

As suggested, some of the core principles of Islamic economics can be understood in a secular light. To see how, we can start by defining economic development, because in this way we can identify the cornerstones of a capitalist economy and the conditions necessary to bring such an economy into being, while describing the mechanism through which it operates. From a historical overview of the development processes undertaken by the top ten advanced economies (Romagnoli and Mengoni 2014, 11–39), we can see that development takes place as a path of transition from a traditional society toward capitalism. This process is characterized by seven elements as follows:

(1) The temporal dimension, meaning that such a transformation needs to take place over an arc of time, since it brings structural changes to all social spheres.
(2) The creation and growth of new social classes replacing those that structure traditional society.
(3) The emergence of new classes and positions tied to labour—the salaried worker, the entrepreneur, and the unemployed—creating a drastically new condition for humans in society, considering that in this transformation the working and social lives of humans changed once and for all.
(4) The introduction and the spread of technological advances in productive and consumption activities, with improved material conditions.
(5) The building and spread of new institutions suited to introducing and running the new economic and social activities like the mechanisms coordinating the economic activities and subjects, the rules governing the disposal of productive resources, the arrangements of the decision-making mechanism, and the procedures governing the public choices.
(6) A systemic atmosphere of fast-growing links among subjects, goods, and organizations, producing continuous change through competition and adaptation.
(7) The intervention of the state to design and support this transformation through the creation of markets (the mechanisms coordinating the economy), rules governing the labour markets, industrial relations, and firm governance; through the provision of the common interest protection and of a welfare system; and through the establishment of the economic activity of the state.

We can think of this list as a watermark revealing the broad features of a capitalist economy, and what it highlights is that the transition toward a capitalist economy needs the support of a government establishing a legislative and regulatory framework designed to facilitate the emergence of new social and economic actors, as well as the creation of capital resources with which to develop new technologies and spread them. Within such a framework, the capitalist economy operates on the basis of individual freedom—the freedom of individuals to use their skills and the assets they own as they see fit to engage in productive activities aimed at making a profit and their freedom as consumers to choose the goods and services that best satisfy their own needs. Just by skimming this list—looking at it next to the list of Islamic economic principles and business ethics—we can appreciate that the two are consistent, showing that Muslim societies could theoretically sustain capitalist development.

Once we have ascertained that Islamic economics satisfies this precondition—this test of its ability to understand the emergence of capitalist economies—the question becomes: to what extent have Islamic principles affected the structure and operation of the economy in Muslim countries? Indeed, there is a relation here, at least an implicit one, and an argument can be made for it, but then we have to contend with "the fact that throughout most of the past fourteen centuries, members and officials of Muslim communities have had a tenuous link with Islam's behavioral norms, even when they have more or less agreed as to what these norms mean" (Kuran 1986, 158). Even so, we can answer that question by analysing the institutions and economic policies that Muslim countries in the Middle East and North Africa have adopted under the social contracts outlined in their constitutions.

The social contract can be defined as "the entirety of explicit or implicit agreements between all relevant societal groups and the sovereign (the government or any other actor in power) defining their rights and obligations towards each other" (Loewe, Zintl, and Houdret 2021, 3). All the official documents in which international economic institutions have dealt with development in the Middle East and North Africa confirm that the development model adopted in the region is based on a social contract. In fact,

> across the Middle East and North Africa (MENA) region during the 1940s and 1950s, societies developed social contracts with a distinctively interventionist and redistributive character. These contracts were expressed and institutionalized through explicit commitments from MENA governments that were articulated in constitutions, basic laws, and other documents that established the state as an instrument of social transformation, mass political mobilization, and economic redistribution. Although the form and content of the contracts varied, they reflected a widely held understanding of the policies for economic and social development.
>
> (World Bank 2004, 23)

Despite this variability, the structure of the social contract expresses some functions that represent the commitments of the authority responsible for the interests of the community (political authority) and for the people belonging to it (citizens). The responsibilities of the state are to protect the community against external threats and individuals against criminal acts, as well as against arbitrary state action; to provide basic services (such as health and education), infrastructure, social protection, economic opportunities, and access to resources; and to enable society to participate in political decision-making processes. The duties of citizens are to recognize the state's legitimacy, pay taxes, and serve in the military.

As the state is the agent entrusted with the interests of citizens, it has two tasks: on the one hand, political action within the state must be aimed at unity rather than resolving itself into a power struggle; on the other hand, the state's economic action must prioritize income redistribution and wealth transfers so as to achieve economic and social fairness, including by intervening in production and regulating markets. As to the first instrument, states have enacted agricultural reforms, nationalized private and foreign assets, and adopted import-substitution industrialization (ISI) so as to protect local markets from global competition. As to the second instrument (market regulation), we need to bear in mind that, under a social contract model, the market is understood not as a means by which to achieve efficiency but as the operating mechanism enabling the capitalist economy to work, as was the case with traditional Muslim economies.[2] The state's provision of social welfare and social services is achieved by extending the welfare state on the model of the European countries; the state, in other words, provides education, housing, healthcare, and food. Under the MENA region's social contract, states even gave out generous fuel and food subsidies. To be sure, this was counterbalanced by authoritarian governance, coupled with government control of labour unions set up as centralized, hierarchical organizations, so as to ensure political stability. Such kind of stability has been appreciated and favoured by Western economic powers (Richards and Waterbury 2008; Noland and Pack 2007; Romagnoli and Mengoni 2014).

A review of the constitutions of Muslim countries can show that the distinctive elements of the social contract overlap to a significant degree of detail with constitutional principles. A case in point is the Egyptian Constitution enacted in 1971, where the state's social responsibility is configured as follows:

> **Article 16**
>
> The State shall guarantee cultural, social and health services, and work to ensure them for the villages in particular in an easy and regular manner in order to raise their standard.

2 In the Muslim tradition the effectiveness of the economy derived from the efficiency of the exchanges that increased business volume. Thus, "they tried to make them more certain, safe, and equitable between the 8th and the 14th centuries. Such features of the market resulted from the implementation of the general principles of the commercial contracts that were: the compliance of the obligations, which made the market activities indisputable, was guaranteed by the binding strength of the contract towards both the contracting parties (contractual constraint); the validity of the exchange made under the freedom of contract was provided by analogy with the typical sale contract, on condition that the exchange was not forbidden; and the equity of the contract was ensured in the absence of fraud, violence, error, market power mistreatment, and imbalance of the obligation of one part" (Romagnoli 2024, 220).

Article 17

The State shall guarantee social and health insurance services. All citizens have the right to pensions in cases of incapacity, unemployment and old age, in accordance with the law.

Article 18

Education is a right guaranteed by the State.

It is compulsory at the primary stage, and the State shall strive to make it compulsory at the other stages.

The State shall supervise all branches of education and guarantee the independence of universities and scientific research institutions, with a view to linking all of them to the requirements of society and production.

And this is how the 1971 constitution configures the economic foundations establishing the features of the economy:

Article 23

The national economy shall be organized in accordance with a comprehensive development plan which ensures the growth of the national income, fair distribution, raising the standard of living, solving the problem of unemployment, increasing work opportunities, connecting wages with production, fixing a minimum and maximum limit for wages in a manner that guarantees lessening the disparities between incomes.

Article 24

The people shall control all means of production and direct their surplus in accordance with development plan laid down by the State.

Article 25

Every citizen shall have a share in the national revenue to be defined by the law in accordance with his work or his non-exploitative ownership.

Article 26

The workers shall have a share in the management and profits of the projects. They are committed to the development of production and the implementation of the plan in their production units, in accordance with the law. Protecting the means of production is a national duty.

Workers shall be represented on the boards of directors of the public sector units by at least 50% of the number of members of these boards.

The law shall guarantee for the small farmers and small craftsmen 80% of the membership on the boards of directors of the agricultural co-operatives and industrial cooperatives.

Article 27

Beneficiaries shall participate in the management of the services projects of public interest and their supervision in accordance with the law.

Article 28

The State shall look after the cooperatives in all their forms and encourage handicrafts with a view to developing production and raising income.

The State shall endeavor to consolidate the agricultural cooperatives according to modern scientific bases.

Article 29

Ownership shall be under the supervision of the people and the protection of the State. There are three kinds of ownership: public ownership, cooperative ownership and private ownership.

Article 30

Public ownership is the ownership of the people and it is confirmed by the continuous support of the public sector. The public sector shall be the vanguard of progress in all spheres and shall assume the main responsibility in the development plan.

Article 31

Co-operative ownership is the ownership of the co-operative societies. The law guarantees its protection and self-management.

Article 32

Private ownership shall be represented by the non-exploitative capital. The law organizes the performance of its social function in the service of national economy within the framework of the development plan without deviation or exploitation. The ways of its utilization should not contradict the general welfare of the people.

Article 33

Public ownership shall have its sanctity, and its protection and consolidation is the duty of every citizen in accordance with the law, as it is considered the mainstay of the strength of the homeland, a basis for the socialist system and a source of prosperity for the people.

Article 34

Private ownership shall be safeguarded and may not be put under sequestration except in the cases specified in the law and with a judicial decision. It may not be expropriated except for the general good and against a fair compensation in accordance with the law. The right of inheritance is guaranteed in it.

Article 35

Nationalization shall not be allowed except for considerations of public interest, in accordance with a law and subject to compensation.

Article 36

General sequestration of funds shall be prohibited. Private sequestration shall not be allowed except with a judicial decision.

Article 37

The law shall fix the maximum limit of land ownership with a view to protecting the farmer and the agricultural laborer from exploitation and asserting the authority of the alliance of the people's working forces in villages.

Article 38

The tax system shall be based on social justice.

Article 39

Saving is a national duty protected, encouraged and organized by the State.[3]

There is further evidence showing that the social contract represented a capitalist development model (Romagnoli 2022, 719–20): in modern economies, there are different kinds of institutions that carry out the same functions, with traditional and differentiated institutional arrangements that evolve according to relations of complementarity, hierarchy, and path dependency; these

3 The Constitution of Egypt of 1971 as amended on 22 May 1980, https://bit.ly/constitution-egypt-1971-1980-wikisource (now superseded by the 2014 constitution).

arrangements are referred to as models of capitalism, and since the social contract corresponds to such an institutional arrangement, it has been possible for it to be outlined by the authors of a famous handbook on economic systems in the 21st century as an Islamic model of capitalism (Gregory and Stuart 2004, 32–34).

4. Economic and Socio-institutional Divides in the Mediterranean Space

The economic policies carried out in the Mediterranean since the 1980s have occasioned four divides, to understand which we need to look at the structural conditions of the economies for which these policies have been devised. In this respect, we can point to three groups of countries whose present-day economies differ but which have similar institutions or structural conditions. These groups are as follows:

(1) The European Union's Mediterranean countries, namely, Portugal, Spain, France, Italy, Slovenia, Croatia, Greece, Malta, and Cyprus. They are members of a common market sharing the same economic institutions and a single currency.
(2) The Balkan-Anatolian countries, namely, Bosnia and Herzegovina, Serbia, Montenegro, Macedonia, Albania, and Turkey. These are all lower-income countries, with Turkey, the economically most advanced in the group, ranking below any other economy in the EU.
(3) The southeastern Mediterranean countries, namely, Syria, Lebanon, Israel, Jordan, Egypt, Libya, Tunisia, Algeria, and Morocco. With the single and notable exception of Israel, the countries in this group have the lowest income of any Mediterranean country. This is also the Mediterranean area with the most widespread conflict and political instability. Because of this instability, coupled with the bad economy, we do not have reliable statistical data for Libya, Syria, or Lebanon.

For an overview of economic conditions in the Mediterranean, we can look at these countries' per capita GDP rankings in 2022 (adjusting GDP for purchasing power parity (PPP) at constant 2017 international dollars).[4] This index takes the per capita GDP of the best-performing country—namely, Malta, at

4 The per capita GDP index measures a country's nominal average value for gross domestic product per person, a value that in international statistics is generally expressed in US international dollars for a given year (here, 2017). When the per capita GDP of a nation measured in its nominal currency of a certain year is expressed in terms of purchasing power parity (PPP), the exchange rate used to convert it is that resulting from the value of US international dollars of a given year equalizing the price for the same "basket of goods" in both currency units. Even if this index doesn't consider income distribution within an economy, it does make it possible to compare economic conditions and standards of living between countries.

100—and uses this value as a benchmark against which to rank the other Mediterranean economies. The table shows that EU Mediterranean economies rank in the top-third tier of the per capita GDP values recorded in the area, the Balkan-Anatolian countries in the middle tier, and the southeastern Mediterranean countries apart from Israel in the bottom-third tier. Within this picture, we find some particularly significant positions: the largest EU economies rank between France's 95.4 percent and Spain's 82.6 percent; Turkey (with 68.4 percent) does slightly better than Greece (with 65.3 percent); and none of the three most populous countries in the southeastern Mediterranean group, namely, Egypt, Algeria, and Morocco, can account for much more than a quarter of the per capita GDP of the best-performing EU Mediterranean country, namely, Malta: compare Egypt's 26.5 percent, Algeria's 23.2 percent, and Morocco's 16.7 percent (a mere one-sixth of Malta's 100 benchmark value). Thus, the main economic divide in the Mediterranean space lies its degrees of economic upgrading. In other words, it lies in the gap between developed economies and developing ones.

Such a divide sharpens if we consider that in 2016

> EU Mediterranean countries produce just over three quarters (75.24%) of the whole value for the area, the Balkan-Anatolian economies little more than one tenth (11.70%), while the South-Eastern Mediterranean countries account for 13.06%. This is a crushingly different weight for the three economic groups of countries as well as between the four "Mediterranean economic powers" and all the other economies. . . . The divergences in the economic structures reviewed earlier show a dichotomy in the "Mediterranean economy" between the EU economies and all the others: high-income countries and a few large economies attract

Table 8.1 The Mediterranean countries' per capita PPP GDP values in 2022 expressed as percentages of the Malta benchmark value (constant 2017 US international dollars)

EU Mediterranean countries	*Per capita GDP*	*Balkan-Anatolian countries*	*Per capita GDP*	*Southeastern Mediterranean countries*	*Per capita GDP*
Croatia	70.5	Albania	32.1	Algeria	23.2
Cyprus	90.4	Bosnia-Herzegovina	34.6	Egypt	26.5
France	95.4	Montenegro	45.8	Israel	91.8
Greece	65.3	Serbia	42.5	Jordan	19.3
Italy	90.8	Turkey	68.4	Morocco	16.7
Malta	100			Tunisia	21.9
Portugal	74.1				
Spain	82.6				
Slovenia	87.4				

Source: Author's elaboration on the World Bank's 2022 world development indicators

> international trade flows on the northern shores; lower-income countries, many small dependent economies, characterise the other shores. Due to this dichotomy, the "Mediterranean economy" presents unbalanced bargaining power between a set of large economic subjects (acting as one under a common market and currency) and many unrelated small economic partners.
>
> (Romagnoli 2019, 241–22)

A second divide in the Mediterranean space, a divide that on the surface appears to be of little interest for the economy, is the demographic transition: trends in the rate of population growth change the demographic structure over the long run by affecting the ratio between the nonworking population and the working or economically active population, while also affecting the welfare pie. The high rates of population growth in the southeastern Mediterranean countries have so increased the youth population that when these people entered the labour force they overtook the dependent population (the young and the old), all to the benefit of production, consumption, and pension systems. On the contrary, in the EU Mediterranean economies the dependency ratio is tilting in the opposite direction, with a below-replacement fertility rate that, coupled with an increasing life expectancy, is projected to bring about a situation in which the dependent population will exceed the active one, and the declining working population is already creating worker shortages that are decreasing both the productive potential and social welfare.

So, despite the greater economic power of the EU Mediterranean countries, the dynamic owed to the dependency ratio is slowing down their growth relative to the southeastern Mediterranean countries, highlighting a third divide but in the opposite sense: between 2000 and 2016, the EU Mediterranean economies recorded annual average rates of growth ranging from 1.1 percent (Spain, France, and Croatia) to 2.8 percent (Malta), with Greece and Italy even sliding into negative territory (–0.8 percent and –0.2 percent respectively), and they were therefore outperformed by the southeastern economies, whose growth rates ranged from Serbia's 2.9 percent to Algeria's 6.7 percent. This performance tracks with the annual rate of population growth, highlighting a trend where the welfare pie in the EU Mediterranean countries is growing at a slower pace than along the Mediterranean's southeastern shore (see Romagnoli 2019, 244).

A fourth institutional divide in the Mediterranean space is the one created with the accession of some northern Mediterranean states to the European Union, as contrasted with the malfunctioning of some economic agreements among Arab states, most notably in the Maghreb. This has resulted in the southeastern countries losing bargaining power to the EU. Even so, the economic dynamics sustained by the aforementioned demographic trends hint at a possible complementarity in the ability to manage Mediterranean problems.

5. Euro-Med Policies and Southeastern Mediterranean Development

The complex and colliding socioeconomic reality previously outlined forms the backdrop against which Euro-Mediterranean policies have been put into effect since the 1990s. This is a succession of programmes that over the course of three decades have piled problem upon problem in the Mediterranean rather than advancing toward a solution of these problems, and the reason for this lack of progress, as I have suggested, is that these programmes are all based on a new, broad-brush economic paradigm that fails to recognize the distinguishing traits that differentiate a developing economy from a developed one, treating all alike. The paradigm is that of the free-market economy that informs trade agreements under the World Trade Organization. Consistently with that model, Euro-Mediterranean policies

> [d]rastically reduce the role of the state from a driver of the economy to a guarantor of stable economic conditions, through significant reductions in taxes and spending, the deregulation of markets, and the curtailment of trade unions. Behind these policies there was an interpretation of the economic mechanisms centred on the market as the engine of the economy and the most efficient organiser of economic activities, associated with the efficiency of private entrepreneurship and the harmfulness of state intervention in the economic domain. Such a neoliberal approach disseminated the idea that the alignment of economies with this model would have made them more efficient, upgraded, and on-stream, provided that they underwent the implementation of a "structural adjustment process."
>
> (Romagnoli 2022, 718)

European policies for cooperation in the Mediterranean got underway in the mid-1990s with the Barcelona Declaration (1995), establishing a political partnership between the EU and twelve southern Mediterranean countries. This partnership rests on three pillars:

(1) *Political and security partnership.* This is the partnership's first objective, promoting a common area of peace and stability in the Mediterranean, where the partners undertake to respect human rights, the principles of the rule of law and democracy, the sovereignty of states and their territorial integrity, and the principle of nonintervention in internal affairs. They also commit to fighting terrorism, organized crime, and drug trafficking; promoting regional security; eliminating weapons of mass destruction; and adhering to international and regional nuclear nonproliferation agreements, as well as to arms-control and disarmament agreements.

(2) *Economic and financial partnership.* The objective here is to create an area of shared prosperity in the Mediterranean through a sustainable and

balanced socioeconomic development of neighbourhood countries; the creation of free-trade areas, to be achieved by gradually eliminating trade barriers (fiscal as well as nonfiscal) for manufactured products; and the promotion of economic cooperation.

(3) *Social, cultural, and human partnership.* This pillar is mainly about establishing a security partnership to protect the EU's southern borders under a common scheme designed to coordinate the immigration policies enacted in each state. Beneath this strategy we can see its neoliberal underpinnings, since not much thought is given to the problem of promoting the development of lower-income countries, and no effort is made to camouflage its primary objective, which, on the contrary, is to bring the southeastern Mediterranean countries into the fold of the European market.

The European Union continued to work on the Euro-Mediterranean Partnership established under the Barcelona Declaration (1995) but did little to move away from this neoliberal template. This was the template at work when the Euro-Mediterranean Partnership was first rebranded as the European Neighbourhood Policy (ENP) in 2004—"a bilateral policy between the European Union and 16 partner countries (the EU's closest neighbouring countries), further enriched and complemented by three regional and multilateral cooperation initiatives" (EC 2024a)—and then as the Union for the Mediterranean (UfM) in 2008 with a view to achieving "economic and social development" (CE 2008, 8) and "regional stability and security through regional cooperation and integration" (CE 2008, 9, point 2) under "a Union of the EU Member States and 16 Southern Mediterranean countries built on cooperation agreements that aims to promote economic integration and democratic reform across the EU's neighbours to the south in North Africa and the Middle East" (EC 2024b).

Although we cannot enter into a full discussion of these policies for economic cooperation in the Mediterranean, what they reveal is a one-sided strategy narrowly tailored to advance the interests of the EU member states, so much so that under this strategy there is little, if any, communication between these states and the other Mediterranean partners; neither is there a shared understanding of the problems they have in common or of the economic policies best suited to dealing with these problems. In summary, I would submit that if the EU strategy were instead framed with an eye on the problem of promoting the development of the southeastern Mediterranean countries, this would at the same time offer solutions to the problems plaguing the northern Mediterranean countries, such as the previously discussed problem of an aging population reducing productive capacity and whittling away at pension systems and the social safety net, as well as the energy problem and the problem of end-markets for technological equipment.

Works Cited

Aoki, Masahiko. 2007. "Endogenizing Institutions and Institutional Change." *Journal of Institutional Economics* 3 (1): 1–31. https://doi.org/10.1017/S1744137406000531.
Askari, Hossein, Zamir Iqbal, and Abbas Mirakhor. 2015. *Introduction to Islamic Economics: Theory and Applications*. Singapore: Wiley and Sons.
Barcelona Declaration. 1995. "Barcelona Euro-Mediterranean Conference (November 27–28, 1995): Declaration and Work Programme." European Commission, DOC/95/7. https://ec.europa.eu/commission/presscorner/detail/en/DOC_95_7.
CE (Council of the European Union). 2008. "Joint Declaration of the Paris Summit for the Mediterranean (Paris, 13 July 2008)." Brussels, July 15, 2008, 11887/08 (Presse 213). www.consilium.europa.eu/uedocs/cms_data/docs/pressdata/en/er/101847.pdf.
Clark, Barry. 2006. *The Evolution of Economic Systems: Varieties of Capitalism in the Global Economy*. Oxford: Oxford University Press.
EC (European Commission). 2024a. "European Neighbourhood Policy (ENP)." https://home-affairs.ec.europa.eu/networks/european-migration-network-emn/emn-asylum-and-migration-glossary/glossary/european-neighbourhood-policy-enp_en.
EC (European Commission). 2024b. "Euro-Mediterranean Partnership (EUROMED)." https://home-affairs.ec.europa.eu/networks/european-migration-network-emn/emn-asylum-and-migration-glossary/glossary/euro-mediterranean-partnership-euromed_en.
El-Ashker, Ahmed, and Rodney Wilson. 2006. *Islamic Economics: A Short History*. Leiden: Brill.
Gregory, Paul R., and Robert C. Stuart. 2004. *Comparing Economic Systems in the Twenty-first Century*. Boston: Houghton Mifflin.
Hifazatullah, H., S. N. Badshah, H. Farooq, R. Shafiq, and Nasir-ud-Din. 2011. "Islamic Society: A Conceptual Framework." *International Journal of Education and Social Sciences* 2 (1): 1–6.
Kuran, Timur. 1986. "The Economic System in Contemporary Islamic Thought: Interpretation and Assessment." *International Journal of Middle East Studies* 18 (2): 135–64. https://doi.org/10.1017/S0020743800029767.
Kuran, Timur. 1997. "Islam and Underdevelopment: An Old Puzzle Revisited." *Journal of Institutional and Theoretical Economics* 153: 41–71. www.jstor.org/stable/40752985.
Kuran, Timur. 2004. "Why the Middle East Is Economically Underdeveloped: Historical Mechanisms of Institutional Stagnation." *Journal of Economic Perspectives* 18 (3): 71–90. https://doi.org/10.1257/0895330042162421.
Kuran, Timur. 2018. "Islam and Economic Performance: Historical and Contemporary Links." *Journal of Economic Literature* 56 (4): 1292–1359. https://doi.org/10.1257/jel.20171243.
Laybourn-Langton, Laurie, and Michael Jacobs. 2018. "Paradigm Shifts in Economic Theory and Policy." *Review of European Economic Policy* 53 (3): 113–18. http://doi.org/10.1007/s10272-018-0737-4.
Loewe, Marcus, Tina Zintl, and Annabelle Houdret. 2021. "The Social Contract as a Tool of Analysis: Introduction to the Special Issue on 'Framing the Evolution of the New Social Contracts in Middle Eastern and North Africa Countries.'" *World Development* 145 (September): 1–18. https://doi.org/10.1016/j.worlddev.2020.104982.
Mirakhor, Abbas, and Hossein Askari. 2010. *Islam and the Path to Human and Economic Development*. New York: Palgrave Macmillan.
Noland, Marcus, and Howard Pack. 2007. *The Arab Economies in a Changing World*. Washington, DC: Peter Peterson Institute for International Economics.

North, Douglass C. 1990. *Institutions, Institutional Change and Economic Performance*. Cambridge: Cambridge University Press. https://doi.org/10.1017/CBO9780511808678.

Rice, Gillian. 1999. "Islamic Ethics and the Implications for Business." *Journal of Business Ethics* 18: 345–58. https://doi.org/10.1023/A:1005711414306.

Richards, Alan, and John Waterbury. 2008. *A Political Economy of the Middle East*. Boulder, CO: Westview Press.

Rodinson, Maxime. 1973. *Islam and Capitalism*. Translated by Brian Pearce. New York: Pantheon Books. Orig. pub. as *Islam et le Capitalisme* (Paris: Éditions du Seuil, 1966).

Romagnoli, Alessandro. 2019. "Bound to Share Aims and Instruments: The Future of Euro-Mediterranean Migration Policies." Chap. 11 in *Mediterranean Migration and the Labour Markets: Policies for Growth and Social Development in the Mediterranean Area*, edited by Salvatore Capasso and Eugenia Ferragina, 238–56. Abingdon, Oxon: Routledge.

Romagnoli, Alessandro. 2022. "The Emergence of the 'Sovereign Debt Crisis' in 1970s MENA Economies." *Middle Eastern Studies* 58 (5): 712–27. https://doi.org/10.1080/00263206.2022.2081555.

Romagnoli, Alessandro. 2024. The Structure and Operation of Modern Economies. Abingdon, Oxon: Routledge.

Romagnoli, Alessandro, and Luisa Mengoni. 2014. *The Economic Development Process in the Middle East and North Africa*. Abingdon, Oxon: Routledge.

Sirageldin, Ismail. 2002. "The Elimination of Poverty: Challenges and Islamic Strategies." Chap. 2 in *Islamic Economic Institutions and the Elimination of Poverty*, edited by Munawar Iqbal, 25–46. Leicester: The Islamic Foundation.

Sombart, Werner. (1911) 2017. *The Jews and Modern Capitalism*. Translated by Mordechai Epstein. Abingdon, Oxon: Routledge. Orig. pub. as *Die Juden und das Wirtschaftsleben* (Leipzig: Duncker & Humblot, 1911).

Suar, Abi, Meirson Meirison, and Zerly Nazar. 2020. "Islamic Economic Redefinition and Its Methodology Among Contemporary Thinkers." *Kawanua International Journal of Multicultural Studies (KJIMS)* 1 (1): 7–17. https://doi.org/10.30984/kijms.v1i1.3.

Taheri, Mohammad R. 2003. "The Basic Principles of Islamic Economy and Their Effects on Accounting Standards-Setting." *Accountancy*, September 11, 2003. www.isfin.net/sites/isfin.com/files/the_basic_principles_of_islamic_economy_and_their_effects_on_accounting_standards-setting.pdf.

Tripp, Charles. 2006. *Islam and the Moral Economy: The Challenge of Capitalism*. Cambridge: Cambridge University Press. https://doi.org/10.1017/CBO9780511617614.

Weber, Max. (1904/05) 1992. *The Protestant Ethic and the Spirit of Capitalism*. Translated by Talcott Parsons, introduction by Anthony Giddens. London and New York: Routledge (first published in 1930 by Allen and Unwin). Orig. pub. as "Die protestantische Ethik und der 'Geist' des Kapitalismus." *Archiv für Sozialwissenschaft und Sozialpolitik* 20 (1904): 1–54 and 21 (1905): 1–110. Reprinted in *Gesammelte Aufsätze zur Religionssoziologie* (Tübingen: J. C. B. Mohr / Paul Siebeck, 1920), 17–206.

Wilson, Rodney. 2015. *Islam and Economic Policy*. Edinburgh: Edinburgh University Press.

World Bank. 2004. *Unlocking the Employment Potential in the Middle East and North Africa: Toward a New Social Contract*. Washington, DC: The World Bank. https://doi.org/10.1596/0-8213-5678-X.

Index

Note: Page numbers in **bold** indicate a table on the corresponding page.

Kolibri 360 GmbH
Ferdinand-Jühlke-Straße 7
99095 Erfurt, Deutschland
produktsicherheit@kolibri360.de